T0277182

# WHEN THE
# BRITISH
# MUSICAL
# RULED THE WORLD

# WHEN THE
# BRITISH
# MUSICAL
## RULED THE WORLD

## FROM *EVITA* TO *MISS SAIGON*

### ROBERT SELLERS

**APPLAUSE**
**THEATRE & CINEMA BOOKS**
*Essex, Connecticut*

# APPLAUSE
**THEATRE & CINEMA BOOKS**

An imprint of Globe Pequot, the trade division of
The Rowman & Littlefield Publishing Group, Inc.
4501 Forbes Boulevard, Suite 200, Lanham, Maryland 20706
www.rowman.com

Distributed by NATIONAL BOOK NETWORK

**Library of Congress Cataloging-in-Publication Data**

Names: Sellers, Robert, author.
Title: When the British musical ruled the world : from Evita to Miss Saigon
    / Robert Sellers.
Description: Essex, Connecticut : Applause Theatre & Cinema, 2023. |
    Includes bibliographical references and index. | Summary: "A definitive
    account of how Evita, Cats, Starlight Express, Les Misérables, Phantom
    of the Opera, Chess, and Miss Saigon changed the business of musical
    theater across the world" —Provided by publisher.
Identifiers: LCCN 2022057947 (print) | LCCN 2022057948 (ebook) | ISBN
    9781493071333 (cloth) | ISBN 9781493071340 (epub)
Subjects: LCSH: Musicals—England—London—History and criticism. |
    Musicals—Production and direction—England—London—History—20th
    century. | Musicals—England—London—Anecdotes.
Classification: LCC ML2054 .S35 2023  (print) | LCC ML2054  (ebook) | DDC
    782.1/409—dc23/eng/20221212
LC record available at https://lccn.loc.gov/2022057947
LC ebook record available at https://lccn.loc.gov/2022057948

∞™ The paper used in this publication meets the minimum requirements of
American National Standard for Information Sciences—Permanence of Paper
for Printed Library Materials, ANSI/NISO Z39.48-1992.

For Percy, a beloved friend now gone but never forgotten.

# CONTENTS

# ACKNOWLEDGMENTS

The author wishes to express his sincere thanks to the following people, all of whom gave their time and assistance with great generosity of spirit.

Jonathan Allen, Leo Andrew, Julie Armstrong, Graham Bickley, Michele Breeze, Andrew Bruce, Rebecca Caine, John Cameron, Judy Craymer, Janet Devenish, Susannah Fellows, David Firman, Rosemarie Ford, Larry Fuller, Zoe Hart, Alan Hatton, Martyn Hayes, Murray Head, David Hersey, Finola Hughes, Seeta Indrani, Lynn Jezzard, Bonnie Langford, Paul Leonard, Gary Love, Martin McCallum, Siobhan McCarthy, Robin Merrill, Claire Moore, John Napier, Andreane Neofitou, Paul Nicholas, Timothy O'Brien, Simon Opie, Elaine Paige, James Paterson, Arlene Phillips, Peter Polycarpou, Caroline Quentin, Sian Reeves, Sir Cliff Richard, Frances Ruffelle, Mark Ryan, Myra Sands, Jeff Shankley, Ray Shell, David Soames, Richard Stilgoe, Christopher Tucker, Chris Walker, Chrissy Wickham.

# "DON'T CRY FOR ME ARGENTINA"

One night in 1973, driving to a dinner party in London, Tim Rice caught the tail end of a radio documentary about Eva Peron. Tim knew next to nothing about her, just the bare essential facts. Rising from impoverishment to become wife of the Argentinian fascist dictator Juan Peron and one of the most powerful people in south America, Eva Peron was dead before her thirty-fourth birthday. This was a Cinderella story of operatic tragedy: what a great subject for a musical.

With their controversial rock opera *Jesus Christ Superstar* playing successfully in several countries, it was always going to be tough for Tim and Andrew Lloyd Webber to come up with a project to match it. What they did eventually choose was unexpected to say the least. Fans of P.G. Wodehouse, they had somehow convinced themselves that setting music to the exploits of uber-toff Bertie Wooster and his manservant Jeeves was a good idea. It very well might have been, but the book and lyrics weren't going well for Tim, and he wanted out. Before leaving he mentioned the Eva Peron idea to Andrew. It didn't appeal; Andrew's problem with it was the lack of a single character you could emphasize with: "hardly a great premise for a successful musical."[1] Instead Andrew wanted to persevere with Jeeves and brought in playwright Alan Ayckbourn as Tim's replacement.

Tim decided to research the life of Eva Peron on his own, curious to find out why she became this cult figure. He read the few books that had then been written about her and sat through repeated viewings of a 1972 television documentary called *Queen of Hearts* by Argentine filmmaker Carlos Pasini Hansen. There was a trip to Buenos Aires in early 1974, where Tim maintained a low profile after the theatre scheduled to present *Jesus Christ Superstar* was fire-bombed. It probably wasn't a good idea to announce himself as tackling Eva Peron next, whose legacy was both revered and reviled in equal measure by the populace. Thanks to a few contacts, Tim met with journalists prepared to talk, shifted through documents, and was excited to visit some of the places important in Eva's life, notably the Casa Rosada, the presidential palace, scene of many of Eva's melodramatic speeches. All of this added to Tim's increasing knowledge and fascination for his subject, and he began to build up a basic plotline.

He'd figured the best way to tell the story was through a narrator, someone cynically watching proceedings from the sidelines. At first, he hit on the idea of this being Eva's hairdresser until research pointed him in the direction of Argentine-born Marxist revolutionary Che Guevara. Both of these historical figures existed in the same timeline, although they never actually met in real life. Tim didn't think that mattered. "I thought: Hang on—Che would be much more interesting than some unknown hairdresser. That way, I get two icons for the price of one."[2]

In the spring of 1975 *Jeeves* opened at Her Majesty's Theatre and was a resounding failure, closing after just a few weeks. With his confidence severely bruised, Andrew began to show a keener interest in the Eva Peron idea and telephoned Tim suggesting they reignite their partnership. Tim was delighted. Much had changed in the interim, both were now independently wealthy since *Jesus Christ Superstar* first launched in 1971 and both had homes, wives, and solo careers, but it was a comfortable fit working together again. It would also be for the very last time on a major production. And the result was a show that changed the landscape of British musical theatre forever.

Tim was never really into the theatre or musicals growing up; he was much more interested in going to the movies and pop music. He was born in Amersham, Buckinghamshire, in 1944 and privately educated. He studied law, believing that's what his parents wanted, and hated it. Instead, he rather fancied life as a singer/songwriter.

While an apprenticed clerk at a law firm, Tim made numerous attempts to crack into the music biz, failing badly. His next idea was to write a book about pop history and approached an independent publisher by the name of Desmond Elliott. Not interested, Elliott was more impressed about Tim's budding songwriting career, mentioning how he knew another young musical wannabe that was looking for a collaborator. His name was Andrew Lloyd Webber, and he was four years younger than Tim and about to go up to Magdalen College, Oxford, to read history. But what he really wanted to be was a composer. At

Elliott's suggestion Tim wrote to Andrew requesting a meeting. This took place toward the end of April 1965 at the Webber's family home in South Kensington. Tim was hardly through the door when Andrew began bashing out his tunes on the piano. Tim recognized his talent immediately, and the meeting finished with the promise to collaborate on something.

As people, Tim and Andrew couldn't have been more different. Andrew spent money on things like Georgian wine glasses, paintings, furniture, and classical records. Tim was more likely to buy the latest Rolling Stones album. Andrew was steeped in all thing's theatre, with a particular love for American musicals. As a kid, when he should have been practicing Chopin, he was knocking out *Oklahoma!* on the piano. His boyhood idols weren't some long dead classical composers but Rodgers and Hammerstein. However, it was these very

Andrew Lloyd Webber and Tim Rice, the child prodigy and the cricket-loving, wannabe popstar combined their talents for the ground-breaking *Evita*.
*Credit*: Trinity Mirror / Mirrorpix / Alamy Stock Photo

differences that helped the two men as writing partners. As Tim was to say, "my comparative ignorance about musical theatre helped because I wasn't so concerned about doing what you *ought* to do."[3]

As the subject for their first collaboration Tim and Andrew chose the life of Dr. Barnardo, the Victorian philanthropist who founded the orphanages that still bear his name. *The Likes of Us* turned out to be a very strange, hybrid thing. "Half of it is Rodgers and Hammerstein and the other half sounds like Lionel Bart,"[4] says musical director and composer Chris Walker, who did the orchestrations when *The Likes of Us* finally received its first public performance in 2005. Back in the 1960s, no producer wanted to touch it and Tim and Andrew, feeling desperately sorry for themselves, wondered what they were going to do next.

Alan Doggett was head of the music department at Colet Court, an independent preparatory school for young boys. He had previously taught Andrew's brother, Julian, now a rising star cellist. Doggett asked Tim and Andrew if they fancied writing a musical entertainment for his choir to sing at their end of term concert. "We had visions of the West End," said Tim, "and here we were, writing for a school. But at least we had a guarantee that our work would be shown."[5]

A religious subject seemed to be the safest option, and they chose Joseph and his coat of many colors, which had always been Tim's favorite bible story. The result was a "pop" cantata lasting just twenty minutes, and it was performed in front of an invited audience of children and parents in March 1968. It would be another five years before a fully staged production of *Joseph and the Amazing Technicolor Dreamcoat* reached the West End.

Staying on religious territory, the story of King David was considered as a possible *Joseph* follow-up, until Tim returned to an old idea of doing a contemporary musical about Jesus Christ. He raised it with Andrew, who especially liked the idea of telling the story of Christ's final week on earth from the viewpoint of Judas Iscariot. What emerged was a radical departure from traditional musical theatre; *Jesus Christ Superstar* owed more to the Beatles and rock and roll than it did to the likes of Rodgers and Hammerstein or Irving Berlin. The problem was every theatre producer turned it down.

In a bid to drum up interest, a decision was made to bring *Jesus Christ Superstar* out as a concept album. The recording took place at the Olympic Studios in London in late 1969 and featured the talents of Deep Purple's Ian Gillan, Murray Head, Yvonne Elliman, and Joe Cocker's former backing group The Grease Band. On release, the album courted some mild controversy when it was briefly banned by the BBC for being sacrilegious. Despite that, it was a modest hit in the United Kingdom. However, it was in America where it really took off, reaching number one on the billboard album chart.

This unexpected success drew the attention of Australian-born Robert Stigwood. A former booking agent and manager, working with The Who and Cream, Stigwood brought the Broadway production of the hippy rock musical *Hair* to London, where it generated big box office returns. After hearing a demo of *Superstar*, Stigwood agreed to invest in the show and signed the boys up to a management deal.

*Jesus Christ Superstar* opened first on Broadway in 1971, then at the Palace Theatre in London in 1972, catapulting Tim and Andrew into the big time. Ultimately the show never made its second birthday on Broadway, but it ran for a record-breaking eight years in the West End. Its influence is undeniable. "Those musicals of the 80s could not have happened without *Superstar*," claims conductor and musical arranger David Firman. "It was so out of left field, and it sort of broke all the rules. It also emboldened British producers to think, well, we'll give it a go, whereas before they'd have all run away saying, no, no, that's not something we do, we put on Maggie Smith and Derek Jacobi. Tim and Andrew wouldn't have done *Evita* but for *Superstar*."[6]

The musical theatre landscape in the West End before *Evita* was a strange one. Most theatres put on straight plays rather than musicals or imported them from the States. Musicals weren't really something that the British did much of. There was a view back then, a latent inferiority complex perhaps, that the musical was an American artform, and they did it much better. There was the odd big British musical like *Oliver!* but culturally our background was music hall and variety. Broadway had jazz and the Great American Songbook.

British musical theatre wasn't viewed with any great seriousness either; they were mere entertainments, not real theatre at all. And if you appeared in them, you weren't a real actor—you were a musical theatre person. As a result, musicals in London tended to be done on the cheap. It was left to the Americans to bring in the big guns to the West End. *A Chorus Line* breezed into town in 1976 with a huge budget, a huge cast, and an incredibly well-drilled Broadway production team; homegrown musicals didn't stand a chance. But the wind was changing.

In the summer of 1975 Tim and Andrew felt good vibes about *Evita*. Employing the same writing process that had served them so well before, the plot came first, then the score, followed by the lyrics. Andrew really hit it out of the park with the first piece of music he composed for the show, a beautiful tune that eventually went by the title of "Don't Cry for Me Argentina."

In a bid to get away from the hustle and bustle of London, and a climate of mild bewilderment from friends and colleagues who couldn't fathom why they were doing a musical about someone nobody really knew much about, the pair decided to go off somewhere. Biarritz was chosen, for no other reason that Tim could discern other than Andrew, a big foodie, knew a couple of nice restaurants there. "By the time we came back not only had we had three or four really good meals," Tim recalled, "we'd written 30–35 minutes of the show. And we felt it was going well."[7]

Early in the process a decision was reached to follow the same innovative course as *Jesus Christ Superstar* and launch *Evita* on record first in order to create hype. At the time these concept albums were how those musicals got exposed and known, while at the same time becoming part of pop culture, getting played on Radio 1 or going on *Top of the Pops*. With hit songs in the charts, it led to a strange phenomenon of audiences walking into the show whistling the tunes instead of walking out whistling the tunes. Also, the concept album was a great way for the creators to work a project through.

Returning to the Olympic studios, *Evita* was recorded over the hot and airless summer months of 1976. Singing the role of Eva was Julie Covington, who Tim and Andrew spotted in the television drama series *Rock Follies*, about a trio of aspiring female singers. Paul Jones, formerly of 1960s pop group Manfred Mann and now an established actor, played Peron. After considering Murray Head and The Small Faces' Steve Marriott, Irish singer Colm Wilkinson was asked to perform the role of Che Guevara. Colm had recently played Judas Iscariot on *Superstar*'s British national tour. Other vocal roles went to the up-and-coming Barbara Dickson and popular crooner Tony Christie.

*Evita* follows the life story of Eva Peron reasonably faithfully. It opens in 1952 in a cinema where the performance is suddenly interrupted and a voice announces her death. After the funeral the story flashes back some twenty years to the young Eva, determined to leave home and make something of her life. She'd been born in Los Toldos, a village 150 miles west of Buenos Aires, the youngest of five illegitimate children. At school she was shunned because her mother was not married. That sting of rejection never left her. At fifteen, she arrived in the city of her dreams, Buenos Aires, where she became a stage and radio actress, something that taught her valuable lessons about how to present a persona to the public. We then follow Eva's faithful meeting with Peron and rise to power.

All of this is underpinned by a score that interweaves pop, rock, jazz, Broadway, Latin, and other elements into a potent brew. There's a maturity and sophistication in *Evita* lacking in *Jesus*, which at times was primal and visceral, and quite straightforward in rock opera terms. *Evita* is more layered, more complicated with moments of bravura that saw Andrew at his best. Like *Superstar*, *Evita* is not a musical in the conventional sense, telling its story entirely through music and song. Andrew had always dreaded that moment when the orchestra lurches into life and someone starts to sing in the middle of a dialogue scene, it's what convinced him that *Jesus* and *Evita* should be written with continuous music. As he has said, if the music structure is right, it renders unnecessary a good deal of exposition.

Highlights of the *Evita* score include "Oh What a Circus," in which Che's role as narrator is established as he mocks his country's national grief and savages Eva's legacy, "Buenos Aires," a funky samba number, "Another Suitcase in Another Hall," sung by Peron's rejected mistress, "High Flying Adored," Che's denouncement of Eva's rise to the top of Argentinian politics, and "Rainbow High," which is something of a vocal tour de force.

All these songs are eclipsed, however, by "Don't Cry for Me Argentina," one of Tim and Andrew's most famous compositions. At first neither considered it even a candidate for a single. That changed when the marketing boys at the record company MCA listened to the finished track, the power and beauty of Julie Covington's vocals and the mastery of Andrew's arrangement, and proclaimed it to be a certain chart topper. And they were right. Released as the debut single off the album, it was the first song from a musical to reach the top of the UK chart, selling almost a million copies. As for the album, released at the beginning of 1977, it went gold in Britain and sales exceeded those of *Jesus Christ Superstar* in many European territories. For some reason it failed to take off in America. Even so, it had more than served its purpose, and Robert Stigwood was able to secure funding from private sources for its theatrical production. In the meantime, though, Stigwood's focus had shifted to film; he'd be responsible over the next couple of years for mega hits like *Saturday Night Fever* and *Grease*, so left much of the producing chores on *Evita* to his line producer Bob Swash, a capable theatre man and ardent left-winger.

Now came the search for a suitable director.

Because nobody had done anything quite like *Evita* before, there were few directors working in musical theatre capable of pulling it off. Hal Prince was probably top of that list. He was the undisputed king of Broadway: *West Side Story*, *Cabaret*, and *Fiddler on the Roof* were just some of his successes. But could Tim and Andrew actually get him, and why would he leave his home patch and work in London with two semi-rockers, not yet established in the theatre? Andrew had in fact already sounded Hal out, flying to his holiday home in Mallorca to play him the album. "Overall, I think it's a fascinating project," he later wrote to both Andrew and Tim. "You fellows deal in size, and I admire that."[8]

Andrew firmly believes Hal always wanted to direct *Evita*, but it's also true that the director took other people's opinions on board before committing. One of those was choreographer Larry Fuller who at the time was working with Hal in Europe on the screen adaptation of Stephen Sondheim's *A Little Night Music*. Larry was assistant choreographer on the film and recalls Hal telling him that he'd been sent demo tapes of the *Evita* album. "He said, 'I want you to listen to it and tell me what you think.' Never, ever thinking that I would be involved in creating it. I did listen to it, and I was quite flattered that Hal wanted my opinion, so I said to him, if you direct this it could be really something special."[9]

Ultimately, it was the opening funeral scene that drew Hal in. "I thought, that's the damndest thing in the world. There's a funeral on stage with 200,000 mourners in front of the Casa Rosada, how in hell do you do that. I was hooked immediately."[10] There was just one problem, after finishing *A Little Night Music* Hal was committed to doing the musical *On the Twentieth Century* on Broadway, which ruled him out until the spring of 1978. Despite concerns that the impetus might be lost following *Evita*'s album success, Tim and Andrew were prepared to wait.

Meanwhile cracks were starting to show. Andrew had held discussions with Ronald Neame, the veteran director of *The Poseidon Adventure* and *The Odessa File*, which Andrew had scored, about turning *Evita* into a film rather than a stage musical. Tim was vehemently against the idea and during a US publicity tour for the album the two men almost came to blows over it in the foyer of the Regency Hotel in New York.

There were also vibes emanating from the Covington camp that she wanted nothing to do with reprising the Eva role in any stage version. Tim was chosen to take Julie out for a slap-up dinner and charm a yes out of her. She turned up with an unannounced date, a young Irish actor called Stephen Rea. All through the meal Tim waited for the most appropriate moment to pop the question. The food kept coming, the bottles of wine, then finally as he paid the bill Tim asked, "Er—any chance you might like to play Eva?"

"'No thanks.' And that was that."[11]

The reason Julie gave at the time for rejecting the role had to do with not being tied down to a long-running show; there were also rumors of artistic differences. As it was, what could have been a bitter blow turned into a publicity coup. *Evita* was now a star vehicle looking for a star, and press speculation as to who that might be started to grow.

Auditions began during the autumn and winter of 1977. Hal, although busy with his Broadway show, did pop across the Atlantic several times to join Tim and Andrew as they shifted through literally hundreds of candidates, including some established names. It was such a difficult part to cast and so important to get the right person.

No serious contender emerged from this process, although the number was whittled down to about twenty possibilities. Better luck was had with some of the other roles. Paul Jones was thought to be too young to play Peron, instead the distinguished character actor Joss Ackland was chosen. Indeed, no artist survived from the album. Barbara Dickson had scored a top twenty hit with "Another Suitcase in Another Hall" but was never even considered for the stage version. Instead, casting calls went out to find a singer with more acting experience. It was a search that took Bob Swash and musical director Anthony Bowles to Dublin. Siobhan McCarthy read about the auditions in a local evening newspaper and decided to try her luck. There was something like forty or fifty singers there, some quite well-known. As she waited to be called, Siobhan could hear her mother's advice ringing in her ear, "Only sing one verse of the song, don't bore them."

Making an impression, Siobhan was one of just three girls asked to go to London. It was desperately exciting. Siobhan had done amateur dramatics and cabaret, as far as she was concerned the West End was this faraway glamorous place. Her audition was held at the Palace Theatre, "and afterwards Hal Prince came up to me and said, 'I think I've found her.'"[12] Amid a buzz of excitement, Siobhan was asked to sing again. After that she headed out the stage door to grab a break, "and they ran after me, dragging me back in saying I had to sign the contract. So, I was offered the part there and then."[13]

For Magaldi, Eva's first lover, a tango dancer and singer in Buenos Aires, another unknown was chosen after a barnstorming audition. Mark Ryan was in his early twenties and began his career as a singer in Northern working men's clubs. Coming to London in 1976 he appeared in a troubled musical production about the life of James Dean. "I had a very quick education of being in Soho, being in the West End and being in a gigantic flop."[14] Things turned round when his singing impressed the screenwriter and composer Ronnie Cass, who'd written the Cliff Richard vehicles *The Young Ones* (1962) and *Summer Holiday* (1963), and he was signed up to a management contract.

Out of the blue Cass told Mark he wanted him to go up for the part of Magaldi in *Evita* and he wanted him to sing an old show tune called "Old Man River." Mark was unsure about the choice, but Cass had done a remarkable jazz/blues arrangement of it. Feeling confident, and with nothing to lose, Mark arrived for his audition. "And I was in great voice. And you know when you're in good voice because you can hear it resonate off the back wall of the auditorium. At the end Hal Prince stood up and said, 'You are my Magaldi.' His second line was, 'And that is a super arrangement.' So, for the rest of my relationship with

Ronnie Cass he would always go, never mind the voice, what about the super arrangement. It became a private joke between us."[15]

Hal Prince got up to talk briefly with Ronnie, who then left the stage with Mark. Waiting in the wings was Bob Swash. "Ronnie, you'll be hearing from us in the next 48 hours." Mark walked out into the crisp daylight of a Soho afternoon. Cass looked at him and said, "Have you any idea what just happened."

"Not really," said Mark.

"Your life has just changed."[16]

Elaine Paige had just about had enough of musicals. After years of doing them, she'd reached a point where she felt stuck in a rut. Making her West End debut at the age of twenty in *Hair* back in 1968, she'd gone on to play small roles or to be in the chorus. "I was making my way, learning my craft as I went along, just trying to make that extra leap."[17] She went on to appear in *Jesus Christ Superstar* and then the lead role of Sandy in *Grease* and *Billy*, co-starring with Michael Crawford. By the mid-1970s things began to stall a bit. She seemed never to be out of work for very long. "I just couldn't get the roles that I really wanted to play. At auditions I'd always get down to the last two or three people for most things that I went to, particularly in musical theatre, and then I'd get the big elbow. I think a lot of it was due to my height."[18] Elaine was a diminutive four foot, eleven inches. "It was my father that said to me, you must have something. You must have some kind of talent because you always get down to the last three. He gave me huge encouragement, telling me to persevere and that I should stick it out. But I was on the brink of thinking, I can't do this much longer."[19]

Elaine had already begun to change course in her career, having accepted a small part in a television drama about the British singer and striptease artist of the 1940s and 1950s, Phyllis Dixey. In Blackpool filming at the time, she told her agent she wasn't interested in auditioning for *Evita*. "I want to be a dramatic actress," she stated. "I don't want to do any more musicals." This was different, her agent stressed, and she urged Elaine to go out and buy the album. "It's a fantastic part. You're perfect for it." Elaine went out the next day and bought the LP. "I played it and on first hearing I knew I wanted the part. I read the liner notes that Tim had written inside the album and that was my introduction to Eva Peron and that life and her politics. I knew nothing about Argentina or this era. And I wasn't alone in that. Not many people did."[20]

Returning to London, Elaine prepared for her first audition and was determined to make an impression. She wore a genuine 1940s frock bought in Kensington market. It was blue and white. She had her hair pinned back in a style that again echoed the 1940s period and ankle strap shoes. "I always wore the same thing, every time I went back to audition."[21] In another bid to stand out she decided not to sing "Don't Cry for me Argentina," which practically everyone else chose to perform, instead choosing "Yesterday" by the Beatles. "I sang it like a three-act play, very dramatic."[22] That went down very well, as did two other songs she was asked to sing. They thanked her and Elaine left. "They called me back the next week and this went on for something like eight or ten weeks."[23] If she was going to win the role it was going to be after a marathon, not a sprint.

Meanwhile in New York Hal Prince was putting the finishing touches to *On the Twentieth Century*. He'd asked Larry Fuller to choreograph it and after working together for a few weeks invited him to do *Evita* with him next. "I was thrilled because I thought it was such an interesting and magnificent piece of material."[24]

With scarcely a break after the launch of *On the Twentieth Century*, Hal was on a plane to London with his assistant, the vastly experienced, unflappable, and efficient Ruth Mitchell, who'd been with him since *West Side Story* in 1957, and Larry. It was going to be a fast turnaround, with just two months of planning before rehearsals were due to start.

Hal's first job was to whittle down the last remaining Evas and choose his leading lady. Larry was there every day for those final auditions. Already, the press scrutiny around the show was gathering pace. "Every day, on the page of this newspaper that usually had a very attractive woman with her boobs out, they replaced that with a picture of some actress who'd just come out the stage door having auditioned and they would interview her about what it was like. We had to put security on the entrance to the theatre because reporters would sneak in and watch the auditions. I remember once we had to stop and kick somebody out."[25]

By the end of it all they were no nearer making a decision, each of the final few candidates was capable of doing the job, and no one really stood out. It was now that Hal threw in a curve ball. There was an American singer/dancer called Bonnie Schon that Hal liked and had already got Andrew and Tim to meet and see perform while they were in the States. It was decided to bring her over to London. "Within two days she was on a plane, learning her songs," recalls Larry. "She came in and auditioned and just blew us away. She was terrific. At the end of that day, which was the final call backs, all the production team was sitting in the theatre and Hal said, 'Well, I mean, can it be denied, it's got to be Bonnie,' and one by one the British contingency said yes—but—and gave some reason why they weren't quite sure about her."[26]

It was now a two-horse race, Elaine versus Bonnie.

Things fell silent as the Easter weekend approached. Elaine went down to the south coast to stay with her parents. On the Tuesday, her agent called. They wanted to see her again, one last time. Elaine said she couldn't make it. "You've got to get on a train now and come back." Elaine said she wasn't prepared. "Tell them I'll come tomorrow afternoon at two o'clock." Elaine preferred not to audition in the morning because she liked to warm her voice up. "You can't make all these demands," said her agent. "Everybody in the world wants this part. You're going to lose it." Elaine was adamant. "Just tell them you can't get hold of me and that you know I'm out of town for Easter."

On the Wednesday afternoon Elaine arrived at Andrew's apartment in Eaton Square. She was asked to wait in the study, which was a small room full of books and a baby grand piano. Then the door opened and in walked Hal, Tim, and Andrew, who sat at the piano. "They asked me yet again to sing practically the entire score."[27] The one song Andrew particularly wanted Elaine to sing was "Rainbow High." It was the one that separated the men from the boys, he said, because it had such a huge range to it. Then Elaine left. It was going to be an anxious wait.

Back home in her flat in West Hampstead, Elaine and her mother, who had returned to London with her daughter to stay a few days, were about to go to bed. It was almost midnight. The doorbell rang. Outside on the doorstep was Elaine's agent, resplendent in evening wear, with a long flowing cape. "Whatever are you doing here at midnight," asked Elaine. "Have you come to deliver the bad news personally? Is that what it is? Are you going to let me down gently?"

Elaine's agent was Canadian and had this very slow drawl. "Elaine, I have come to tell you . . ."

"Yeah, yeah, go on, just say it, spit it out."

"I have come to tell you . . ."

"Yes, yes, just get on with it."

". . . to tell you that the part of Eva Peron . . ." she began to go through a list of all the other people that had been up for it, very famous people, the world and his wife, ". . . Barbra Streisand, Bette Midler, Liza Minnelli . . ."

"For God's sake, just tell me. Have I got it or not?"

". . . the part of Eva Peron . . . is . . ." she opened her cape to reveal a magnum of Dom Perignon champagne, ". . . is yours."[28]

Elaine couldn't believe it. After all those years, finally the right part at the right time had come her way. And she was ready.

With Elaine experiencing so many emotions, she knew one of the first things she had to do was call her dad, on his own at home. "Guess what."

"Why are you ringing so late?" he asked.

"Well, I've got some news." On the other end of the line Elaine could hear him almost gasp. "It was so fantastic for him," says Elaine, "and my mother, but particularly for my father because he'd been such a support and always encouraged me not to give in."[29] As Elaine was telling him the news, her agent uncorked the champagne and everybody celebrated together. "It's a moment I will never forget," says Elaine. "And my life changed from that moment on."[30]

The first indication of this new life happened before six o'clock the following morning. The phone rang. It was a reporter from the *News of the World*. Elaine put the receiver down. Next to call was the *Daily Mail*. Then it was *The Times*. And *The Telegraph*. In the end she had to take the phone off the hook.

By seven thirty, when she looked out of the window of her flat, the press was camped outside in the street. "I pulled the blinds down and realized that my mother and I were trapped in my flat. I couldn't get out."[31] That morning Elaine had a recording session to go to; she earned a bit of extra money as a studio backing singer. How was she going to get there with half of Fleet Street on the front porch? Over the years Elaine made a habit of keeping bits of costumes from some of her other shows. One of the first things she ever did was called *The Roar of the Greasepaint – The Smell of the Crowd*. "I played, don't ask me why, a Chinese urchin, and so I had this black cut wig they'd given me which I'd stolen as a memento. I put it on, along with a pair of sunglasses and a scarf round my head, and I said to mum, 'You're just going to have to stay here, there's food in the fridge, and I'll get back to you somehow, but don't talk to anybody.'"[32]

Elaine opened the front door, and there was a sudden rush toward her and a barrage of questions: "Does Elaine Paige live here?" "What floor is she on?" Elaine feigned ignorance on the matter, explaining that she was from China and had no idea what they were talking about. Her beloved Mini was luckily parked nearby, and as she reversed to get out of the parking space and was about to speed off, she whipped off the wig and glasses. "And I looked in the rearview mirror and these reporters were literally all running after the car with their cameras and microphones. It was mad. I thought to myself, I'm in a film. It was like a scene in a movie."[33]

Long before touching down at Heathrow airport, Hal and Larry had already begun work on *Evita*. Because there was no script, Hal took the lyrics from the concept album and made a book out of them, and this became their main source of reference. "Because of the way it was written," says Larry, "I referred to *Evita* as a documentary revue because it was a series of musical numbers depicting somebody's life, with very little dialogue."[34] An early concept of Larry's was that whenever Eva and Peron are seen in public everything was in black and white, like a newsreel. When the couple are in private, everything is color. Hal saw

*Evita* as a way to comment on fame and life in the public arena, but discarded Larry's bravura notion. "But Hal never put you down for an idea that he didn't think worked," says Larry. "He'd just say, no, I don't think so, let's think of something else."[35]

For Larry, Hal was great to work with because he really collaborated. "He didn't just say, choreographer, go in the other room and do some steps. I was truly collaborating in the creative vision."[36] Together both men went through each and every number and came up with visual styles of staging to help tell the story in metaphors, poetic movement, and so on. "Every single thing that we staged had total conceptual thought behind it," says Larry. "Every move was meant to impart information."[37] It was a challenge, but a wonderfully creative one. Larry thinks there were something like fourteen variants of the "Buenos Aires" dance sequence before he fixed on the right one.

As for the song "Goodnight and Thank You," rifling through some research notes Larry came across a list of Eva's lovers before she ended up with Peron. It was obvious she was sleeping her way to the top, and Larry came up with the device of a revolving door as a metaphor for these multiple affairs; each time emerging dressed in a more expensive robe.

Larry's work on the show was meticulous, and how he moved the crowds and extras on the stage was visually stunning. "He really gave that show a language," says *Evita*'s production manager Martin McCallum. "He did the most exquisite job and so many elements of that show have been ripped off since."[38]

With this being Hal's first show in London, *Evita* marked the pivotal moment when Broadway met the West End musical. "And there were quite a few birthing pains," recalls David Firman, who'd come into the show as assistant to the musical director Anthony Bowles. "It was a bedding in process."[39] It was clear there was a different approach between the Broadway crowd and the Brits, a different way of doing things. "The musical had always been the vernacular of Broadway," says David. "They'd been doing it for a hundred years; they knew how to put on a show. Andrew and Tim came from a very different tradition. Andrew's father was a classical musician and a church organist, so Andrew had a whole lot of English musical influences, and soft rock, the Everly Brothers and those sorts of people, in his brain."[40] In a way, *Jesus Christ Superstar* was emblematic of that. While not a stage concert, it was a lot grander than that, and it nevertheless sat in the heritage that Andrew, and also Tim, were part of. "Then along comes Hal from Broadway," says David, "and suddenly there are different expectations."[41]

From the outset Hal wanted to make changes. The most substantial was the removal of the song "The Lady's Got Potential," which was all about Che's unlikely brush with capitalism by attempting to market an insecticide. Andrew and Tim came up with a hurried replacement, "The Art of the Possible," which was about Peron's rise to power. One day Larry heard Hal mumble to himself, "No, that won't work."

"What won't work?" asked Larry.

"Musical chairs for 'Art of the Possible.'"

"Hal, that's brilliant. We have to do that, using a childhood game to find out who gets to be at the top."[42] In the end, Hal staged it with rocking chairs so there was some movement. It was a tour de force of theatrical staging.

Hal also insisted on a heavier political tone. David Firman recalls rehearsing Eva's final lament, when close to death she wonders what life might have been had she chosen a simpler path. "Elaine was singing the bejesus out of it and sounded gorgeous. I'm going through it with her and Hal leaned over to me and in a very loud voice said, 'Is she dead yet?' Because Hal was more interested in what Che Guevara was going to say about the death rather than the death itself. Hal's view, and it's very clear in the production, he wanted to make it a musical with real muscle and with a real political intent."[43]

The all-important role of Che Guevara actually ended up being the very last to be cast. Colm Wilkinson was magnificent on the record but, according to Andrew, "did not cut it with Hal."[44] It was Tim's wife Jane who mentioned David Essex. Better known for his pop career, Essex had successfully dabbled in acting, although Hal didn't really know him at all. "David was always strongly in the frame for Che," says David Firman. "There were others, more theatre names, who were also under consideration. David arrived and Hal loved the look, the bright blue eyes and the sardonic smile."[45] One dissenting voice was Robert Stigwood. "He was worried that David's fame as a rockstar would make him less believable as the character of Che," claims Larry. "All the way to the last-minute Hal and Stigwood were battling about that."[46] A final meeting took place between the two at Claridge's Hotel, and Hal got his way.

The day Essex first arrived at rehearsals there were gasps from all the female cast, "and quite a lot of the male cast, too," recalls singer Robin Merrill.[47] What Robin most admired about David was his professionalism. "Although he was the popstar, he was absolutely fully open to everything and was quite prepared to make mistakes or make a fool out of himself in front of us."[48]

While Elaine undoubtedly had the lead role, Essex was undeniably the star of the show and received top billing. He also had the largest dressing room, along with the biggest salary and a percentage of the box office. It was hoped that Essex would sign on for a year, but he'd already committed to going out on tour with his new album and so his commitment to *Evita* was to be just five months.

Tim liked David Essex enormously and the two became friends. At one rehearsal Tim asked David who his understudy was. "It doesn't matter," David replied. "He won't be doing it." And he didn't. David never missed a single performance, even at one point when he was suffering from appalling flu. "I will never forget standing near him on the side of the stage," recalls Robin Merrill, "and sweat was pouring off him. He was like that for three or four days, as sick as a parrot, but insisted on going on. His minder told me that David didn't want to miss a show because he thought people had come to see him."[49]

Supporting the leads was an ensemble made up of actors, singers, and dancers, among them Myra Sands, Michelle Breeze, and Susannah Fellows. Susannah was a native New Yorker and came to London in 1969 when her father, actor Don Fellows, was cast in the West End production of the Neil Simon musical comedy *Promises, Promises*. At the time of *Evita* Susannah was doing *Cabaret* with David Firman in Sheffield and unable to get an audition. Perhaps David was able to pull a few strings when he went to work on *Evita*, and Susannah got her audition.

Susannah had trained as an actress at the London Academy of Music and Dramatic Art, and although her mother was a singer (she was in the original Broadway production of *My Fair Lady*) she'd never had a singing lesson. She just loved to sing. The audition was held at the Palace Theatre. "My father always said to me, 'never sing a song from the show unless they ask you to,' so I sang Cole Porter's 'Ridin' High.' I remember the girl before me sang 'Don't Cry for me Argentina' with lots (lots) of gestures. I remember muttering under my breath, and now for something completely different, and belted out 'Ridin' High.' My recall was the final audition day. I sang 'Buenos Aires' and Hal made me take my boots off to see how tall I was."[50] Susannah landed a role in the ensemble and was made first cover for Elaine; Michelle Breeze was second cover.

David Essex's understudy was a young actor and budding comedian by the name of Nigel Planer. Susannah had been at drama school with him, "and I loved his dry deadpan humour. He used to perform, with his guitar at parties, his early prototype of Neil, the hippy character he created and played for years in the TV sitcom *The Young Ones*, and he was hilarious."[51]

Robin Merrill was in his final year of study at the Guildhall School of Music and Drama. At his audition he sang a Mozart aria and got the job, necessitating him having to leave Guildhall early. Robin was more of a singer than an actor, and because he could read music was usually the one out of the chorus that Anthony Bowles asked to sing a short solo. Being somewhat green, Robin jumped at each opportunity. "I ended up having something like ten costume changes. I was busy the whole bloody night."[52] He was a peasant, a worker, policeman, marching soldier, you name it. At one point he was required to accompany Elaine onto the stage dressed as a colonel. It had to look as though he were talking to her, but because Elaine was listening out for her cue, Robin said the same thing every night. This he did, for months. "She could be a bit feisty, Elaine," admits Robin, "and one day I was called down to her dressing room and she said, 'Can't you bloody well think of anything else to say.' Whoa, I thought, ok. And so, I started telling her a joke every night. Then one night the joke was too good, and she missed her cue. She called me down again and gave me a right good talking to, and I said, 'What the fuck do you want!' We became quite pally after that because I stood up to her."[53]

Rehearsals began at the end of April 1978 at Cecil Sharp House in London's Primrose Hill, home to The English Folk Dance and Song Society. Scheduled for five weeks, even Hal Prince got nerves the night before. "I thought, oh God, this is so off the wall, what the hell are we embarking on."[54]

For Elaine rehearsals came as a blessed relief from all the press attention and demands that had fallen on her since she landed the part. "I was suddenly having to go to interviews, photo sessions, everybody wanted a piece of me and suddenly there was no time for myself, every hour of the day I was somewhere, doing something for somebody. And at the end of that first week, I burst into tears with my mother. 'This isn't what I signed up for,' I explained. 'I just want the job. I just want to play the part. I don't want all this other stuff that goes with it.' Maybe I was naïve. I hadn't expected that kind of attention. And I suppose it finally sank in how life was going to be from now on."[55] Rehearsals almost had a calming effect on Elaine—at least she was in a safe place surrounded by other people working towards the same goal. "And I was shielded to some degree."[56] Although it was long hours: starting at ten o'clock in the morning, Elaine might not finish until ten at night. "Even when rehearsals finished at six, I'd have to go off for a costume fitting and I'd have to stand sometimes for three or four hours while they measured me up and fitted all these clothes on me."[57]

Hal's plan was to rehearse the show chronologically, which meant starting with the funeral scene first. "So, every day for, it seemed forever, we were singing a funeral, which was fairly gloomy," recalls David Firman.[58]

The company quickly bonded. Myra Sands was a favorite and kept everyone supplied with bottles of Copella apple juice made on her family's farm. Myra cycled in every day and always arrived, with her wild black hair, looking like she'd come through a storm. "My favourite moment," says Susannah, "was when we were on stage in the tech rehearsal, Hal giving notes, and Myra came sailing in soaking wet, with her bicycle clips still on, saying, 'I'm very sorry I'm late Hal, the wind was against me.'"[59]

For Susannah it was enough at times just trying to deal with this whirlwind of an experience at twenty-one. It was her first West End show. One supposes that raised in a theatrical family was adequate preparation. "But, of course, the politics of each job are always different, the nuance of what things mean, the managing of one's self, aside from simply performing the role, were all new to me. I had a lot to learn. And this was HUGE."[60]

Likewise, Siobhan McCarthy was making her West End bow at just twenty. Arriving in London from Ireland she was made to feel immediately at home. "It wasn't like you were left to your own devices, and wondering how to make friends, I was put in an instant family."[61] She found Tim and Andrew very generous, too. "Tim would hold cricket matches with the cast and there were parties at Andrew's house."[62]

One of the things that first struck Siobhan was the outstanding nature of the entire ensemble. "To me they all sounded like stars. Normally in shows you have the chorus and they're not quite as good as the leads. But this was something else. I had never heard voices like them."[63]

Tim and Andrew were usually around, keeping an eye on things. What struck many in the company was what an odd combination they were. "Tim is debonair, sophisticated, gregarious, and great company," says David Firman. "Andrew was, at that stage, less comfortable in big groups and more insular."[64] Set designer Timothy O'Brien, who referred to Tim and Andrew as "the boys," also recognized their contrasting personalities. "Andrew was far less convinced about himself, while Tim was good fun all round."[65] As alluded to already, this disparity was perhaps why they worked so well together. "They brought different sensibilities to any project they did," says David Firman.[66]

As they watched rehearsals, both Tim and Andrew appeared content to take a back seat to Hal. "He was often cutting music and Andrew seemed to take it well," says Susannah. "I think they wanted a Broadway hit and Hal was the king of Broadway directors, so what he wanted was what we did."[67] Larry Fuller has another simpler view: "They were in awe of him."[68] Much of the cast, too, held Hal in high esteem, just his reputation. "Hal was extraordinary," says Robin Merrill. "He seemed to know exactly what he wanted. I was watching a master at work."[69] There was certainly a dynamism to him, creating this incredible excitement around everything. "He brought an energy into the rehearsal room that was completely charismatic," says Mark Ryan. "And when he was in the room directing, there was nobody else. Hal in charge was mesmeric. He brought a pizazz, that Broadway punch into a British musical."[70]

During the entirety of rehearsal professionalism was paramount. "With so much to do, so little time to do it in, there was no time for egos," recalls Michele

Breeze. "And there was one boss, Hal Prince."[71] What Susannah loved about Hal was his clear vision. "And he had the shortest attention span of anyone I've ever met. His mind was always working 10 times faster than anyone else's and if you didn't hit him straight with what you wanted to say, within two seconds, he had already dismissed you and moved on to something else."[72]

For Mark Ryan the rehearsal period was particularly grueling as he faced rumors of being replaced, perhaps because of his relative inexperience. Hal waved off the concerns, backing his man, and drove him hard as a consequence. "Harold Prince gave me hell for six weeks," says Mark. "I think that he felt that he'd taken a big gamble with me and once he'd taken a big gamble, he had to ensure that it worked."[73] Mark readily admits that he was a little green and really did need help with the whole process of building his character. Just before Hal Prince died in 2019, Mark wrote to him and they entered into a short correspondence. "I told him, everything I learned from you during the course of that rehearsal I've applied again in my career. I learned so much from him."[74]

Of course, the greatest pressure was on Elaine; this was her big chance, and she was understandably apprehensive and very much in awe of Hal Prince. "I was slightly terrified of him, but at the same time I trusted him implicitly because I knew he had a vision for the piece. And from that very first day of rehearsals, I knew this was something different and special and unusual."[75]

Hal was to spend a lot of one-on-one time with Elaine, helping her to bring Eva Peron alive. He did this by not overwhelming Elaine with the whole character of who this woman was but by helping her discover her scene by scene. Elaine didn't know anything about Eva Peron. Unlike today, there wasn't an awful lot of material out there on her. Before rehearsals began it was suggested she read *The Woman with the Whip*, one of the very few biographies written about Eva Peron. That was her main source of research. "After the event I found out more about her and indeed went to Argentina and visited the Casa Rosada palace and saw a lot of film footage of her. But at the time I had to make a lot of it out of my head and reading that book was a great help because there was a lot of photographs of her."[76]

Gradually the character started to come to the surface, and Elaine got better and better as rehearsals went on. Although Larry Fuller always felt that Elaine was holding back, not really grabbing the role. "It wasn't that she didn't sing it beautifully or acted ok, the character itself wasn't really there until the first preview. In front of an audience, she just let it rip. And I think of all the Eva's, she was the best."[77]

One of the keys to unlocking Eva Peron was the song "Don't Cry for me Argentina." Hal repeatedly stressed that Elaine look upon the song more as a political speech; "Forget about the beauty of the melody," he'd say. Eva is speaking to her working-class voters, the people that she claimed to represent, trying to get across her political message. Hal first had Elaine speak the lyrics, rather than sing them, and got her to stand on a rostrum to get the feeling of looking down from the balcony of the Casa Rosada. "And when you start," Hal would say. "I want you to lock eyes with some of the people in the first few rows of the audience. Even if you can't see their faces, they'll think that you're looking at them, make them feel uncomfortable, stare them out, and take your time before you even utter a sentence."[78] It was about establishing the character and determination of this woman and the fact she's going to win these people over. Elaine never sang that song again without thinking about that simple yet highly effective piece of direction.

It was agreed that *Evita* would open at the newly refurbished Prince Edward theatre. This was not anybody's ideal choice, but at the time the only place available. Formerly a cinema, it was tucked away from theatre land in the center of Soho and had never housed a long-running musical hit, which didn't bode well. When the company moved into the place for final rehearsals, they were in for a bit of a shock. The stage in any theatre is a built-up area, created for every show that is put on. Some have rakes built in, some are flat—it depends what the designer envisages. The stage for *Evita* was a one in sixteen rake. "And that's a very steep stage," says Martin McCallum. "And I don't think there has been a stage as steep as that since."[79] A raked stage can be very powerful, just the way it can serve to present the piece to the audience and the way actors can be positioned to completely change the dynamic. But it presents a whole set of practical problems. "We had a lot of trouble with it," recalls Robin Merrill, "but Hal Prince was determined to have that slope."[80] Getting on from the side was always a bit tricky, with the stage area being higher at the back. Equity, the actor's union, did raise concerns about its members having to dance eight shows a week on it.

When *Evita* traveled to Broadway the set designer Timothy O'Brien put his back out and went to see a chiropractor. "We were having a chat and he asked what I did. I told him I was a theatre designer. 'What have you designed,' he asked. '*Evita*,' I replied. Suddenly he savagely attacked my back. 'What did you do that for?' I asked. It turned out that a lot of the dancers had been coming to see him after dancing on that severe rake and it hadn't done their backs any good. 'So, I'm just getting even,' he said."[81]

It was Hal's choice to bring in Timothy O'Brien, who was ably assisted by Tazeena Firth. Timothy had designed many productions for the Royal Shakespeare Company and at the time was working at the London Coliseum, home of the English National Opera, when he took a phone call from Bob Swash. "He said he wanted to talk to me about doing a musical, and for a split second my future hung in the balance, because I was on the point of saying, stop right there, I don't do musicals."[82] Timothy had barely survived a musical flop many years before and saw them as nothing but trouble. "What you get are a lot of people drinking whisky in a hotel room at four in the morning, tearing their hair out. But when I learnt that the director was going to be Hal Prince, I was a lot more interested."[83] Timothy had worked with Hal before, on a Broadway production of a Jean Anouilh play back in the mid-1960s, "and I had found him engaging, worldly."[84]

From the outset Hal wanted a "magic box," a set that delivered and did everything. Time and money put an end to that hope, along with a few disasters. One idea was that people and things could be brought into the stage area on sliding trucks from the wings. However, when these small trucks moved, because of the height the stage had been constructed, they left gaps, and in certain places in the wings these gaps were huge and deep. "They were so dangerous," recalls Myra Sands especially when the stage was in semi-darkness.[85] Susannah remembers taking a look at these trucks and thinking, this is never going to work. During one technical rehearsal, where nothing seemed to go right, Michele Breeze heard a distressed voice crying out for help. It was Jimmy Cassidy, one of the singers. He'd wandered upstage and fallen fourteen feet down a gap vacated by one of the platforms, breaking a bone in his foot.

A little later, Elaine Paige fell down one, too. Luckily this was downstage and only four feet deep. She didn't do any damage to herself and managed to crawl out unaided, but that was the last straw for Hal. "It's not rocket science," he bellowed. "You know they are there, even if you can't see them. Use your brains for God's sake." At which point he turned round and immediately disappeared down one of the holes. "We all burst into hysterics," recalls Michele Breeze, as he clambered out, "while trying desperately not to laugh at Hal who was still clutching his privates."[86] Hal saw the funny side of it, maybe to hide his own embarrassment. "Fill 'em in," he said, and the platform idea was no more.

Other things were stripped back, until the production had a minimalist, almost Brechtian feel. The only big piece of scenery was a two-level gantry that could move up and down the stage and served, among other things, as the balcony of the Casa Rosada. Because this was a very different subject matter for a musical, Timothy O'Brien was determined that *Evita* should be seriously presented. "And be convincing in terms of its ideas and the political acumen of the piece. I was always very pleased when Indira Gandhi came to see it, and she really admired it."[87] Neither did he want the show to be, in his words, "customarily beguiling." As Tim Rice commented, "The set always served the show, rather than taking over the show."[88]

Saying that, the production was often spectacular, with rousing moments such as the first act closer "A New Argentina" with the working poor's calls to arms, carrying placards and flaming torches. There was also clever use of film projection. Timothy was so intrigued by the fact the story began in a picture house that he took the idea of a movie screen as a way of telling the narrative, not only by using historical footage but also taking the place of expensive backdrops. The screen was impressive in size (thirty-four by twenty-three feet) and also mobile, hand-cranked by a stagehand. Its movement was heightened by a bank of lights set into its base which shone directly downward cutting a brilliant swath across the stage whenever it moved.

Working closely with Timothy was lighting designer David Hersey. Both had collaborated on several productions at the National Theatre, and it was Timothy that expressly asked for David to join him on *Evita*. "The relationship between the set designer and the lighting designer is crucial," says David. "You can have the best set in the world but if it's not lit properly, it loses impact. The lighting designer is really part of the storytelling. I like to think we can influence very much how an audience reacts to a specific moment. For example, we can guide your eye around the stage so you're looking at the right place at the right time."[89]

Born in New York, David arrived in the United Kingdom in the late 1960s and always had a real interest in developing the technology of lighting; on *Evita* he pioneered the use of the Light Curtain. "*Evita* was a project that everybody couldn't help but respond to," he says.[90] One felt almost beholden to try new things and push the envelope. "It was very intense. And we certainly were aware fairly early on that something special was going on, that was clear."[91]

Another talent that came to work on *Evita* from the subsidized theatre was Martin McCallum. He'd been production manager for Timothy and Tazeena on several shows at the National, but he had recently left the company after several disagreements. With his colleague Richard Bullimore, he set up the Production Office. This was a new concept at the time and comprised a team of technical specialists that provided a production management and design service for West End shows. This was a service that didn't really exist prior to *Evita*, shows were really run, in the physical sense, by the designer, a carry-over from the 1950s, and they were built very traditionally with standard painted scenery and canvas. "*Evita* really showed the opportunity for that to change," says Martin. "It was a much more modern production in the way design, technology and materials were used. As a result, the theatre absolutely modernised itself, having done nothing really for 25 years."[92]

As *Evita*'s production manager, Martin oversaw the entire physical production and from the start it was a tough slog for his team, largely because there just wasn't enough money. A good example was the large mural that hung across the proscenium arch. This was Hal Prince's idea, that the proscenium be flanked by artwork depicting the struggles of the Argentine workers. "That was a massive job," recalls Martin. "Richard and I put those canvases up ourselves one night because we couldn't afford the overtime for the crew."[93]

One morning Hal sat everyone down in the auditorium and asked each member of the chorus to select somebody from the mural and to be that person. "I want you to go home tonight and create a character for yourself," he said. "I want to know who you are, where you come from, if you've got brothers or sisters, do you have a job." It was a brilliant way of making everyone feel emotionally invested in the piece. "The power in that show is the ensemble, really," believes Larry Fuller. "If they don't give you their guts, then it doesn't have that epic-ness."[94]

As for costumes, they were brought in from a leading costumiers, racks and racks of them, all original from the period and in different colors. When the ensemble cast put them on, Hal said he didn't like any of them. "He wanted the costumes to be dyed into a sort of sepia colour," recalls Myra Sands. "And so, these beautiful costumes were all dyed this horrible colour. I think he had in mind that we were from a documentary film of the time."[95] When everyone paraded around in their new costumes, Hal didn't like those either and at further expense they were discarded. In the end the ensemble costumes were sourced from secondhand shops and set up on rails in the stalls bar where the actors were allowed to go and pick what they wanted. "We then did a costume parade for Tazeena," recalls Susannah, "and she would say, 'that needs a hat, that needs a pair of gloves, that needs a cardigan . . .' and that was how we were costumed. It always amused me that when the Broadway production was being planned, they meticulously photographed every costume and replicated it. It all came from a charity shop!"[96]

As Peron's mistress, the costume department had put Siobhan in something akin to a sailor's dress, with a big bow and collar, and little sandals. "I do remember thinking, would a mistress wear something like this? I felt like a schoolgirl."[97] When she went on stage for the dress rehearsal Hal took one look and yelled out, "What the hell have you got her in! Stick her in a negligee for God's sake!"

Siobhan's big number, "Another Suitcase in Another Hall," always stopped the show, but it was short and sweet, lasting just a few minutes. Elaine comes into the room to turf her out, she packs a suitcase, sings the number, and then leaves. Worried she'd have nothing to do for the rest of the night, Siobhan asked to be involved in the ensemble and so featured in many of the other scenes.

To complement Andrew's score, *Evita* was to be one of the first musicals to use radio mics. To handle the sound Hal brought in Abe Jacob, one of the pioneers of sound design and reinforcement in modern musical theatre, and the man known on Broadway as the "Godfather of Sound." Abe began in the music industry, working with the likes of Jimi Hendrix, and was responsible for bringing a rock music aesthetic to the theatre for the first time, beginning in 1970 with the musical *Hair* and then *Jesus Christ Superstar*. In 1976, Abe brought his talent to the West End for the production of *A Chorus Line* and it was here that he first came into contact with Andrew Bruce, when he asked his sound company Autograph to install and operate sound for the show at Drury Lane.

It's rather obvious to state that sound is one of the most important, if not *the* most important, aspects of producing a musical. You can have the best costumes, brilliant sets, wonderful lighting, the finest artists, but if the sound sucks, if the singing voices are dismal or ineffective, that's a disaster. Andrew Bruce started his career as a sound technician at the Royal Opera House, operating under good budgets and achieving authentic sound. The same quality did not exist in the West End of the early 1970s, and renowned theatre producer Michael Codron was increasingly fed up with it. He invited Andrew and his colleague Phil Clifford to check out his shows and advise how to make things better. "It was quite obvious that the equipment they were using was so antiquated and poor," recalls Andrew. "Some of it was actually war-time."[98] After writing a report they went to see Codron, and he politely took their criticisms. Just as Andrew and Phil were leaving Codron said, "By the way, if you ever think of starting a sound company do be sure to let me know." It was only a short walk back to the Royal Opera House and by the end of it, Andrew and Phil had decided to take up what was an obvious offer of work. They set up Autograph, which is still going strong today half a century later and is the premier sound design and equipment rental company in the world. Back when it first started in 1972 Andrew and Phil had to prove their worth, but Autograph quickly acquired a good reputation and led to Abe's invitation to work on *A Chorus Line*. This was their first proper musical and led to an association with Abe that lasted for several years. Inevitably, when Abe landed the *Evita* job, Autograph was brought on board.

Doing *Evita* was a great experience for Andrew, but he was rushed off his feet. Six radio mics were being used, certainly the most ever used for a musical up to that time and a huge innovation. All the principles had them throughout, and a couple were shared around. At this stage, they were placed on the performer's chest or hidden within a costume, such as a lapel. These were very unsuitable locations. "And for many reasons," says Andrew. "It was too far from the mouth, it was subject to all kind of clothing noise, and worst of all as the person turned their head they went off-mic, because they don't turn their body necessarily. But that's the way it was done."[99] And that's the way the performer wanted it done. No one had plucked up the courage to ask them to wear mics on their heads, which was closer to the mouth. "Sound was a very poor relation at that time," says Andrew. "It was in its infancy and people were very suspicious of us. It was a dark art, and they didn't know what we did."[100]

As the date of the first previews edged closer, the media buzz surrounding the show ratcheted up several notches. "The expectation was immense," says Robin Merrill.[101] Behind the scenes the pressure was enormous. "There was a lot of stress," recalls Mark Ryan. "Everybody was vocally whacked, tired and feeling the stress. And there was a lot of worried people, and Andrew Lloyd Webber was one of them."[102] This was breaking new ground. "Nobody had ever done anything like this before," says Larry Fuller. "We really were testing the waters, and we had no idea what the audience reaction was going to be."[103]

That very first preview turned out to be a resounding success. "The audience absolutely loved it," recalls Myra Sands.[104] As the curtain came down, Hal and Larry were walking up the aisle. At first the applause was just a slow steady rhythm, not overly enthusiastic, then it picked up in intensity and turned into cheers as the whole house, the stalls, the circle, and the upper circle, rose to its feet as one. Hal turned to Larry, "Well, I guess it works."

By now Elaine and the rest of the company had taken their bows and left the stage, Elaine to climb the several flights of stairs up to her pokey little dressing room. "I was just about to get out of everything when the stage manager came running up telling me to get back on. 'They won't leave,' he said. 'They're still on their feet. And they're chanting: Evita! Evita! Elaine! Elaine!' I said, 'By the time I get down those stairs they'll be gone.' He said, 'No, come on,' and he yanked me out of my dressing room, pulled me down the stairs, very reluctant I was to go because I genuinely thought it would all be over by the time I got there and how embarrassing would that be. When I arrived in the wings, I could hear for myself this chanting, and he pushed me on. I literally got pushed back on the stage and the audience went mad again."[105] The applause lasted for five minutes. Elaine knows this because at the end of the week she was presented with a privately pressed vinyl recording of it.

There was now a palpable sense of excitement among the entire company, a feeling they were headed for success. "There was no doubt about it," says Myra. "The advance booking was incredible. We knew it was going to be a hit and that we were going to be in work for a long time."[106]

Things were only soured by a financial dispute among the cast when it was discovered that the dancers and the singers were on different wages, but everyone was doing the same work. Equity became involved and it got a bit messy. "We had a little strike before they sorted it out," recalls Myra. "Robert Stigwood went straight to the point and said, look, pay everyone the same."[107]

As previews continued things were worked on and tightened, notably the final montage sequence when all these echoes from Eva's past appear on stage before she dies. "It went on way too long, just on and on," admits Larry Fuller. "I kept begging Hal, please cut some of that, please, we all know the bitch is dead. Come on. And he did, he cut it down. And that's the main thing that was done."[108]

*Evita* opened on June 21, 1978. So much had been written in the months leading up to its launch that a full-page ad in that day's *Evening Standard* required just two words: "Tonight . . . *Evita*." Just days earlier the *Sunday Times* proclaimed it, "The most heralded musical of the Seventies."

The atmosphere was electric at the theatre, all day long flowers, telegrams, fruit baskets, and cards arrived at the dressing rooms. Everyone in the company was presented with a full case of champagne and a set of four crystal glasses etched with the *Evita* logo. Elaine was given a gold *Evita* necklace. Mark Ryan was in his dressing room with his parents when Tim Rice came in with a present of a gold *Evita* medallion and a musical box that played "Don't Cry for me Argentina." "I didn't see Andrew," says Mark. "He was not very visible on opening night, worried whether it was going to work. But Tim went round all the dressing rooms, he was much more positive."[109] Hal was feeling fairly relaxed, too. "He sent me a lovely note on the opening night," reveals Martin McCallum. "It said: 'Martin, smile,' because I didn't smile. I was so stressed."[110]

Act 1 seemed to fly by. As Act 2 got underway, Elaine was busy getting into her ballgown ready to sing "Don't Cry for me Argentina," when Myra Sands came rushing over with some news. Sitting in the stalls was Dustin Hoffman. The company was rife with rumors that Elaine had enjoyed a short fling with Hoffman the previous winter, when the Hollywood star was in England shooting the film *Agatha*. Elaine confided in Hoffman the despondency she felt about her career. He heard her sing, recognized her talent, and told her not to consider giving up. And now there he was in the audience on opening night, and what a moment for Elaine to find out, just before her big moment.

That opening night turned out to be a sensation. "I knew right away there was a kinetic excitement in the house that I could feel while the show was unfolding," Hal recalled. "And I had felt that only once before, and that's when I produced *West Side Story*."[111] Andrew Lloyd Webber would call the opening night of *Evita* one of the most unforgettable of his career.

For Elaine it was the very definition of overnight stardom. David Firman, who had taken over as musical director from Anthony Bowles, witnessed it. During previews he used to go and see Elaine in her dressing room before curtain up, just to say hi and see how she was doing. They had a very good

**Dustin Hoffman celebrates with Elaine Paige at the after-show party for *Evita*.**
*Credit*: **Trinity Mirror / Mirrorpix / Alamy Stock Photo**

relationship. "The day after the opening night, I tapped on the door and somebody opened it that I'd never met before. I said, 'Hello, who are you?' And he said, 'Who are you?' I said, 'I'm the musical director.' And he said, 'I'm the assistant to the chief press representative for Miss Paige.' And suddenly this dressing room was absolutely full of people I'd never seen before, all preening and cossetting and cuddling. It was just extraordinary the life change."[112]

The after-show party took place on the SS *Tattershall Castle*, a boat moored off Victoria embankment. It was a rainy night. "It was unbelievably glamourous but we were tripping over ourselves with the wet on the boat," recalls Siobhan McCarthy.[113] That didn't dampen the mood as several hundred guests crammed inside. "That was a fabulous party," recalls David Firman. "The world and his wife were there."[114] Susannah recalls that the DJ played mostly the Robert Stigwood–managed Bee Gees all night. "And I wore a virtually transparent dress (what was I thinking!) I spent the entire night fighting off Ginger Baker, the drummer from Cream."[115]

At 1 am, someone took a cab to Fleet Street to buy all the newspapers hot off the presses, and there was Elaine's face splashed all over the front pages. In his review in *The Sunday Times*, Derek Jewell called the show, "Magnificent, original, compelling," and "A masterpiece." After what he called the "ludicrous ballyhoo," *The Guardian*'s Michael Billington feared the show itself would be an anti-climax. "But the first thing to be said about *Evita* is that it is an audacious and fascinating musical."

There were some dissenting voices, like John Peter in *The Times*: "*Evita* is a superb musical, but its heart is rotten. It is a glittering homage to a monster." Bernard Levin of *The Sunday Times* disliked it intensely, calling it an "odious artefact" and "one of the most disagreeable evenings I have ever spent in my life." No one ever found out why Levin loathed it so much. It didn't matter anyway, *Evita* was indestructible. "When it got going it was a ship that was uncapsizable," says David Firman.[116]

After the trauma of previews and opening night, *Evita* settled into its run and the company went from strength to strength, secure in the knowledge of playing in front of packed houses every night. "There was a real sense of excitement that you were in a hit," recalls Siobhan McCarthy, "which is the most incredible feeling."[117] Sadly for Siobhan, the thrill of being in a smash West End show was tinged with tragedy. Julie, her younger sister, was one of the dressers and had only been working there for a few months when she was killed in a motorbike accident. "The company paid for her body to be flown back to Ireland; they couldn't have been nicer," says Siobhan. "The support I got from the company was just incredible."[118]

Not surprisingly, *Evita* became the hottest ticket in town and VIPs and celebrities were often in attendance, the likes of Sylvester Stallone, John Travolta, Margot Fonteyn, and Princess Margaret. Paul Newman and Joanna Woodward turned up one night and afterwards the cast lined up on the stage to meet the couple. Everyone had been told not to ask for Newman's autograph, as he was notorious for refusing. Robin Merrill either ignored the advice or didn't hear it, and asked for a signature. "And he got pissed off with me, and then of course the cast thought I was a complete wanker for about two days."[119]

One politician caught a performance and was so impressed she sent a letter to her speech writer about it: "It was a strangely wonderous evening yesterday leaving so much to think about . . . if they can do this without any ideals then if we apply the same perfection and creativeness to our message, we should provide quite good historic material for an opera called Margaret in 30 years' time."[120] The Member of Parliament in question was Margaret Thatcher and just six months after penning that letter she became Prime Minister. When in 1982 Britain went to war with Argentina over the Falkland Islands, "Don't Cry for Me Argentina" became the unofficial anthem of the British task force.

Things went wrong during performances, of course, as they often do. One night a new stagehand took over operating the giant screen and wound it the wrong way so it moved down instead of up. "And it literally swept everybody either into the wings or into the orchestra pit," recalls Mark Ryan.[121] On another occasion, when Mark took over as Che, he slammed the lid of Eva's coffin so hard during the funeral sequence that it fell off its legs and started to slide down the raked stage; fellow actors leapt after it to stop the thing going into the middle of the orchestra.

Night after night Elaine needed bags of energy and stamina to play what was an incredibly demanding role, physically, emotionally, and mentally. "It was truly exhausting."[122] Andrew Lloyd Webber always felt the role of Eva was too much for one performer to sing eight shows a week, and so it proved. After the long endurance of rehearsals and a few weeks into the show's run, all without a break, it finally took its toll on Elaine. "Eventually I just collapsed. I was done."[123] In truth, the role of Eva Peron was operatic in scale and no opera singer would even think of singing that number of performances. The decision was made that Susannah Fellows, as first cover for Elaine, would become the "Alternate" Eva, as well as continuing in the ensemble. Thus began the tradition of two actresses playing the role. "In the end I only did six shows," reveals Elaine, "because I physically couldn't do it."[124] Indeed, any of the big shows today have alternates, but at the time it was something new.

The first time Susannah went on as Eva her head was a tangle of all the notes that she'd been given and the mental notes she'd made to herself. "The front cloth had a gap either side so we, onstage, could see the audience very well; and we had to be careful that they didn't see us. When the announcement went out there was an enormous groan and lots of hubbub, seats flipping up. Strangely, it didn't really bother me and, in a funny way, it made me more determined to do a good job. I remember some of the cast saying, 'don't let it bother you' and being so supportive."[125] The performance passed in a blur and at the end there was a standing ovation and cheers. Susannah could see Andrew and Tim at the back of the auditorium. "I was just pleased to have got through it without it all grinding to a halt!"[126]

Quite early on there was talk that both Elaine and David Essex would reprise their roles on Broadway. When Elaine found out that the American equivalent of Equity had refused permission, she gave one of her most explosive performances in the role. "It was absolutely electric," recalls Mark Ryan. "She was on fire."[127] At one point Mark had to physically restrain her. "She almost smacked me in the face and I actually took hold of her and she was shaking, shaking with rage."[128] For the most part Mark got on very well with Elaine. "I liked her. I respected her. She was a grafter."[129]

The absence of its two leading players wasn't the only change when *Evita* made its way across to Broadway. One of the key criticisms leveled at the show was that Tim and Andrew had ended up turning Eva into an attractive figure, or at the very least adopting a tone of fence-sitting neutrality. Tim always countered this accusation by saying that if your subject happens to be one of the most glamorous women who ever lived, you will inevitably end up glamorizing her. Indeed, the political message he and Andrew hoped to convey was that extremists are dangerous, and attractive ones even more so. Despite that, Hal Prince responded to these criticisms by hardening the character of Eva for the Broadway version and giving the production more edge. "A little too far," thought Tim. "In London the balance between the enticing glamour and the vicious ambition was just about right."[130]

Hal also changed the character of Che. Casting a largely unknown musical theatre actor in the role, Mandy Patinkin played the anger and rage much more, rather than Essex's more sardonic interpretation. It is Patinkin's characterization that subsequent actors have followed.

For his Broadway Eva, Hal Prince wanted Patti LuPone, but from the start she had problems vocally. Instead of opening cold on Broadway, it was decided to do some try outs first, at the Dorothy Chandler Pavilion in Los Angeles, which was a barn of a place, seating just over three thousand, and in San Francisco. In Los Angeles, Patti lost her voice, giving too much in rehearsal, and her understudy went on in the early previews. Patti was not a singer as such; rather, she regarded herself as an actress that could sing. When she returned to the show it was to face a string of negative reviews, some vicious, and tensions began to rise within the company as rumors spread that she might be replaced.

Moving to San Francisco, Patti asked Larry Fuller to stay behind after a tech rehearsal when everyone else had gone. They sat on the stage, just the two of them, and before anyone said a word Patti collapsed into tears. Larry asked what the matter was. "I can't control this part," she said. "I never know if I'm going to make it at the end of Act 1. I can't control it because it's controlling me." Larry told Hal, who was anxious to retain Patti. It just so happened that one of the male singers in the show was a respected vocal coach. Hal organized it that he worked with Patti most days during the six-week run in San Francisco. "And by the time Patti got to New York she was singing it standing on her head spinning. No problems," says Larry.[131]

*Evita* finally opened at the Broadway Theatre on September 25, 1979. Tim was a bit surprised by how bad the reviews were and feared they might prove terminal. Despite darkening the character of Eva, the show was still accused of glamourizing a fascist, which Tim Rice considered just ludicrous. John Simon in *New York Magazine* didn't hold back when he wrote, "Stench is a stench on any scale." What made the situation even more laughable was that *Evita* went on to clean up at the Tony awards. It even later won the critics' award, which Tim was of a mind to give back. The naysayers didn't count for much; audiences still flocked to the show, perhaps spurred on by the first ever television advertising campaign for a stage musical, a Stigwood stroke of genius. *Evita* ran on Broadway for four years becoming the biggest British musical hit there since *Oliver!* back in the early 1960s.

Back in London, David Essex was the first principal to leave the show, replaced by Gary Bond. As is the custom when somebody leaves a production, the other members of the cast try desperately to make them corpse during their final performance. All through the first act various ploys were put into action but none of them worked. As the second half got underway, most of the ensemble were up on the scaffolding. Essex came on downstage, his back to the audience, with his dick or something hanging out of his trousers. By the time he turned to face the audience it was neatly tucked away. So, far from the cast making Essex corpse, he corpsed them.

Essex was much missed by the cast. "I loved David," says Susannah. "He was a breath of fresh air. So unpretentious, although he was a huge star."[132] Someone had the brilliant idea of giving him a toilet seat for his leaving present.

On it was written: Be sure when you deposit no one sees you—a twist on a lyric from Che's song "And the Money Kept Rolling In."

After a twenty-month run, Elaine was to leave the show. Her final performance was an emotionally charged evening, with the theatre packed out with her fans, there to see her one final time in the role. When the final curtain calls were over and the theatre drained of people and noise, a fan left a single red rose on the bare stage.

Elaine herself experienced mixed emotions on that last night. This had been a momentous time in her life, incredibly exciting, and yet at the same time a huge strain. It had been comparable to living like an athlete, having to maintain the peak of physical fitness, that meant resting her voice all the time and staying healthy by eating the right food. She was also compelled to entertain in her dressing room the flood of celebrities, VIPs, and royalty that came to see the show, something she found a huge pressure and almost akin to giving another performance. In the end, it all wore her down. "So, there was a mixture of both sadness and relief when it came to an end. A relief that I was going to get some of my life back."[133]

Marti Webb came in as Elaine's replacement and when Gary Bond left Mark Ryan took over as Che, even though he'd been discouraged from trying out for the part. Hal didn't see him making the transition from Magaldi. Mark was determined to prove him wrong. Borrowing a wig from make-up, he bought a false beard and a combat jacket and with the collusion of the stage manager secured an audition. "I was halfway through 'Oh What a Circus' before Hal realised it was me. He stopped me and went, 'You cheeky bastard.'"[134] Mark got the part and played Che for two years. Before he started, Hal gave him a great piece of advice, telling him, "The show is called *Evita*, but it's Che that drives the train."

When Alan Parker came to direct the 1996 screen version of *Evita*, he personally asked Mark to make a cameo appearance. Mark found it amusing to be handed a studio dressing room sandwiched between Madonna and Antonio Banderas.

Both Tim and Andrew knew perfectly well the theatre business didn't take them seriously just on the strength of *Jesus Christ Superstar*. It was *Evita* that turned them both into an entertainment force. "Maybe not quite Establishment at this point," said Tim. "But no longer upstart outsiders."[135] For Tim *Evita* was to remain a personal favorite, partly because everyone told him it could never be a success and it's always fun to prove people wrong. Hal Prince too was to name it among the favorite musicals he ever worked on, and one of the most satisfying experiences of his career.

Broadway meets the West End. Hal Prince directed both
*Evita* and *Phantom of the Opera*; he called the opening night
of Evita his "most thrilling since *West Side Story*."
*Credit*: Clive Barda / Photofest

*Evita* continued to play at the Prince Edward theatre until February 1986, closing after almost three thousand performances. Beyond London and Broadway, its impact was equally spectacular. With his connections in Australia, Robert Stigwood quickly set in motion a production in Adelaide early in 1980, which later moved to Sydney, and there were further productions in Mexico, Spain, and Brazil in the early 1980s. In truth, *Evita* has never really gone away, it's probably being performed right now in some part of the world.

In many ways *Evita* changed musical theatre and lifted the British musical out of its doldrums. "In my opinion," offers Mark Ryan, "none of *Cats*, *Les Mis*, or *Phantom* would have happened if *Evita* had failed."[136] Its staging was ahead of its time. Indeed, if it were put on now as a new musical it would still be seen as innovative. "If I was to do it from scratch today," says David Hersey. "I don't think it would be that different."[137]

There is also much truth in Tim Rice's assertion that the musical did much to turn Eva Peron herself into the pop culture icon she is today. Her grave, with a plaque that has "don't cry for me Argentina" engraved on it in Spanish, is visited daily by tourists and admirers. Tim was there once when a woman standing in front of the tomb began singing the song. This is weird, he thought, and wondered if he should tell her he wrote it. He didn't.

# "MEMORY"

With *Evita* out of the way, Tim and Andrew were all set to work on another project together. It was based around another of Tim's ideas and set during a grandmaster's chess tournament. The main protagonists would be an American and a Russian, and the backstage dramas would act as some kind of metaphor for the Cold War. Andrew was intrigued but found fault in Tim's storyline; it lacked depth, and he suggested getting someone in like John Le Carre or Frederick Forsyth to beef it up. Tim took umbrage with this suggestion, saying how they'd always worked as a duo and why now change a winning formula. Andrew didn't think too much about this impasse and assumed they'd pick things up again later.

What neither of them knew at the time was their relationship, which had produced three successful and ground-breaking musicals, was at an end. Never again would they collaborate on a big show, although their musical paths have crossed occasionally over the years. When they first started working together, Tim had fanciful notions of them being the next Gilbert and Sullivan, doing ten, maybe fifteen, shows together. Whether that would have happened is unlikely, especially given their very different personal taste regarding music and theatre. When the split eventually came, it wasn't a sudden thing either. No definite parting of the ways, like a warring married couple sending in the lawyers; rather, they drifted apart. Tim could see that Andrew was pursuing other projects without him.

One such project was a classical/rock fusion album that Andrew recorded with his brother Julian, the distinguished cellist. Called *Variations*, it reached number two in the pop album charts in the United Kingdom, and one of the pieces was adopted as the theme tune for ITV's arts program *The South Bank Show*. It didn't take long for approaches to be made about putting *Variations* on as some kind of show. It would work well, Andrew thought, as a double bill with another current project of his, based around one of his favorite books from childhood, T.S. Eliot's *Old Possum's Book of Practical Cats*. Written for the poet's godchildren in the 1930s, this collection of light poetry had long fascinated Andrew, ever since his mother used to read them to him at bedtime; he loved their whimsy, their ingenuity.

But before anything could move forward, Andrew needed to sort out his professional affairs. The ten-year management contract with Robert Stigwood was up, and Andrew could now take control of his own artistic destiny. This he did by handing over all business dealings to his own Really Useful Company, which Andrew ran with entertainment entrepreneur Brian Brolly.

Andrew was also to make another important decision. In search of a new collaborator, he sent a note to Cameron Mackintosh asking for a meeting. This was a strange choice given the fact that Cameron had almost punched his lights out at a recent awards bash. Andrew had been appalled at the shambolic ceremony, with its sound problems and technical glitches, and announced how it was a shame that Hal Prince wasn't around to direct it. Producing the event for television was Cameron, who took the words as a personal affront. It took all his self-control not to walk across to Andrew's table and demand an apology, forcefully if necessary. The next day the London theatre fraternity lapped up news of the feud.

Andrew decided to make peace by inviting Cameron to lunch at the Savile Club on Brook Street, ironically just next door to Robert Stigwood's Mayfair office. This was January 1980. It turned out to be a momentous encounter for Andrew discovered in this boyish looking thirty-three-year-old a passion for musical theatre that rivaled his own. He had, in effect, found his "soulmate," as he was to describe it. And over several bottles of fine burgundy, and a lunch that dragged on to the early evening, "we had sorted out the future of British musicals for several generations."[1] Andrew raised, too, what he openly admitted was a "crazy" idea about doing a musical based on *Old Possum's Book of Practical Cats*.

It was at a matinee performance of *Salad Days* aged eight that Cameron Mackintosh realized what he wanted to do for the rest of his life. After the performance, instead of leaving with the rest of the audience, he marched purposefully down the aisle, with his mother and aunt in tow, to wander on to the stage and ask questions of the director. After leaving school he got a job as a stagehand at Drury Lane. Keen to be a producer, Cameron set about learning every aspect of the business, from handling bookings, publicity, and touring. By the late 1960s he had a small office in Charing Cross Road and was putting on low-budget shows in suburban and provincial theatres. His first attempt to break into the West End, with a revival of Cole Porter's *Anything Goes*, was a disaster when it closed after two weeks. Licking his wounds, Cameron went back to touring plays, mainly old West End successes with the backing of the Arts Council. In 1976 he finally made a name for himself when he picked up the revue *Side by Side by Sondheim*, after a number of producers had turned it down. Its success finally made people take note of him. After that, things started to pick up with successful revivals of *Oklahoma!*, *My Fair Lady*, and *Oliver!*

Andrew had already made approaches to Eliot's widow Valerie about the possibility of doing something with her late husband's work. The two of them were to become good friends over time but at their first meeting Andrew found her to be a forbidding woman. As custodian of the estate nothing was done without her strict say so. "We had this conversation," Andrew recalled, "which kicked off with her saying, 'You realise don't you that Tom turned down Disney.' And I thought, this is not going to go very well."[2] Eliot's fear regarding Disney was that they would turn his cats into cute and cuddly kittens, insipid pussycats. "So, he thought of them as quite earthy street cats?" asked Andrew.

"Yes," replied Valerie. "They're proper cats, they're people, they're not pussy cats at all."

Feeling a bit more emboldened, Andrew asked if Valerie had ever seen a dance troupe on television called Hot Gossip.

"Oh, you mean that raunchy lot," she said.

"Yes, the ones that Mary Whitehouse doesn't like. Well, I'm thinking of going in that direction."

"Oh, Tom would have liked that."[3]

The idea to do some kind of double bill, with *Variations* forming the first part of the show, followed by *Cats*, now formulated in Andrew's mind. Cameron agreed to send out a few feelers. The result wasn't very reassuring. While there was a degree of positivity about *Variations*, there was no interest whatsoever in the T.S. Eliot cat piece. Cameron reported this a few weeks later to Andrew who admitted he'd no bites, either. Undeterred, Andrew decided to put something together anyway.

Back in 1973 Andrew used the royalties from the *Jesus Christ Superstar* album to buy Sydmonton Court, a grade II listed mansion in Hampshire. Surrounded by five thousand acres, there was a small deconsecrated sixteenth-century church on the grounds which Andrew quickly converted into a modest workshop theatre. 1975 saw the first of what became The Sydmonton Festival, a totally unique private arts event where Andrew can trial run shows in very rough form. "When it first started it was more like a country house party," says David Firman. "And that's what makes Andrew so quintessentially English."[4] It was a gathering of like-minded people, theatricals and neighbors, the sort of crowd that might go to a David Frost party at Berkeley Square, out to just have fun; "Andrew creates a wonderful atmosphere there," says Bonnie Langford.[5]

Gradually over time it became more serious and more carefully put together, a place where producers hung out, looking for product. "The great thing is that Andrew can try out shows there almost in private," says Richard Stilgoe, "with what he calls a cross section of the British public, almost all of whom are multi-millionaires. They come along for the party and they all say, that was wonderful Andrew, which is fairly unhelpful, really."[6] Nevertheless, the festival has managed to retain a unique personal quality, thanks to it being put on in the grounds of Andrew's home: "It's sort of momentously huge but also quite low key at the same time," says actress Janet Devenish who has performed there.[7] Paul Leonard did several workshops, including the one for *Phantom of the Opera*, and always had an enjoyable time. All the great and the good of the entertainment world would attend, and Paul's fondest memory is of staying over one night and coming down to breakfast to see Stephen Sondheim sat at the other end of the kitchen table.

Andrew decided to put on a few early numbers from his proposed *Cats* musical at Sydmonton that summer of 1980. The first person he contacted was Paul Nicholas, his original Jesus in the London production of *Superstar*. "I'd just come back from living in America and didn't have a lot of work. Andrew called me up and asked, 'Have you read *Old Possum's Book of Practical Cats?*' to which I replied, 'Er?' He told me he'd put all these poems to music and would send me a tape, which he did. I listened and really liked it."[8]

Together with Gemma Craven and Gary Bond, Paul performed some of those early numbers at Sydmonton. "And Andrew seemed very buoyed by the reaction. I don't think he was entirely sure that it was going to be a show, but I think that helped convince him that he had something."[9]

Among the stagehands at that year's Sydmonton was a die-hard musicals fan called Judy Craymer who had recently left the Guildhall School of Music, having done a stage management course and music. This was her first introduction to the world of Andrew Lloyd Webber, but she knew Cameron, having worked on several of his productions at the Leicester Haymarket Theatre. Back in London, working on dancer Wayne Sleep's one-man show, the Sydmonton opportunity came up. "Somebody called me and said that Andrew needed a person to go down and put some plugs on some sound equipment and things like that. So, I volunteered and spent two days there, hiding behind a speaker or something, and somebody said, this is going to be a big West End show one day, and I was like, really!"[10]

Andrew made a point of inviting Valerie Eliot to that Sydmonton performance. "You've got a marvellous sense of street Andrew, in the music," she said after the performance. "And I know that's what Tom would have liked."[11] *Cats* now had the official seal of approval. As further proof of her faith in the project, Valerie allowed Andrew unprecedented access to some unfinished fragments and unpublished verse from the *Practical Cats* book. One poem in particular piqued Andrew's interest. It told the story of Grizabella, a once-beautiful cat, the center of attention, now old and frail. She has been cast out, abandoned. Eliot never included this section in the original publication because he thought it might be too sad for children, but it set Andrew's mind racing; it added a key emotional dimension to the project and convinced him not only to continue with the show but to turn *Cats* into a full-blown musical.

Andrew was going to need a special kind of director to bring this odd concept to life on the stage. He'd already asked Hal Prince but had been turned down. His next choice was brilliantly left field: Trevor Nunn, the artistic director of the Royal Shakespeare Company, who had never worked on an original musical before. The choice shouldn't have been a surprise to anyone. "Andrew has a track record and a history of looking at the world in a different way," says David Firman, "and hiring people who might bring something different."[12]

Nunn himself was slightly perplexed by the approach. He imagined it was because Andrew wanted to put music to some grand piece of literature like *War and Peace* or Ibsen. After being told it was T.S. Eliot's cat poems, Nunn was slightly taken aback. "I had a marvellous meeting with Andrew, thank you so much for arranging it," he told Cameron. "But what a shame that he offered me the only bad idea he's ever come up with."[13] As he tossed the offer around in his head a few more times, Nunn found his interest growing, but still thought it wasn't for him. Finally, after further overtures from Andrew, Nunn was forced to admit that he'd simply run out of excuses not to do it.

Nunn was in. He did have one overriding concern, though. *Cats* was to be almost completely told through music, song, and dance. There was no book. There was no storyline. All Nunn had to go with was a collection of isolated numbers that he was certain would lose an audience's attention very quickly. There needed to be some kind of narrative thread, however tenuous, to connect everything together. The answer came once again from the Eliot archive. It was a letter describing an unpublished poem about a cat version of heaven known as the Heaviside Layer. Nunn expanded on this concept by conceiving of an

**Webber gambled bringing in Trevor Nunn from the world of classical theatre to direct *Cats*, but his talent for storytelling saved the show and Nunn went on to direct *Starlight Express*, *Les Misérables*, and *Chess*.**
**Credit: Brian Harris / Alamy Stock Photo**

annual ceremony, the Jellicle Ball, where the choice is made which out of the tribe of cats will ascend to the Heaviside Layer and return to a new life. This was to form the climax of the show, while the element of rebirth cleverly played on the idea that cats have nine lives.

This element of dance was going to be something new for the West End: "Which is why people thought we were stark raving mad," Andrew said. "At the time, we didn't do dance musicals."[14] Those came courtesy of Broadway.

The choice of choreographer, then, was a crucial one. Gillian Lynne, or Gillie as everyone called her, had been a principal dancer with the Royal Ballet until she discovered Broadway musicals during an American tour and turned to jazz dance and choreography. It was this intoxicating mix that worked so well for *Cats*, with its ballet moves combined with elements of modern dance, jazz, and vaudeville. "Her choreography was so interesting," says Finola Hughes. "And it was abstract as well. I think it was that abstract feel that removed it from the norm. If it had just been straight up Broadway or straight up dance or ballet, we'd all seen that, but she put a twist on all of those movements, and it was that slight twist that made *Cats* different and made it eye catching for the audience."[15]

Finola was among the very first dancers to be hired and, together with John Thornton, worked with Gillian for several weeks prior to the start of rehearsals building up some of the choreography. Thornton ended up originating the roles of Mungojerrie and Macavity, while Finola got the part of Victoria, an uninhibited and inquisitive kitten who is coming of age, dressed in an eye-catching white costume. "I think that they thought the character of Victoria was pure of heart," says Finola. "She's the one who goes up to Grizabella at the end. Perhaps that's why they chose her to be dressed all in white."[16]

One morning Gillian arrived at rehearsals and told Finola she'd watched her own cat resting by the fire doing this long stretch, "and there's this little refrain that's going to play throughout the whole show and I want to try and choreograph something on it for you." There was no one else in the room except for Andrew, as Gillian explained to Finola that it was very much about a cat stretching, and enjoying herself, and being into her own body, "and then Andrew just started to play that on the piano," recalls Finola. "That was a really special moment for me because I was so young, just 21."[17] Finola had a good working relationship with Andrew, who worked individually with the singers and wasn't averse to giving the odd pep talk. "He would sometimes say what he felt about the music, what it meant and what it meant to him."[18]

In the search for the best dancing talent in the country, general auditions took place in November and December. A number of people were recruited from the recent West End production of *A Chorus Line*, as well as young talent like Seeta Indrani, a graduate from the London Contemporary Dance School, making her professional stage debut, and sixteen-year-old Bonnie Langford. Bonnie was already an experienced performer, with a couple of West End appearances, when her agent told her to go up for *Cats*. She ended up doing five auditions in total, including one where Trevor Nunn made her recite a piece of Shakespeare, something all the dancers were subjected to and complained about. "I didn't mind because I'd just left stage school and done my O Levels so all that stuff was still fresh in my head. Mind you, I was running out of songs by the last audition."[19]

Others brought in, like ex–Royal Ballet dancer Wayne Sleep and Ken Wells, one of the principal dancers at the London Festival Ballet, were used to holding a show on their own but here were being asked to be part of an ensemble. It was all very egalitarian. "We were very much a group that if it was somebody's moment to shine you were there to support them," says Bonnie. "And that's what I loved about that show, everybody got their moment."[20]

What Andrew and Trevor ended up with was an incredibly diverse group of people with different styles and background in dance, along with singers and actors who couldn't really dance at all. "We were picked because we were all so different," recalls Finola, "because they wanted the cats to be individual."[21]

Paul Nicholas certainly didn't classify as a dancer and had to talk Gillian into letting him play Rum Tum Tugger, with the proviso he undertook extensive dance classes before rehearsals began. As did renowned television and stage actor Brian Blessed, cast as Bustopher Jones and the patriarchal figure of Old Deuteronomy. Jeff Shankley had recently returned from a German tour of *The Rocky Horror Show*, playing Frank N. Furter, when he attended the *Cats* audition. Trevor Nunn was so impressed by his rendition of "Sweet Transvestite" that he promised if *Cats* didn't work out, he would take Jeff into the Royal Shakespeare Company. "I floated out of the audition on cloud nine."[22] Jeff was to originate the role of Munkustrap, the leader and protector to the Jellicle cats.

Because Jeff, along with others like Myra Sands, was one of the few actors in a cast predominantly made up of dancers and singers, Trevor also requested he cover the featured roles of Growltiger, Rum Tum Tugger, and Bustopher Jones. "I got gold glitter embedded in my cornea from playing the Tugger. Twice. I also think I'm the only actor to have played Munkustrap in Act 1 and Growltiger in Act 2, returning at the end as Munkustrap for the Macavity fight and finale. That's when I was fit!"[23]

The most far-reaching appointment, certainly where Andrew was concerned, was ex–Hot Gossip dancer Sarah Brightman, who'd scored a top ten hit in 1978 with "I Lost My Heart to a Starship Trooper." She auditioned privately at Andrew's flat, arriving in a blue wig. It was the first time they'd ever met. However, the casting coup was Trevor's decision to bring in Judi Dench to play the dual role of Grizabella and Jennyanydots; both of them had worked successfully together at the Royal Shakespeare Company. The idea of putting a classical actress of the stature of Judi Dench into a musical just didn't happen. But then, who would put Brian Blessed and Wayne Sleep in the same show. "It was very inclusive," says Bonnie. "It was a real moment of individuality. We were all shapes and sizes, ages and styles, strengths and weaknesses, and that I think was really important and perhaps quite innovative."[24]

Rehearsals began in March 1981 in a church hall in Chiswick with the production in a state of uncertainty. "We went into that first rehearsal absolutely with a blank canvas," recalls Bonnie, "not knowing anything about it."[25]

On that first day Trevor Nunn assembled the cast and for most of the morning talked about the life of T.S. Eliot and the world in which he lived. Then, as it was going to be very much a case of working things out as everyone went along, Trevor declared a period of improvisation, as he put it, "getting everyone to make fools of themselves to the point where there were absolutely no barriers to invention."[26] These included workshops where the whole cast improvised being cats. Brian Blessed spent most of his time lifting his leg up to pee and other sundry naughty cat activities. "He behaved extremely badly," recalls Bonnie, "and it was hilarious."[27] Finola recalls seeing Judi Dench sitting under a table just bobbing her head in the manner cats sometimes do. "I thought that was so cool. That was awesome observation right there. Judi was just the best."[28] And because they spent that time improvising, playing trust games and bonding, the company feeling was strong. "And Trevor watched intently," says Jeff Shankley. "Like any good director he made each cast member feel that their individual contributions were valuable and vital to the whole piece."[29]

The biggest challenge was to "imply" more than was written. To create a subtext. That was certainly a greater challenge to the dancers in the company. "Perhaps they got a little frustrated with the few actors in the piece constantly asking: What's my motivation for this?!" says Jeff. "But it was time well spent and certainly helped to sustain me through the long run. Creating an inner life for the role."[30]

Trevor was prone to giving the cast homework, asking them to research aspects of some of the songs and poems and present their findings to the company. For "Skimbleshanks the Railway Cat," their homework was to research trains of the era. It was all a bit vague, and no one really bothered. It was evidence that Trevor was probably more comfortable with the actors and was having to adapt his way of working for the dancers. "He had to really learn how to speak to us," recalls Seeta Indrani. "A dancer functions in a different way. It's not all cerebral and information."[31]

A lot of things that ended up in the show were created in that rehearsal room. "Trevor Nunn didn't mess with anything we came up with and that was incredible," says Finola. "And once you've given performers that sort of space to improvise and create, and you're allowed to and encouraged, then those performers interact in such a way we completely drop our cynicism and our guard is down, we're believing all of it."[32] While the principal actors had been mostly designated a specific role, everyone else found and created their own character during the rehearsal process. And so many of those famous characters are what they are today because of a certain interpretation or something that was done in rehearsal that stuck. Or in the most extreme case even the emotional state of the actor. "One of my friends," says Bonnie, "wasn't sure about this job at all and spent most of the time as her cat being moody in the corner, and that stuck as her character. So, anybody that's played that cat since, which is Demeter, has had to basically be that character, based on the fact my friend was thinking, what the hell is all this, I don't want to be in this show."[33]

At one point Trevor collected everyone together and asked them to queue up in front of him. "He then called each of us up individually," recalls Myra Sands, "and whispered into our ear three words that described our characters. And that was a clue as to how we would behave as the cat that we were going to be."[34]

Another challenge was to evoke the physicality and behavior of actual cats, not to make them come across as cartoony, and to incorporate that feline quality into the movement. That task fell to Gillian Lynne who worked individually with each artist, correcting them, even down to the way they moved their fingers. She was incredibly exact, and her chorography was expected to be executed down to the last detail. "Although there were some members of the cast who did like to go their own way a little bit," recalls Myra, "and she had to accommodate that because they weren't going to budge."[35]

Gillian's reputation certainly went before her. She was known as a hard taskmaster and her classes, which everyone had to attend at the beginning of each day, were tough. "Gillian was a dynamo of a talent," recalls Jeff. "I don't know what she plugged into every morning but her energy was spectacular."[36] In her mid-fifties at the time, Gillie would say, "Darlings, if I can do it, you can do it." One dancer was worked so hard he threw up on the rehearsal floor. Gillian turned to a stagehand and said, "Go and get a bucket, clean it up, and we'll start again."

Paul Nicholas worked with Gillie years later on the London production of *Dear World*, a musical she directed. "Even then, and she must have been in her 80s, she took a class in the morning and it killed you and we'd all be trying to keep up with her."[37]

Originally Trevor conceived *Cats* as something very intimate, almost a chamber piece to reflect the rather charming and slightly offbeat prose of Eliot. Andrew had a much broader vision in mind and pressed him to think again. His inclination now was to stage the production in a very different environment to a regular theatre, with the view of making *Cats* an experience rather than a conventional show. "It was important that the audience should think, immediately upon entering the space, that they had arrived in cat territory."[38] Andrew and Cameron Mackintosh were immediately sold on this bold new concept. The problem was finding the right venue.

The New London Theatre was a thousand-seat house that opened in 1971. It was designed by Sean Kenny as "the theatre of the future" and acted as both a proscenium theatre and theatre-in-the-round. Perhaps because of its location, tucked away from the West End at the top end of Drury Lane, it had never put on a really successful musical and was dubbed the kiss of death by theatre producers. In recent years it had been turned into a television studio and as a site for business conferences. And it was here, back in November 1980, that Andrew was the subject of *This Is Your Life*. As filming concluded, and everyone was urging him to join the after-show party, Andrew made his excuses saying he had to do something first. He put a rushed call through to Trevor, who fortunately wasn't too far away at the Royal Shakespeare Company's then-headquarters at the Aldwych Theatre, telling him to get over quick. With no one else around, the two men scouted the place out. Finding the floor manager, Andrew asked if the revolve that changed the audience configuration still worked. "I think it does," the man said, not sounding too convinced. Anyway, the next day Andrew and Trevor returned to test it out, and it did work. *Cats* had found its home.

The building's owners, however, were not convinced. Why should they give up their steady income from television and conferences for the high risk of putting on a musical? In the end a "terrifying deal," as Andrew was later to refer to it, was brokered by theatrical impresario Bernard Delfont, who just happened to sit on the board of the New London. The deal was that if the show only ran three months, which the building's owners assumed would be the most likely outcome, the production would face no penalty at all. However, if *Cats* ran longer than three months, and for any period up to two years after that, there was going to be a payment required of two hundred thousand pounds. "And of course, nobody could afford that," said Andrew. "Cameron didn't have money in those days. I got a second mortgage on my house, and that's how we got in there."[39]

There was also the expense of converting the building's interior and front of house back into a proper theatre, as well as bringing in new staff. All of that was combined with extensive renovation of some sections of the seating and stage area to accommodate what was going to be a highly imaginative and spectacular set. John Napier had worked with Trevor on the latest Royal Shakespeare Company production, a highly acclaimed adaption of Charles Dickens' *Nicholas Nickleby*. More relevant was their collaboration on the Royal Shakespeare Company's 1976 production of Shakespeare's *The Comedy of Errors*, which was reworked into a musical comedy, and had musical staging by Gillian Lynne and also Judi Dench in the cast. "That production was on Andrew's mind I'm sure," offers Napier, "and the work we'd done at the Royal Shakespeare Company, that we might be up to doing something as bizarre as *Cats*."[40]

It's important to note here that the likes of Trevor Nunn, John Napier, Andrew Bruce, David Hersey, and Timothy O'Brien all came from subsidized theatre, places like the Royal Opera House, the Old Vic, the National Theatre, English National Opera, and the Royal Shakespeare Company. "That was our training ground," says John Napier. "Where we learnt to make ends meet and do things on a budget and be inventive because you didn't have the resources."⁴¹ This development, of people arriving from the subsidized sector into the world of commercial theatre, proved to be one of the most important elements in the success of British musicals in the 1980s. Where traditional designers and technicians perhaps relied too much on the past and on how things had always been done, these new talents came in with fresh ideas and didn't use conventional scenic devices to solve problems. All of which led to a huge leap forward in both a technical and creative sense.

John Napier arrived on *Cats* without their being a book and some of the songs not yet written. "What I had was T.S. Eliot and trying to be true to his original material."⁴² But where to place the story? Somewhere, he thought, where the cats could gather to have this Jellicle ball frolic. "So, I chose to set a musical in a junkyard."⁴³ It actually made sense, was true to Eliot's vision, and meant the cat characters could make use out of all this rubbish lying around. Andrew and Trevor were "a bit gobsmacked," recalls John when he pitched the idea, "but also completely delighted because I think they both understood that the show needed to do something that wasn't risible, that wasn't pantomimic. There were a lot of people at the time giggling at what we were doing, so I tried to make it funky and punky, and a bit rough, not too refined, but in a way that was engaging, to take people on a journey into another world."⁴⁴

In many ways John's set for *Cats* was revolutionary, this garbage dump of tires, bicycles, broken old cars, trash cans, and oil drums, all oversized props to give the illusion that the performers were the size of actual cats. It spilled over into the front row of the theatre; it was in your face, making *Cats* one of the first truly immersive musicals. When the audience first arrive and sit down, they are faced with the back of the set. As the overture starts, the revolve is put in motion and the lights come up on the set. In newspaper ads they teasingly announced: "Latecomers will not be admitted whilst the auditorium is in motion."

During the overture, the cast was encouraged to move and mingle amid the audience. "We would sit on people's laps," says Finola. "It was fun. You got to really interact with them."⁴⁵ This was an innovation of Trevor's. "Do whatever you want," he instructed, "but respectfully."

Paul Nicholas obviously didn't get the memo. When Princess Grace of Monaco came to see a performance, he went and sat on her lap. He also enjoyed going up to members of the audience and ruffling their hair. "One evening we were told Princess Diana would be at the show," recalls Jeff. "Paul Nicholas was told not to ruffle the hair of the Royal party as he usually did when he ran around the auditorium. Of course, he did. But was alarmed that when he ruffled her bodyguard's hair, his toupee came off in his hand. Princess Diana dissolved into a fit of giggles."[46]

Trevor only had himself to blame when it came to Paul. "One of the words Trevor gave me as Rum Tum Tugger was capricious, which absolutely suited the character, so I acted in a capricious way."[47] Most memorably, the Crown Prince of Jordan's younger brother came to see the show one evening, bringing with him a large retinue of bodyguards that positioned themselves at each entrance. Paul was expressly told not to approach Prince Jordan's brother. Of course, he didn't take any notice and went over and ruffled his hair. Everyone's heart missed a beat as the bodyguards reached for their concealed guns.

John was also responsible for the costumes and had fixed ideas about what he wanted and what to steer clear of. "There was no attempt to dehumanize people. It was taking the Eliot principle but saying, these are dancers, actors."[48] This was the main failing of Tom Hooper's 2019 film. The performer was totally lost amid all the computer graphics. John knew there couldn't be any hint of a pantomimic cat. "In the main they err towards human with an essence of cat."[49] Had just one critic written "this is Puss 'N' Boots to music," they were dead. "That's why I made the girls very punky and gave everyone a bit of style."[50]

The result was one of the most iconic theatre costumes ever created, consisting of skin-tight Lycra with patches resembling body fur, along with arm and leg warmers. It was while attending some of the early rehearsals that John noticed several of the dancers wearing leg and arm warmers. What struck him the most was how these gave off a sense of bulk and fluffiness. "Cameron Mackintosh has often said to me, of course if we ever do *Cats* again, you won't be doing it John because leg warmers are out of fashion."[51]

The whole effect was topped off by the performer tying a tail onto their costume just before they went on, "which if you happened to forget to put on or if it dropped off for some reason during a performance you really felt naked on the stage," says Myra.[52]

Each costume was different and brought out an individual character's distinct personality. Bonnie recalls John Napier spraying orange stripes onto her costume with fabric paint. And each performer had just the one costume. "I don't think they expected it to run very long, so it was a case of, only make people one costume," says Bonnie. "And the amount of dancing we were doing they started to fall apart quite quickly."[53] It was a few months into the run before new costumes were made. "But they were never quite the same as those first ones," laments Bonnie.[54]

With no makeup supervisor, John Napier took on the job himself by taking photographs of all the members of the cast and drawing a design of how he thought they should look. Then after a swift lesson, each of the actors did their own makeup. These were quite basic. Bonnie had some stripey lines and tendrils painted in using an eyebrow pencil, then three dots on each cheek and a little nose. In subsequent productions, the makeup became so extensive and elaborate you couldn't see the person underneath, which went against what Trevor Nunn originally envisaged. "He always wanted this weirdness of not knowing whether we were human or cats,"[55] says Bonnie, who used her own hair, strung up in bunches, with little knots to make ears and just a half wig to make her hair look stripey; other people had full wigs on. These were made by a wig maker but there was no stylist. Again, John took on the duties. "At those early performances I was in the stairwells as people were coming out of their dressing rooms heading towards the stage, running round with lacquer and bits of paint."[56]

It was John Napier that was responsible for bringing Martin McCallum and Richard Bullimore into *Cats*. John was a regular visitor to their offices in London and explained he was doing a new show called *Cats* and got them involved. Martin and Richard carried out the same job they'd done on *Evita*, although it was Richard who largely took charge of production as Martin was busy with a touring production of *Jesus Christ Superstar*.

Cameron also brought in some of his own people including Bob West. Known affectionately by all who knew him as "Uncle Bob," his career in showbusiness began working for the British singer Matt Monro before he joined Cameron in the 1970s as a stage manager, then a company manager, then a production coordinator. Bob had a knack for quietly, quickly solving problems, never losing his temper, and just being a calm, reassuring presence in the mad world of the theatre. Bob continued working for Cameron until his retirement.

Crucially, too, Judy Craymer, who remembered working on the *Cats* workshop at Sydmonton, was asked to leave her current job at the prestigious Old Vic theatre to join the stage management team. "I wasn't at all sure. Is it really going to work?"[57] In the end she negotiated an extra ten pounds out of them— not per week, but overall—and took the plunge.

Of all the songs in the show, Andrew identified "Magical Mister Mistoffelees" as the perfect lead single and got Paul Nicholas into a studio to record it. Paul did some television promotion with the song, but it didn't chart. In any case, Paul always felt there was something missing. "The thing I felt about *Cats* was that it did need a killer song. Although 'Mr Mistoffelees' was a good song and became very popular in the show, I didn't think it was *the* killer song."[58]

It was clear almost from the start that Grizabella deserved her own strong melody. Andrew felt he had just the thing. Back in the 1970s, he'd made a stab at a musical about the rivalry between Puccini and fellow Italian opera composer Leoncavallo. The idea didn't go very far but out of it came one knock out tune which Andrew put away in a drawer; never waste a good melody. Digging it out again, it was so evocative of Puccini that Andrew feared accusations of plagiarism and so he played it to several people, the last of whom was his father. "Does this sound like anything to you?" Andrew asked. "Yes," replied his father. "It sounds like one million dollars!"[59]

Paul was at the rehearsal when Andrew showed up and sat at the piano. "He had this tune. At that point it didn't have any lyrics. But I remember thinking, yeah, that's the killer song, that's the one."[60] Trevor Nunn was so moved he turned to the assembled in the room and announced, "Remember the date, remember the time, we have just heard a melody that is going to go round the world."[61]

All the thing needed were some suitable lyrics; easier said than done. Andrew and Trevor dug out some lines from Eliot and also brought in a lyricist to have a go at it, but nothing seemed to work. All they had was a vague idea of a title—"Memory."

Meanwhile, rehearsals continued but in a somewhat sporadic fashion. There were so many disparate elements to the show that progress was painfully slow, and many began to wonder whether the whole thing was going to come together in any kind of presentable form. "It was pretty chaotic," remembers David Hersey, the lighting designer.[62] There was a lot of tough and difficult work to be done on the technical side, involving ground-breaking experimentations in lighting and audio technology, along with complicated optical effects, some not done before. "There were a lot of hours," says David. "I had a couple of electricians who I don't think left the theatre building for weeks on end. They were actually sleeping in the seats. There was a lot to do. It was a long and intense process."[63]

People in the industry had said they were stark raving mad to do it in the first place, a musical about cats based on a bunch of poems, who was going to go and see that! "Everybody expected it to be a disaster," says Martin McCallum. "We used to get ribbed about the show all the time. I can remember people coming to our office and saying, 'You're doing *Cats*.' And we said, 'Yes.' And they said, 'Well, we're doing dogs.' And it became this joke."[64]

Some members of the company even had reservations. Chris Walker had been asked to come in as musical director. His take on the show was that it was an interesting, "if slightly barmy idea."[65] Chris' first task was to teach everyone the entire score in a week, which for such a complex and large-scale musical was a bit of a tall order. The score was all there, at least in some shape or form, and Chris managed to get it to a pretty good standard vocally in the allotted time.

"And then Andrew decided he wanted to change the first number, so that added an extra day."[66]

Chris could relax a bit now, thinking he could take a slight back seat, at least for a little while, as other people took the reins and moved the thing forward. It didn't quite work out that way. "I was very young and a bit green at that stage and wasn't really emotionally prepared for the shenanigans that quite often go on with a new musical," he says. "And it was also quite apparent that Trevor, this being his first musical, was learning as things went along, and so a period ensued where rehearsals were actually quite chaotic. Members of the cast kept coming up to me saying, what's going on? Where are we going? And I found myself unable to answer those questions."[67]

There were problems elsewhere, too. Abe Jacob, who handled the sound on *Evita*, was brought in to work on *Cats*, bringing with him Andrew Bruce and his company Autograph. This time the difficulty was the sheer cast number and the fact they were dancing and on the move most of the time. In all, twelve radio mics were used, more than Andrew had ever employed before. Even with that number, not everybody had one and a few were shared or swapped in the interval. A big issue turned out to be the sweat of the dancers under the hot lights, which played havoc with the transmitters, hidden generally in the small of the back. "We tried several solutions," recalls Andrew, "but the favourite was to put all the transmitters in condoms. So, the last thing you did before you put the transmitter on the performer was you stuffed it in a condom and that protected them very well."[68]

For the show Abe had insisted that Andrew buy a new mixer that was so expensive he'd had to put his house up as collateral. The thing weighed a ton, and it was a huge effort getting it into the New London Theatre. In the foyer was an escalator that took you up to the auditorium. The service lift was out of action and remained so for years. The only way to get this mixer up to the back of the auditorium was to put it on the handrails of the escalator. It took six people to lift it, and Andrew breathed a huge sigh of relief when the job was done. He then headed back to a truck parked outside to bring up the power supplies. "As I walked back into the auditorium, five minutes later, I looked up towards the mixer and there was a fire right in front of it."[69] Somebody had been welding on the front of the circle above and had forgotten to put a welding blanket across the seats, and one of them had caught alight two rows in front of the mixer. "There was quite a lot of smoke, and my heart sank because I could see people running towards it with fire extinguishers, and I thought, please, please, not over my mixer. I've just mortgaged my house for this. Anyway, they put it out, but it was a bit of a shock."[70]

As rehearsals continued Andrew detected a power struggle going on between Gillian Lynne and Trevor Nunn. Gillian was determined *Cats* be this dance spectacular, while Trevor was equally determined the show have T.S. Eliot at its center. Most of the direction, to be honest, was dance direction because everything involved dance and in the early days Trevor let Gillie get on with the choreography. "Everyone was a bit like, well where's Trevor," recalls Bonnie. "But actually, he came in basically when we got into the theatre and pulled the whole thing together."[71]

Relations were odd between Trevor and Cameron Mackintosh, too. Used to being his own boss at the Royal Shakespeare Company, it didn't sit well with Trevor having another center of power above him. "At times it was obvious he tolerated Cameron at best," observed Webber.[72]

There were also financial problems behind the scenes. Having severed his connection with Robert Stigwood, Andrew was looking for new financial backing. The agreement he'd made with Cameron was that they would raise 50 percent of the capital each. While Andrew was by then internationally known, Cameron had yet to really make his mark and found it tough going raising any money; the interest just wasn't there. Andrew too was facing similar problems and so the pair turned to Brian Blessed for help. "You've got the gift of the gab," they said and asked him to go off and see the head honchos at all the big city banks. There was never any difficulty getting an appointment—it was huge kudos having a famous actor pop in, and these bankers would listen dutifully to his rehearsed pitch. "It's a fantastic show," Blessed would start. "T.S. Eliot, one of the greatest writers. This is going to change the West End, transform it. Trevor Nunn, we've got one of the best directors in the world, fantastic music by Andrew Lloyd Webber. It's visionary and you can be part of this."[73] The execs appreciated the enthusiasm but not the concept: A bunch of cats! T.S. Eliot! I don't think so. It was the same story at every financial institution.

The capital required to put on the show was £450,000. *Evita* cost four hundred thousand pounds, which had been easier to raise on the back of the hit album. *Cats* was a gamble, a big gamble. And a tough sell. Andrew was still relatively untested, his two big hits, *Jesus* and *Evita*, had been with Tim, his only other effort, *Jeeves*, had flopped. Cameron, too, was untested. Trevor had never directed a musical in the West End, and there had never been a successful British dance show. No wonder people didn't open their checkbooks.

Despite all that, Andrew had decided to forge ahead regardless, "on a wing and a prayer." Looking back years later he was amazed he did it, "no way would I announce a musical in such an unready state today."[74]

Bonnie Langford, Elaine Paige, and Finola Hughes in Andrew Lloyd Webber's *Cats*; right up to the first preview, the cast was convinced the show was going to be a disaster.
*Credit*: Trinity Mirror / Alamy Stock Photo

In the end Cameron decided to advertise in the financial press to solicit small investments: £750 per unit. In this way three-quarters of the capital required was raised. He also went round the cast and crew looking for investments. "Cameron asked me if I wanted to put any money in," recalls Paul Nicholas, "and I said, oh no, I don't think so, thank you."[75] This was pretty much the reaction he got from most people.

Some investors turned out to be normal members of the public, including a man who wagered his life savings. The majority of these people had never put money into a theatrical venture before. Cameron got letters from people pledging five thousand pounds, a lot of money in those days. He'd write back asking if they were sure and if they were prepared to lose it. One potential investor wrote that he couldn't send a check straight away because he was taking it out of his Post Office account and needed three months. Cameron wrote to him warning that if it was that securely locked up, he shouldn't be doing this. He got a reply back: "No, I have faith in Trevor Nunn, I have faith in Andrew Lloyd Webber, and I have faith in you." For Cameron it really was a remarkable and totally unexpected public response. "I have no idea to this day why so many people, who had no track record at all, suddenly thought that this was something to do;

hundreds of investors."[76] Had sufficient funds not been raised, Andrew would surely have had to underwrite the whole enterprise. As it was, there was a point where he had to personally put in an extra fifty thousand pounds to keep the thing going.

Soon there was an even more urgent matter to deal with. One morning Judi Dench was rehearsing a scene as Jennyanydots with Wayne Sleep. "And literally there was this sound like a gunshot," recalls Bonnie, "and she went, aww, you kicked me. She thought Wayne had accidentally kicked her. But it was her Achilles, it had snapped."[77] Judi landed in a heap on the floor, writhing in agony. "And I was crawling around on the floor with her," says Finola. "I knew what it was instantly. You're a dancer and we know that sound. It was not good."[78]

Wayne picked up Judi and carried her over to the nearest chair. Instead of calling an ambulance, the decision was taken that it would be quicker to drive her to the nearest accident and emergency. Judy Craymer got the job. "We put Judi in the back seat of my beaten-up old car and I set off trying to find my way to the nearest hospital. We got stuck in this terrible traffic jam and I was swearing like mad at whoever was holding up the traffic and there was Judi Dench lying in the back, in terrible pain, going, poor man, poor man. I thought, what a wonderful person, she's in all this pain and she's sympathetic to the man who was causing the traffic jam."[79]

At hospital, Judi faced an operation and a two-week convalescence. Among her first visitors were Andrew and Cameron. There she lay, leg in plaster, profusely apologetic and telling them to recast her. Andrew and Cameron refused; they were prepared to wait.

Judi's sudden departure was a devastating setback for the whole company. Everybody looked up to her. "We all hoped she would be back," says Finola. "Andrew was really concerned. Everybody was crushed. We didn't know what was going to happen."[80]

For Chris Walker, the loss of Judi Dench was the final straw. Working with her had been pure joy. "She was the first person to say, I can't sing. And I had to explain, 'You're maybe right, but you can put the song over and make people cry.' And we had a wonderful time together. So, it was a point of great sadness to me when she left the cast, she was the one light really that was keeping me there."[81] For Chris, rehearsals were getting no better: "they were not a pretty sight."[82] This was all completely alien to him in terms of his previous experience of doing shows. "They were all happy experiences, with everybody heading in the same direction, nobody going off-piste. And everybody going into it with a quite solid game plan, of knowing how we were going to get from A to B."[83]

There didn't seem to be too much of that going on with *Cats* as far as he could see, and the stress of it all made Chris ill. "I went for something like 19 days without proper sleep. And nobody can sustain that."[84] He decided to leave.

Walking out on such a high-profile show was a big decision to make, and Chris wondered if he would ever work again. It took something like six weeks of him lying in a darkened room, metaphorically speaking, to recover from the ordeal and to be in any fit state to resume his career.

Chris was replaced by David Firman and Harry Rabinowitz. Firman was quick to size up the situation. "The show had a mountain of difficulties and issues to overcome."[85] The first clue that things were not going well was when Alan Franks, the orchestral fixer (the guy that contacts and books the band), who David knew from other shows, stopped to tell him, "I've put a thousand pounds into this. I've lost that, haven't I?" That one moment summed up what a lot of people were beginning to feel. "Many times, we thought, we're going to be able to say we were in the show that closed after the first night," recalls Bonnie.[86] Some of the cast had even begun to telephone their agents in a panic. "You could hear them in the corridor," recalls David, "where there were several pay phones, asking, 'Is there a pantomime?' They were desperately trying to find work come the winter because sure as eggs are eggs this is going to be off."[87] Others, like John Napier, were more sanguine about the show's chances. "I thought it was so bizarre in its conception that if we stuck to our guns then we would have a huge hit on our hands."[88]

While all this was going on, Cameron had brought in the theatrical advertising agency Dewynters to come up with a publicity campaign. One afternoon he invited all the creatives, Andrew, Trevor, Gillie, and John Napier to go along with him to a meeting at their office. "A lot of posters came out that were, to be quite frank, vaudeville and pantomimic," recalls John, "with pink pussycats and a lot of rainbows everywhere. We had all agreed that this production had to be something unique and original and unmusical and so Dewynters were sent away with a week to come up with something else."[89] A few days later the agency's head, Robert De Wynter, gave John a call. "I'm having terrible problems, I don't know what to do and Cameron's being an absolute ****. Can you tell me about the set, and the costumes, can we use any of it?"

"No," replied John. "What you don't want to be doing is anything literal. It has to be dark and have its own kind of mystery and magic."[90]

De Wynter asked what he meant by that. Recently John had seen a tin of cat food with a white cat's face on a white background with piercing blue eyes. "I think you've got to go dark, dark," he said. "It's the eyes. It's cat's eyes, that thing of driving along at night and seeing those lights in the road. It's something that simple that will actually draw people's attention rather than a carnival of images and mishmash."[91]

At the next meeting the agency people arrived with about a dozen posters, variations on what they'd done before, "except this absolutely stunning one of these cat's eyes on black," John recalls, "with just the word Cats written on it in white."[92] After the presentation Cameron lent back in his chair, scanning the faces in the room. "What are we going to do," he sighed. "I mean, what are we going to do! Has anyone got anything to say?"

"Yeah, I have," said John. "You missed it. I've just seen the best poster for this musical that we're ever likely to see."

"What do you mean?" Asked Cameron.

John stood up, pulled out the poster, and put it on the easel. "But it's black," said Cameron.

"I know, but isn't it mysterious?"[93]

John won the argument. That poster with those two yellow cat's eyes went on to become one of the most iconic theatre posters of all time. "To this day, you couldn't change that poster," claims John. "No more than you can change the costumes or the music."[94]

By now the company had moved into Her Majesty's Theatre to continue rehearsals on a proper stage; John was still putting the finishing touches to his set at the New London. Jeff Shankley, like Judi, had become one of the walking wounded after landing badly and ripping his cartilage. "I thought that was it."[95] Going into hospital for an operation, Jeff received a huge bouquet of flowers and a massive bowl of fruit with a message from Trevor and Andrew saying: You're the one we want. Be there for the opening night!

Given an iron ankle strap, Jeff was told to do leg lifts every twenty-five minutes to rebuild the muscle wastage. "After a few days I returned to Her Majesty's and took notes for the next four weeks, hobbling to the back of the stalls to do my leg lifts, always accompanied by the theatre cat, who watched over me. A good omen."[96]

Slowly but surely, Jeff went from two crutches to one crutch, to two sticks, and eventually one stick. "I was ready by the opening night, but my right leg would still not bend completely, so I developed a long-stretched leg for the creation of Munkustrap. It subsequently became the rather iconic stance that has remained in every production since."[97]

It was hoped that Judi would be able to make a similar recovery, especially given the fact that as the old Grizabella she was not involved in any of the strenuous dance scenes. And early one evening, when everyone had gone home after rehearsals, she arrived at Her Majesty's in a wheelchair. "And on that empty stage, in that empty theatre, sang 'Memory,'" says Myra. "I think only Trevor Nunn and a few other people were there. It must have been heart-breaking to hear her sing that song in that empty theatre. I would have given a million pounds to have heard that."[98]

Moving into the New London Theatre, the cast were excited to be finally let loose on the set. It served as a huge boost. Another huge buzz went around the cast when news broke that Judi was coming to a rehearsal, albeit arriving on crutches and rather unsteady on her feet. "It's great for the character of Grizabella if she's injured," Trevor kept saying. "Even better." He was desperate to keep her on. And Judi was determined to see how much she could do. "The set of *Cats* was very dangerous," says Myra. "We had to negotiate these ramps and planks to go onto the stage, and there was a drop on either side. Judi was walking across one of them when one of her crutches went down a gap, and that was it. She knew she couldn't do it."[99]

Judi pulling out at what was such a late stage was a hammer blow for the company and added to the woes everybody was already experiencing. A feeling went round that maybe *Cats* just wasn't meant to be.

To fix the problem of Judi's departure, her role of Jennyanydots was given over to Myra Sands. It was a character Myra loved playing. There was a line in "The Song of the Jellicles" that went "Jellicles dry between their toes." Myra had heard Judi do that before she left. "And I liked the way she said it, so when I played the role, I used her inflections completely and I always got a laugh."[100] When Myra returned years later to see the show, the actor performing Jennyanydots didn't use that inflection and the laughs were gone.

The role of Grizabella, however, could not be merely passed to another company member, and Andrew and Cameron were forced into a crisis meeting, going through various potential replacements. "I wonder what Elaine's doing?" someone said. The answer was not very much. After a twenty-month run in *Evita*, she was physically and mentally exhausted; more financially secure than she'd ever been in her life, she had decided to take time out to recuperate. After some six months "resting," Elaine was feeling jittery again and so Cameron's frantic call for help came at the perfect time.

Faced with coming into a show so late, Elaine missed out on all the rehearsals and the company bonding. She was like a new girl arriving at a new school halfway through term. Still, she buckled down and got on with it. "I remember being worried because Elaine had such a reputation," says Seeta. "And because we were all very cohesive as a company, with no prima donnas, I thought, oh God, if Elaine comes in and she's like people say she is. And she wasn't at all, she was an absolute pro."[101]

With not much time left before the previews, Trevor sat Elaine down one afternoon and went through the whole thing and his concept for the piece. "What I realized straight away was that this character, Grizabella, who had once been this beautiful and glamorous cat, her glory days were over, and she was shunned by all the other cats. Every time that character went on stage, they all left. And that's how I felt really during my whole time in the show. I felt like I was a bit of an outsider."[102] Part of the reason why Elaine in the end only did nine months in *Cats* was because it was quite lonely, with not that many people to talk to and the chore of spending most of the time off-stage, waiting, for that one big song. "But the fact that I was on my own, both on stage and off, was actually perfect for the part. But for me it was a pretty lonely experience. And not very fulfilling."[103]

After her discussion with Trevor, Elaine decided to play Grizabella with a limp. Not wishing to make it look like a joke she approached Trevor about the idea. "It's not going to look like Richard the III is it," she said. He didn't dissuade her from doing it, and so Elaine always played Grizabella dragging one leg, "because she was a bit beaten up. She'd definitely passed her prime. Lonely, loveless, probably had to go it alone all her life, I just thought a limp would point all those things up in a physical manner."[104]

Help came, too, from Gillian Lynne. The two of them had worked years before on the musical *The Roar of the Greasepaint – The Smell of the Crowd*. It was Gillian's suggestion that when Elaine came on for her big number, "Memory," with her old moth-eaten coat and bedraggled tail, she sees one of the little kittens. This kitten is dancing, and she's beautiful and it reminds Grizabella of her youth. That's really what the song "Memory" is about: reflections of a glamourous past that is now lost. Gillian got Elaine's Grizabella to try to copy the young kitten's dance, but she can't quite do it and collapses on the floor, and the opening bars of "Memory" begin. For Elaine that little moment of dance set up the song beautifully.

With the previews fast approaching, the show's disparate elements still hadn't come together. "We didn't even know if we'd get to the first night," recalls Bonnie.[105] Trevor had told everyone, "You will all be able to say that you were original cast members of *Cats*." Whether this was calculated to instill a bit of belief, the result was just a lot of sniggering. "The ice was so thin under us," recalls David Firman. "We were absolutely certain that this was going to be a six-week wonder."[106]

These were dark days, and the strain on everyone was enormous. If anything, it engendered a sort of Dunkirk spirit among the cast. "We were all in the same boat," says Myra, "and we were going to go down with it."[107] Behind the scenes, the tension was palpable with so much at stake, especially for Andrew who faced near financial ruin if *Cats* turned out to be the flop that many predicted. Sometimes the strain was too much, such as when he came into rehearsals one day ranting, "I'm going to lose my house on this!"

As the first preview arrived, Andrew and Cameron had zero confidence. They spent the hours before curtain up sat in a bar across the road from the theatre talking through their career highlights, "and how on the whole we had enjoyed our time in a profession from which we would be barred for all time in a mere few hours."[108] Despite that, they turned up at the theatre to wish the cast good luck. It was a packed house. Andrew and Cameron clutched each other as the overture thundered out, "and waited for the debacle."[109]

John Napier had an inkling of the kind of reception they were going to get just minutes before. "I'd been running around like a lunatic, covered in paint, and sweating; we had no idea how it was going to go. I was standing by the revolve and they'd just opened the doors and a bunch of young people came in, walked right past me, and their mouths dropped open and they looked around and one guy said, 'Oh, he's done it again.' It's those kinds of things that give you a lift."[110]

Incredibly, the cast went on that night having only properly dress rehearsed the first act. In other words, that opening performance was the first time they'd gone through the entire show from start to finish, not stopping for technical issues or anything else. The evening turned out to be something of a mixed bag. The first act went very well; the second act not so well. By the end of it, however, something extraordinary happened. "It was one of those things where you're sitting there waiting to get a slow hand clap," says Martin McCallum. "Instead, the audience just went wild. They loved it."[111]

The cast were just glad to have got through it without any major disasters. "We came off all of us absolutely on an adrenaline high," says Bonnie, "having got through the damned thing apart from anything else."[112] Everyone was exhilarated but exhausted. Backstage, a representative from Equity hurried the cast together to explain that he was going to inform Trevor Nunn that everyone needed rest and couldn't come in for rehearsals at ten o'clock the following morning—it was not possible. After hearing this, the cast went off to their dressing rooms. Suddenly the Tannoy boomed into life. It was Trevor's voice: "My dear, dear, dear company, you were magnificent. But we are not there yet, and I will see you at ten o'clock tomorrow morning." And that was to be the regime until opening night, rehearsing all day long, changing and working on new things—"It never stopped," says Bonnie[113]—and then doing the show in the evening. "People were on their knees," recalls David Firman.[114]

The second preview was also greeted with enthusiasm. Afterwards, Andrew and his wife Sarah Hugill went to celebrate at one of London's trendiest nightclubs, Annabels. The doorman, recognizing him, asked how the club might organize a supply line of tickets to see *Cats*. "That night I realized we just might have something extraordinary on our hands."[115]

Everything was far from perfect, though. "When we had the opportunity to run the entire show you could see bits that didn't work," says Martin McCallum. "But you knew immediately how to fix it, that it would get sorted out. And there was huge energy then to work on it. Everybody in the company was highly motivated and the evenings got better, and it just became clearer and clearer to see one's way through."[116]

The showstopping song "Memory" certainly needed work doing to it. The lyrics were not coming together, despite several lyricists having a go, including Don Black and Richard Stilgoe. Andrew even invited Tim Rice to supply a lyric. All this was rather confusing for Elaine. "I would be asked to sing a bit of one and something of another and kept getting it muddled up. I drove myself crazy for ten nights thinking, what am I singing!"[117]

Every morning following a performance, the heads of each department would gather in a room by the side of the stage for a debrief on how everything was going. It was during such a meeting that a telegram arrived from Tim Rice who had seen one of the previews. It read: "Understand you are using another person's lyrics as well as mine. Stop. This must cease immediately. Stop. Otherwise, litigation will follow. Stop. Tim." David Firman recalls everyone looking at each other and saying, what are we going to do?[118] In desperation that night Trevor went home and re-read Eliot's book from start to finish, jotting down favorite lines. After something like two hours he had come up with a new set of lyrics for "Memory" that have remained ever since.

Fate is a strange thing. Coming in at the eleventh hour to replace Judi Dench, "Memory" has lived with Elaine Paige ever since, becoming her signature tune. She is possessive of it. "I do feel that song belongs to me,"[119] even though over 150 different artists have recorded it over the years, and singing it every night was always an emotional experience. "You could hear a pin drop. Every single night."[120]

But it wasn't just "Memory" that required attention; elements of the score were being reshaped all through previews, contrary to Andrew's usual method of working. "Andrew is one of those composers who will write the show and then he doesn't want anything changed," says Chris Walker.[121] Not so on *Cats*. Andrew would scrap a passage of music he wasn't happy with or alter things. David Firman had a team of three or four copyists sitting in the green room hand copying all these new changes, crossing out stuff or sellotaping stuff onto other stuff. The number would then be performed that night in its new format, only for Andrew the next day to say that yes, he liked most of it, but he didn't like that bit at all, and that's got to go as well and replace it with this bit over here. "And you couldn't commission the copyists to start work until the cast could actually perform that new version of the song," says David. "And at that moment you had to get the fastest copyist to create this new thing and sometimes they'd be unsticking pieces that they stuck on before. It was an absolute nightmare. And you just had to try to remain sane during it."[122]

Things like this do happen when putting on a musical, but for David this was the most extreme example of it he ever encountered. "It was pretty radical surgery every night."[123] It was perhaps toughest on the cast. "They'd be something we were working on, a passage of music or a dance sequence," says Finola, "and then by the next day it wouldn't be there anymore."[124] Some of the cast would be reduced to tears, while others battled through it.

While all this was going on, Bonnie was facing her own private little drama. In the show her character of Rumpleteazer is part of a double act with another cat called Mungojerrie. They share a song and dance number together boasting about their reputation for troublemaking. This was one of the dances already set by Gillie prior to the start of rehearsals, and the dancer cast as Mungojerrie found it difficult to adapt to the preexisting moves and choreography. Then just four days before opening night, he left. "It was a very tricky and unpleasant situation," Bonnie remembers. "By four o'clock that afternoon he was gone and his picture was removed from the programme immediately."[125] He was replaced by John Thornton. For the sixteen-year-old Bonnie, this was a real lesson. "You think, oh, it can be a tough business; we're all very replaceable."[126]

The opening night of *Cats* on May 11 was memorable for all sorts of reasons. As with most opening nights, much of the audience was made up of invited guests, family and friends, agents, and investors, all eager to give out positive vibes. The only anxiety was how the critics were going to react. The performance went without a hitch until the final moment. "We'd finished the show and done our bows," recalls Myra, "when Brian Blessed came down to us and said, 'No panic, but there's a bomb scare.'"[127]

The management of the theatre had rehearsed an evacuation drill, but how were they going to get an applauding audience numbering a thousand people out of the theatre in an orderly manner. The New London's manager Nicholas Allott thought the best way to accomplish this was to get one of the actors to make an announcement. Quickly he grabbed Blessed and told him what was happening, but insisted he not mention anything about a bomb scare or do anything to alarm the audience, just with his authoritative manner ask them to leave. So, on he went, held up his arms and of course there was a huge cheer; everyone thought he was milking the applause. He held his arms aloft again, this time the cheer got even bigger. "No, no, no, no." With the cheering not likely to stop any time soon, Blessed whipped off his wig and said, "Ladies and gentlemen we have to leave now, we've had a bomb scare."

As it turned out the audience behaved with steely detachment; some even tried buying programs and ice cream on the way out. The cast were told not to go back to their dressing room but to leave the building immediately. Jeff Shankley passed his dressing room on the way out, grabbed his coat and car keys, and drove straight home. "I received some very strange looks when I stopped at traffic lights dressed as a cat!"[128]

The rest of the cast congregated outside in the cold night air still in their costume and make up. Finola was one of the first people out into the street, making sure her dad and brother, who'd been in the audience, were also safe. There she stood, shivering in her thin Lycra. "I remember a car pulled up and this woman took out a blanket and handed it to me and I wrapped it round myself. I had it for the whole run, it was underneath my dressing table. I never knew who to return it to."[129] Myra recalls the singer Marti Webb coming over to her, "and she was wearing this thin little gossamer dress, with quite flappy sleeves, and she put her arm round me to keep me warm."[130]

Finally, the all clear came and everyone was allowed back in to change for the after-show party. Even today Finola remembers what she wore for the party. It was the time of punk pirate chic, "and I looked like Adam Ant."[131] Early in the morning someone went out to fetch the early newspapers to read what the critics had to say. It was a mixed bag but there were several outright raves. Michael Billington of *The Guardian* lauded *Cats* as, "an exhilarating piece of total theatre." *The Sunday Times*' Derek Jewell proclaimed it to be "among the most exhilarating and innovative musicals ever staged," while Peter Hepple in *The Stage* declared that with *Cats*, "the British musical has taken a giant leap forward, surpassing in ingenuity and invention anything Broadway has sent us."

It was a stunning turnaround from where things were just a few weeks before. "We thought it was going to be a big flop," says Myra. "But it worked. It was just quite remarkable."[132] No one was more surprised by the success than Chris Walker. "I was absolutely astonished. It could quite conceivably have turned into a train wreck."[133] All that is true, of course. However, it is also true that the ingredients to succeed were already there: a talented cast, a great score that was full of energy and surprise, an innovative set and costumes, and incredible choreography. On top of all that was the guiding influence of Trevor Nunn who managed to bring all of those different elements together to create a unique and original vision. He added a sense of mystery, too, and an element of intellectual wonder that elevated it above just people dancing around in cat suits. And that's where Nunn's strength lay as a director. "He is so good at narrative," says Caroline Quentin, who worked with him on *Les Misérables*. "He's wonderful at staging, he knows where the audience should be looking at every moment. He can keep their affiliation going with a certain character. He's very good at that."[134]

From hardly any advance ticket sales, and seats readily available for all performances, suddenly there were queues round the block. "Ticket touts would stand outside and sell tickets at four times the price," recalls Bonnie.[135] A ticket tout agency even opened an office across the road. "You couldn't make it up," says John Napier. "And it was there for years."[136]

Had *Cats* been done just a few years earlier, it might not have worked. This was very much a 1980s show and seemed to catch the mood of the new decade, especially in terms of how dance was developing. "It tapped into and enhanced and elevated the whole dance industry," says Bonnie. "It caught the imagination. It opened just at the time the dance boom was about to happen."[137]

*Cats* succeeded because of the way it tells its story. As already noted, one of the reasons why the 2019 film version was so spectacularly dreadful was the makers stopped the artists from being human. "That was a real misconception," says David Firman. "The attraction of the theatre show is because you see humans dressed up as cats, but you know they're human. It's the same technique that was done later in *The Lion King*, you're watching human beings being something else, but what you're actually concentrating on is their humanity and identifying with them. They capture your imagination."[138]

When audiences go and watch a play or musical, they want to believe everything that is happening. And theatre is a fabulous place to escape and be taken on a journey. "I think that's why *Cats* worked," says Finola. "You put your disbelief at the door, you leave your cynicism at the door. You come in and you are part of the experience. And that is the beauty of musicals, and the beauty of theatre; just to be a child for a moment."[139]

*Cats* quickly settled into its run, and for the cast it was enormously exciting to be part of a successful show that everyone was talking about and wanted to see. "That's what was rewarding for us, that we always had full houses," says Finola. "Always."[140] Some audiences were better than others. Paul Nicholas often used to pop into Nicholas Allott's office between numbers for a quick cup of tea. One matinee he came in complaining, "This lot are dead, they are absolutely dead," only nobody had turned his mic off and it went booming round the auditorium.

Somebody rushed in and grabbed it and turned it off. Paul commented, "It's just as well they knew."[141]

Just like *Evita* before it, *Cats* became the hottest ticket in London. Every member of the Royal family came to see it at one time or another. Princess Margaret was at one of the previews. At the interval Nicholas Allott had put out some wine and champagne for the VIP guests, but the Princess wanted only whiskey. Allott rushed out of the green room to get some, only every bar was packed and the staff rushed off their feet. Allott knew where the liquor store was, but he didn't have a key. "So, I took a fire axe off the wall and smashed the door to grab the only bottle left. Of course, it wasn't the right brand, she only drank Famous Grouse, this was Johnnie Walker. She took one sip and said, 'Thank you very much,' and put it down."[142]

Myra remembers Margaret Thatcher coming to see the show one evening—she'd been brought by Denis on her birthday. "I had lines that I directed straight to her—Cockroaches need employment. To prevent them from idle and wanton destroyment—because at that time there was a lot of unemployment in the country. I don't know whether she took it on board. In the interval she was directed to the VIP office and that meant going past where the orchestra was, and apparently, she was pissed."[143]

And there were visiting celebrities: Stevie Wonder, swaying to the music in his chair, Elton John, Bette Midler, and Paul Newman. The usual practice was for an announcement to be made backstage before the show started about who was in that night, since most of the visiting celebrities wanted to meet the cast afterwards. "One evening I thought they said Clodagh Rodgers," says Seeta. "By this time, we were all a bit blasé about all these famous people coming and I remember thinking, do I really want to meet her if it means I'm going to miss my bus home. In the end I did, being polite, and I'd misheard, it wasn't Clodagh Rodgers, it was Ginger Rogers."[144] On stage after the show everyone asked if they could have a little dance with her, "because we all wanted to say we'd danced with Ginger Rogers," says Paul.[145]

There was a big brouhaha about Barbra Streisand coming to see the show. She wanted her visit kept as low key as possible, so arrived via the stage door. "When she walked in you couldn't miss her," recalls Bonnie, "she was wearing a gold turban, and you're like, I thought you didn't want to be seen and here she is with this Belisha beacon on her head."[146]

During the interval Nicholas Allott walked into the green room just as Andrew uncorked the champagne, which exploded everywhere, drowning the carefully prepared canapés. It turned out Barbra didn't want champagne; she wanted a glass of milk. Cue another desperate search by Allott, raiding fridges and the like backstage and in offices. Finally, he came across a pack of twenty-four UHT long-life milk sachets and poured them all into a glass. It did not go down well with Miss Streisand. Anyway, she left during the interval complaining of a migraine. She went on to record a version of "Memory."

As for Judi Dench, she waited several months before attending a performance. "Although I suppose I cried a little bit, I saw how wonderful Elaine Paige was and I had no regrets."[147]

As one of the most challenging and physically demanding shows in musical theatre history, the toll on the dancers became clear after the first week when the injuries started piling up. "On one occasion," recalls Jeff, "chasing after Macavity, the iron gate had been accidently left open and as I landed, full impact, with my shins on the iron bar, I put thirty-six stitches in one leg and eight in the other. Cameron Mackintosh carried me out shouting, 'I've always wanted to do this!' It took five hours to stitch me up."[148] Less painful, but more embarrassing was the time Jeff slid down the car boot to escort Grizabella to the Heaviside Layer and a jagged piece of tin ripped his costume, exposing a large amount of white buttock. "As I walked around the stage the entire cast closed in around me, to preserve my dignity and the seriousness of the moment."[149]

To keep things moving along, a full-time physiotherapist, massage therapist, and throat therapist were on hand looking after the cast like athletes. Even so, professional pride meant that it took a lot for anyone to miss a performance or be invalided out for any amount of time. "It was the toughest show ever because everyone was used to being up front and they were dancing to get the focus on them," says Seeta. "We took no prisoners on that stage. It was full out every single night."[150] There was a sign in an elevator backstage which read: "maximum seven people". Somebody had written underneath "or twenty-five cats": "because we all weighed so little by the end," says Finola.[151]

With *Cats* breaking records in the West End, every New York producer wanted a piece of it on Broadway. In the end the Shubert Organization, run by Bernard Jacobs, pounced. The original plan was to replicate what had been done in London—in other words find a venue that was not a traditional theatre. "We were thinking of trying to use a Madison Square Garden type set up," recalls John Napier, "but it was too big."[152] Finally, it went into the Winter Garden theatre, which had recently undergone an expensive renovation. More work was required to accommodate John Napier's junkyard set, and at the insistence of Andrew and Trevor Nunn the whole place was painted black.

Jacobs had seen the show in London and loved it. His only concern was over the choreography which, he declared, "sucks." Cameron was somewhat taken aback by this; it was Gillian Lynne's work with the dancers that was so much a part of the show's appeal. Jacobs waved that away; he wanted to bring in Michael Bennett, the director of *A Chorus Line*, a "genius," said Jacobs, who would do a better job. Bennett flew to London to see the show and thoroughly enjoyed it. Afterwards he met with Cameron and they discussed what Jacobs had said. "Sure, I might come up with a few better steps," said Bennett. "But I'd never come up with a better show."[153] The idea of him taking over as choreographer was quietly dropped.

For months New Yorkers were bombarded by a publicity blitz of newspaper ads, giant billboards, and television commercials asking, Isn't the curiosity killing you? The answer was palpably yes as *Cats* opened in October 1982 to the largest advance sale in Broadway history—$6.2 million. Both Trevor Nunn and Gillian Lynne went over with the production to rehearse the new cast, while Andrew shortened and revised some of the songs. The Broadway version of *Cats* was done on a far grander scale and with a much larger budget. While the London show did push the envelope in many of the things it did, especially in the way David Hersey used gobo lighting to create shapes and shadows, money was tight. The result of that was some of the optical effects were done on the cheap. At one point David had to replicate a pair of car headlights sweeping across the stage picking up a cat on the way. This was achieved by two lights rigged on a swivel over the sound desk with a bit of string that was pulled on cue to move them. In New York this effect was created by use of a machine that cost thousands of dollars to put together: "and it didn't work as well, either," claims David.[154] Things had already reached a point where David began to question in his mind, is more really that much better. "There's an interesting line between what you encourage an audience to imagine and what you show them. I almost felt it went so far in New York it was almost unnecessarily over the top."[155]

Following on from the success of *Evita*, one wonders if a sense of resentment was growing in some quarters of New York's theatre establishment that it was the British, rather than their own native talent, that had come up with what looked like the biggest hit Broadway might ever have seen. Maybe for that reason the notices were decidedly mixed, although critics had to admit the show was both innovative and visually spectacular. Frank Rich, in the *New York Times*, said the show was full of banalities and stretches of boredom, but praised its "theatrical magic" and made the smart prediction that it would "lurk around Broadway for a long time to come."

Rich wasn't wrong, *Cats* ended up running for eighteen years, a Broadway record later surpassed by *Phantom of the Opera*. During that time, it went on to win seven Tony awards. In London the production won the Olivier award for Best Musical of 1981 and in 1996 *Cats* became the longest-running musical in

West End history. It ultimately ran for twenty-one years, finally coming to an end in May 2002, during which time over eight million people had seen it at the New London Theatre. In a wonderful tribute to the enormous contribution Gillian Lynne made to the success of *Cats*, the New London Theatre was renamed in her honor in 2018. A frail and clearly ill Gillian attended the ceremony and some of the original *Cats* cast members were in attendance, including Seeta. "It was wonderful to see her again. And she was carried in on this open sedan chair by these four nubile men. They put her down and danced around her. And I thought, that's exactly what Gillie would love."[156] Andrew and Cameron were also there and must have known she didn't have long. Gillie passed away just a few days later. "Gillie was the greatest leader for dancers," confirms Finola. "A great champion."[157]

Doing much to lift both the West End and Broadway out of something of a current financial slump, *Cats* went global too, with dozens of productions touring the world. With its narrative told through music and dance, no wonder it did so well internationally; it spoke to people of all languages. Pre-*Cats*, if a show was a huge success, whether it was *South Pacific* or *Sound of Music*, a producer bought the rights to put it on and then came up with their own production, using their own designer and concept. *Cats* was the game changer because the scenery, the costumes, the lighting, and the concept was such a whole, was so unique, Cameron, quite rightly, said, if you want to do *Cats*, you do this production, and that then turns into a proper franchise organization as much as Starbucks or anything else.

Taking charge of a lot of these international productions was Martin McCallum. Not long after *Cats* opened, Cameron asked to see Martin and his business partner Richard. He'd liked what they'd done on *Cats* and wanted them both to look at his company, make it all work a bit better. Richard didn't want to do what he saw as a consultancy job, so Martin agreed to handle it himself. He'd only just begun when Cameron said to him, "Once you're here you can do *My Fair Lady*."

"I beg your pardon," said Martin.

"We're going to rehearse *My Fair Lady* and take it to Canada. Go and do the deal. Bob will tell you what to do."

Bob West was Cameron's long-serving stage manager. "So, what's the deal with Canada?" Martin asked him.

"Well, there isn't one," Bob admitted.[158]

Martin got on a plane thinking that he'd never ever negotiated a theatre deal in his life. Luckily Martin knew the American Canadian theatrical impresario Ed Mirvish who guided him through what to do and the show went ahead. "And that experience was actually very good for me," explains Martin, "because I saw how Cameron's company worked, or didn't work, and I wrote this report and Cameron went bonkers, 'This isn't what I want at all!' He was very put out. 'Well, this is what you need,' I said. 'You have to take a decision.' Anyway, I went back to Richard and said, 'That's it, I've completely stuffed up our relationship with Cameron, we'll be lucky to get another show from them, so make the most of *Cats*.'"[159] Two weeks later the telephone rang. Cameron had been thinking. He wanted Martin to join him and put into practice his recommendations. "So, I set up a duplicate of what I had done at the Production Office at Cameron Mackintosh."[160] Martin was to remain an integral part of the Mackintosh group of companies for the next twenty-two years, rising to managing director.

*Cats* was a game changer, too, in terms of marketing. It was the first show to really capitalize on merchandising as a major revenue stream. Before then, the focus on merchandise wasn't a big deal. People bought a program and that was about it. Some bright spark on the production team came up with the notion of making a bunch of T-shirts for the cast and crew emblazoned with the cat's eyes logo. Quite a few were left over, and it was decided to sell them in the theatre lobby. That first day there was a line of punters stretching into the auditorium. Posters and mugs were next and a host of other items. But it all began with that T-shirt, which went on to become the second biggest-selling T-shirt in the world during the 1980s, beaten only by the Hard Rock Cafe.

On a more personal level, *Cats* changed a lot of people's lives. "The success of it gave us all the freedom to go on and do other shows," said Cameron.[161] For many in the cast, it was the turning point in their careers. Seeta stayed with the show for a year, during which time she took acting and singing classes and went to work at the Royal Shakespeare Company. "I'm very grateful to the show. It certainly set me on the path for the rest of my life."[162] For Judy Craymer, too, it was hectic, bewildering, but above all exciting to have been a part of it. "I was looking on and didn't realize how much I was absorbing for later in my career. I met so many people on that show, and some were the people that were going to impact the rest of my life."[163]

Most importantly of all, *Cats* ushered in a golden age for the British musical. For the remainder of the decade, it was London, not Broadway, that was the natural home of new musicals.

# 3

# "THERE'S A LIGHT AT THE END OF THE TUNNEL"

At first glance, the concept of *Starlight Express* must have sounded as crackers as the one for *Cats*: a child's train set comes to life and the engines race each other to be the fastest in the world. Add to that a love story between a steam engine and a first-class carriage, and everyone rushing around singing on roller skates; it looked a recipe for disaster.

The origins of *Starlight* go back to 1974 when Andrew Lloyd Webber approached author Reverend W. Awdry about adapting his Thomas the Tank Engine children's stories into a musical animated series for television. Awdry, then in his sixties, approved the idea and Andrew began work. The material was pitched to Granada television only for the project to amount to nothing. A couple of years later an American television company invited Andrew to compose songs for an animated film of Cinderella. Perhaps with the aborted Thomas the Tank idea still percolating in his mind, Andrew decided to tell the Cinderella story using trains, with Cinderella as a steam train and the ugly sisters as diesel and electric engines. Again, nothing came of the project.

The idea remained dormant until 1982 when during a family trip to a vintage railroad in the States, Andrew saw the look of pure joy and amazement on the face of his young son Nicholas as a big steam locomotive pulled up. Back home, Andrew contacted Richard Stilgoe, the lyricist, musician, and comedy songwriter. At Cambridge Richard had been a contemporary of John Cleese, Graham Chapman, Bill Oddie, and a certain Trevor Nunn at the university's famous theatrical club the Footlights, "which gave me a fatal glimpse of showbiz possibilities."[1] Since then, he'd made a name for himself penning amusing topical ditties on the BBC news program *Nationwide* and the enormously popular Esther Rantzen hosted consumer show *That's Life*.

Richard first met Andrew in the green room between Parkinson shows. Michael Parkinson was recording two of his chat shows that day, because he was going to Australia and needed a stockpile to broadcast while he was away. On one of the shows, Richard was publicizing a tour of his one-man shows, on the other Andrew was talking about the forthcoming *Cats*, which had just gone into rehearsal. It was while both were relaxing after the recording that Andrew asked if Richard fancied having a go at supplying lyrics for the opening number of *Cats*, "Jellicle Songs for Jellicle Cats."

Richard had a reputation for churning out songs quickly. "And Andrew needed something by Monday."[2] Andrew produced a handwritten poem by T.S. Eliot about the Jellicle ball that Valerie Eliot had given him. It was written in blue ink on light blue paper. "It looked wonderfully old fashioned. And my job basically was to write an opening number that T.S. Eliot might have written, which was an interesting brief because Andrew is really good at parody. He's always been good at taking other musical styles and making them his own."[3] That was something Richard was especially good at, too, and he had great fun with the piece and did a fine job. He was offered five hundred pounds but knew the difficulty Andrew and Cameron were in raising the money. "So, I agreed to take a risk along with the rest of them. Just give me whatever tiny percentage of the writer's royalty I'm entitled to, I said—and gosh that was a good decision."[4]

Where *Cats* drew upon people's affection for their moggy, *Starlight Express* aimed to tap into the public's love affair with trains, especially the almost romantic sentiment people have with steam locomotives. Why else do so many of us go on these heritage steam trains while on holiday? "There's something about little steam engines," says Richard. "We think of them as having personalities in a way that we don't think of the Eurostar having a personality."[5] That was one of the routes in for Richard when he sat down with the task of writing the book for *Starlight*, that he didn't necessarily approach it as a show about trains: "It's about a little guy up against two bullies and the little guy wins and gets the girl in the end. It's actually a gender swapping version of Cinderella."[6] Andrew was to credit Stilgoe for making audiences believe that a railway train could be relatable in human terms. And for Richard that was all about turning those bits of metal into characters that audiences could root for and connect with. "Take Dinah the dining car," says Richard. "She is basically a mini-Dolly Parton, she's Karen Black in *Five Easy Pieces*, she's the waitress in the diner, and straight away that gives her a personality."[7]

Working closely with Andrew, Richard found him to be both a perfectionist and "hands on" in every department. "Andrew is just as great a producer as he is a composer. The look of the thing. The way the sound department works.

What props look like. He cares just as much about that. And he's not alone, Sondheim was the same and Oscar Hammerstein was half producer and half lyricist."[8] John Napier was someone else who found Andrew a hard taskmaster. "He gets a bit tense and grumpy sometimes, but I always got on with him very well. He respects what other people can bring to a project because the solutions that we find are to things that are almost undoable."[9] In that respect, Andrew always demanded from someone their best work, and that person never stopped until they themself were satisfied with what they'd done. "When you're working with Andrew don't think, well that's a good bit and that's a good bit, and we'll get away with the bit in the middle," says Richard. "You work on the bit in the middle until it's as good as the other bits."[10]

In July 1982, Andrew previewed a selection of songs from *Starlight* at Sydmonton, with a cast that included Elaine Paige, Paul Nicholas, and Bonnie Langford. At this stage, Andrew envisaged his new show as being quite a low-key affair. It was Trevor Nunn, sat in the audience that afternoon, who had different ideas. "I guess it was inevitable," said Andrew, "that after the success of *Cats* people would see in *Starlight* something different and rather bigger than I did."[11] If *Starlight* had any chance of working, Trevor proposed, it had to move away from a traditional musical theatre setting and offer something audiences had never experienced or seen before. "Trevor had a vision of what *Starlight* would look like," says Richard. "For it to work it needed to be the size it was. It's a series of train races and those train races have to be really exciting. And be big."[12]

Running alongside traditional theatre, there had always been popular entertainments, be they circuses, spectacles, pantomimes, operettas, or vaudeville. For Trevor *Starlight* seemed to fit perfectly into that category, it was, he said, "undemanding in content, novel in theme, inventive in composition and full of opportunity for spectacle and theatre magic."[13] Having worked with Andrew on *Cats*, Trevor knew exactly how he operated and what he wanted from his collaborators, that they were encouraged to find new methods of presentation, in design, dance, light, and sound. "We are all concerned," Trevor explained, "with the pursuit of total theatre, with all the elements coalescing in an experience which is involving, and above all, live—like a sporting event."[14] No other Andrew Lloyd Webber musical more perfectly suited that description than *Starlight Express*.

The first challenge was how to portray racing trains on stage and replicate that sense of motion and speed. "We had many discussions about how to do it," recalls Richard. "And because I work a lot with young musicians in wheelchairs I said, 'Really you should see these guys in electric wheelchairs and the speed that they can go.' And everybody looked at me as if I was mad."[15] In 2004 Richard did organize the first wheelchair production of *Starlight* at a college he has connections with for young disabled people. "And God it was thrilling."[16]

John Napier had joined the creative team very early on and detected a general feeling of "after *Cats* now Andrew's doing a show about trains!" "But you go along with it because Andrew's imagination, it's bizarre and not of this world, but it is original. He chooses subjects that you think, why are you doing a musical about this, and yet, somehow, he pulls it off."[17] John was taking a stroll through Central Park with Trevor Nunn around the time *Cats* hit Broadway when they saw some people on roller skates. "In particular a guy skating with a kind of boom box on his shoulder doing some pretty fancy dance work, and we both looked at each other and went, mmm, epiphany."[18]

So roller skates were the answer. It was then that Andrew recalled a conversation he'd had with the choreographer Arlene Philips in his kitchen. The two of them had known each other for years. "Andrew was a huge fan of Hot Gossip," confirms Arlene.[19] Back in 1979 Arlene was in America choreographing the Village People movie *Can't Stop the Music*. She was in the early stages of pregnancy at the time with her first daughter Alana, and there was a roller skating sequence in the film. Arlene didn't roller skate herself so one of the producers, Allan Carr, got the best skating teacher in Los Angeles to give her a crash course. "One day Allan came in to see what we had created for the sequence and he had totally forgotten I was pregnant and I hadn't got any insurance to roller skate and he was screaming, 'get the skates off! get the skates off.'"[20] Back in England, Arlene and the newborn Alana were guests at Andrew's Sydmonton estate. Over breakfast one morning she just happened to mention the roller skating incident, which obviously stayed with Andrew, and he put a phone call through to Arlene asking if she still skated. Arlene did. "Well, I'm going to do a show and I think it's going to be on roller skates. Can we meet up?" So began one of the most extraordinary experiences of Arlene's career.

In March 1983, Andrew decided to hold a workshop lasting a few weeks to run through some of the material to see if it had any chance of working. A call went out for actors, singers, and dancers that could, or thought they could, roller skate. What came through the door was a motley group of wannabes and chancers. "We saw a ceaseless procession of people lurching out of control," recalled Trevor Nunn, "heading straight for our table or at the pianist, unable to stop until they had become a crumpled heap on the floor."[21] A strict rule was brought in. "If you hit the piano, you were out," says Richard.[22]

The first time the production team actually saw somebody skating with style and skill, they all hugged each other, only for the auditionee to then open his mouth to sing and out came a monstrous noise. "That happened time and time again," says Arlene.[23] It was going to be a challenge, but then everyone knew that already. "It was surprising how many really quite good names turned up," recalls Richard, "and weren't very good because suddenly these new things strapped to their feet made it impossible for them to perform."[24]

It was hurriedly decided to expand the search and place adverts in skating magazines and in roller hockey clubs. The result of that was some of the people chosen to appear in *Starlight* were completely new to the profession. Richard recalls one in particular, Drue Williams. He was a builder from London who'd been an avid skateboarder and skater since his teens and also played roller hockey. He didn't know the first thing about auditions and showed up without any prepared music. Anyway, he managed to perform an Elvis song which went down well. And then he put on his skating boots and set off. "He went round and round the room getting faster and faster and faster," recalls Richard, "and then jumped over the piano. And we all looked at each other, Andrew, Trevor, Arlene, and myself, and we didn't say anything but we all thought, heh, maybe we're going to be able to do this show."[25]

Because of what turned out to be an interesting mix of theatricals and pro skaters, the *Starlight* company wasn't your average West End company. "But it was a lovely gang," says Frances Ruffelle. "And a lot of us stayed in contact."[26]

Frances was only seventeen when she showed up at the audition. She could skate reasonably well but was by no means expert. Frances was brought up around theatre and the arts; her mother, Sylvia Young, was the founder and principal of the renowned Sylvia Young Theatre School in London. Frances' first ambition was to be a dancer and was age fifteen when she was taken to see *Cats*. "And I just thought, oh my gosh, if only I could be in something like this in the West End, an Andrew Lloyd Webber show."[27]

The nearest she'd come so far was playing the narrator in a touring production of *Joseph*, only to be fired: "Luckily, because if I hadn't got fired, I wouldn't have been available for *Starlight*."[28] The tour had a crippling schedule, doing twelve shows a week, which played havoc with Frances' voice so when she turned up at her audition she was suffering from laryngitis. "I sounded like Bonnie Tyler, which they liked because they could hear the sort of country style coming through."[29] Frances was recalled several times. Her final audition is a moment she's never forgotten, "when Andrew said, you're in, you've got the job. I left the building and almost got run over because I couldn't believe it. I called my mum and said, 'mum they think I can sing.'"[30]

Chrissy Wickham had been practicing and practicing on roller skates, without really getting to grips with the notion of how to stop. Arriving at her audition, she did all the routines but carried straight on into Trevor Nunn's table. Asked about herself, Chrissy explained she used to be in Hot Gossip. Andrew, who had been looking constantly down at the table, suddenly sat bolt upright. Chrissy was in.

When Jeff Shankley rolled into the audition, Trevor Nunn was mildly surprised to see him, considering his ruptured cartilage during *Cats*. As a teenager there'd been a skating rink near to where Jeff grew up. "And every weekend a group of us went there and played roller hockey to impress the girls."[31] As an actor you never know what skills are going to come in handy.

Jeff hadn't prepared a song and so Andrew got him to sing "(I Can't Get No) Satisfaction" by the Rolling Stones. "They asked me to skate a bit so I took off around the hall at speed and as I approached the table where Trevor, Andrew, Arlene, and Richard were all sitting I shouted, 'Forward somersault coming up!' They rose from their chairs in alarm and as I sailed past, I said, 'I'll save that for the opening night.' Fortunately, they laughed."[32] Trevor said later that it was game set and match. It was just the quality they required for the role of Greaseball, a diesel engine that's the top dog of the trainyard, the reigning champion of the races.

By comparison Rusty is a somewhat jaded steam train, and although he's a bit of an underdog goes all out to beat his arch rivals Greaseball and Electra to win the hand of the lovely first-class coach, Pearl. He's also the main protagonist of the show. At the time Ray Shell was teaching at Pineapple Studios, a popular dance studio in Covent Garden, and noticed a poster in the corridor that was looking for young dancers that could roller skate. "I didn't go because I wasn't very young," admits Ray. "And I didn't consider myself much of a skater."[33] An American actor, singer, and director, Ray arrived in London in 1978 with his young family and was working in the music industry as well as teaching dance. "One of my students ended up going and didn't get it but said, 'You should go Mr Shell.' I happened to have a pair of roller skates left over from this music promotion thing I'd done. I used to skate as a kid but that was about it. I didn't tell the class that I was going to audition, and they called me back four times. The fourth time Andrew and Trevor came up and put their arms around me and offered me the role of Rusty."[34]

A large rehearsal space at Notre Dame Hall, just off Leicester Square, was taken over for the workshop. Everyone assembled that first morning for an introductory talk by Trevor, who explained the task ahead and asked each member of the cast to describe their first memory traveling by train.

It was on that first day that Frances was told she was playing Dinah the dining car, when Trevor explained to her all about the character. "It was then I realised I wasn't in the ensemble or chorus. I had a major role. I would have been happy with anything. So, I was blown away."[35]

The first two weeks of the workshop was basically a training camp, getting the musical theatre actors to skate proficiently, while some of the pro skaters drafted in were given, "the shortest dance training in history," according to Arlene.[36] It was very much trial and error. "I remember putting the trains together for the first time," recalls Arlene, "just getting everyone to hold on to each other's T-shirts or clothes, just seeing how long we could make this train. It was an extraordinary time of trying to put it all together and seeing what worked and what didn't."[37]

Rising actress and singer Tracey Ullman had been brought in specially to play the role of Pearl, *Starlight*'s female lead. A new coach compared to some of the other clapped-out ones, Pearl was also naive and innocent, and it was this aspect that didn't find favor with Tracey. "She did not like that character at all," confirms Arlene. "Pearl was far too sweet. Tracey kept saying, isn't there anything bad about this character."[38] Tracey also never quite got a handle on the skating. "She hated it," recalls Chrissy. "She never got used to the skating. And you just knew she was never going to cut it. But Tracey was wonderful to work with."[39]

Toward the end of the workshop, the cast put on a show for a group of prospective financial backers. "I think at that time probably the music convinced them most of all," claims Arlene.[40] Andrew, too, was satisfied, confident that it could work. "Although it became very clear early on," says John Napier, "that it was going to be difficult in the extreme."[41]

When the workshop finished, the best were chosen, the likes of Frances, Chrissy, Drue, Jeff, Ray Shell, and Zaine Griff. In the end Zaine Griff, a New Zealand–born singer-songwriter living in London and part of the current New Romantic scene, had to turn a lead role down as he was committed to a European concert tour. Frances was told to get some roller skating lessons; she'd got through purely on her exceptional voice. Conversely, Chrissy could dance but wasn't a great singer. Andrew told her that before rehearsals began proper, she ought to go off and practice singing. "At the time I lived on the Isle of Sheppey [located off the northern coast of Kent] and I found this local man, an old school teacher, who was virtually blind, and he taught me to sing using a skipping rope. He had me lying down on the floor with the skipping rope pulled round my feet, and I was pulling it up with my arms. I guess it did something to my stomach muscles because I could belt out notes that I couldn't do before. When I got back Andrew said, 'Well done, you've come back with an amazing voice. I'm so proud of you.'"[42]

Rehearsals proper began in January 1984 in a large hall in Kensal Rise, North London, "deliciously run-down," Andrew called it. "I remember they were Caribbean behind the canteen and served everybody goat curry," says Chrissy.[43] Arlene had brought in more street and disco skaters. "Some had a bit of dance training, some of them hadn't, and we worked very hard to train them vocally."[44] In subsequent productions, as the show toured the world, it became policy to cast specialist stunt skaters. There were also several new additions to the main cast. Stephanie Lawrence, who took over the lead role in *Evita* in 1981 and played Marilyn Monroe in an ill-fated West End musical, arrived for her audition able only to roller skate forward. Her policy at auditions was always to say "of course I can," even when she couldn't. Stephanie won the role of Pearl and immediately went off to learn how to skate backwards. "She had a voice that was so stunning," recalls Arlene. "Beautiful. I can't say that she was ever really happy with the show. She was so sweet natured. But definitely quite troubled."[45] Stephanie later suffered from depression and alcohol abuse and died at the tragically early age of fifty in 2000.

Jeffrey Daniel brought a touch of authentic music credibility to the show, hailing from the American R&B and soul group Shalamar. He'd even taught Michael Jackson how to do the moonwalk. Frances liked him very much. "He'd drive us all out for lunch in his Rolls Royce."[46] Adding further musical clout was the American soul singer P.P. Arnold. And there was Danny John-Jules, later to find fame as The Cat in television sci-fi sitcom *Red Dwarf*. One of the youngest cast members was eighteen-year-old Gary Love, who had the benefit of already knowing how to skate well. "My dad was a rock musician doing some album in LA and he bought me a pair of skates and I never took them off."[47]

For the entire cast, rehearsals were long hours and hard work. "It was learning how to be a team," says Ray. "A team that would keep each other safe. And a team that would look out for each other."[48] Above all it was tough. Inevitably, there were crashes and injuries, and invariably it fell to Trevor and Arlene to persuade the fallen to get up and try it again. "At first they wanted to see what skills we had," recalls Ray. "We were jumping up and twirling around. One kid did this jump, landed badly, twisted his foot and they took him out screaming. That was our first day!"[49] He never returned to rehearsals. "We never saw him again," says Frances.[50]

Most days started at 10 am and didn't finish until early in the evening. The first week was entirely taken up with dance and skating training. "We practised the skating religiously," says Chrissy.[51] Roy Scammell, a stunt coordinator on movies like *Alien*, came in to help. "He taught us the style, really," recalls Chrissy. "He was wonderful."[52] Scammell had also worked on *Rollerball*, the

1975 science fiction film about a perilous, gladiator-like sport that takes place on roller skates. At one rehearsal a screen and a projector were brought in and everybody sat and watched it. "I understand now why Trevor showed it to us," says Ray, "because the show had to have a dangerous edge to it. At the same time, we had to be able to perform it safely so it could be replicated night after night, eight times a week."[53]

All throughout the rehearsal period Frances hung on to every word Trevor Nunn said. "I was quite nervous, here was one of the world's top directors. We all had private sessions with him for our characters and he made us talk the song before we sang it so that we would really feel it as an acting piece."[54] She also felt quite self-conscious about her own ability to match the dancing and skating quality of many of the other cast members. Something else, too: back then the image for women was to be as thin as possible, and many of the women in the cast fretted about how they looked in a leotard. "And I was a little bit plump, and 18 by this time, and the company sent me to a diet doctor to lose weight, which is absolutely outrageous. The fact they even did that to an 18-year-old, it wouldn't be tolerated today."[55] Frances was on safer ground creating her character, although it did feel odd for everyone playing a train. "We had to bring in our own characteristics as the train. You had to be as real as possible otherwise the audiences wouldn't feel for you. Because I was only 18, I brought that vulnerability and naivety to Dinah, and an honesty."[56]

While *Starlight* certainly tapped into the romance people have with trains, this was a show that first and foremost was about fun and deliberately reached out to a younger audience and those for whom theatre had always been something of a no-go zone. With more of a young audience in mind, Andrew's songs reflected what was going on in the immediate pop chart more than *Evita* or *Cats* did. "Also rap for the first time on stage," says Arlene. "The opening of Act 2 was a huge rap."[57] Each song was written in a style to suit a particular character, be it electro pop for the electric locomotive played by Jeffrey Daniel or a Rock and Roll number for Greaseball. "I think what Andrew was trying to do was bring in as many pop genres of music that wouldn't normally be seen in a traditional musical," says Arlene. "Andrew loved pop music and rock n roll, he embraces all music, and that was his determination."[58] This populist approach is something Andrew has always been criticized for, but *Starlight*, perhaps more than any of his other shows, was made for audiences not critics. "Andrew often creates thinking of the way something will affect the audience," says Arlene. "As a human being he's deeply emotional and sensitive and passionate, and I think within him as he creates and feels the music, he's also feeling what he wants to reach and get an audience to feel."[59]

One big challenge was finding the right kind of performance space that could accommodate races on roller skates. The first instinct was to put it on in something like a sporting arena. Richard Stilgoe recalls spending a day with Andrew, Trevor, and John Napier in the disused Battersea Power Station. "Which at the time had just four walls, four chimneys and no roof. We all stood there in the rain seriously discussing whether Andrew should buy the place and put *Starlight Express* in it."[60] The extraordinary plan was for the box office to be located at Victoria station and the punters to get on a train that took them across the Thames, via Grosvenor Railway bridge, and alight at the power station. "But since nobody knew whether the show was going to run for more than three days it seemed to be an unnecessary investment," says Richard. "However, in hindsight it might have worked."[61]

It's not hard to see why at first the idea of an arena was so appealing. Indeed, *Starlight* works best in an arena or a custom-built stadium. For instance, in Japan it was first put on in one of the arenas from the 1964 Tokyo Olympics. And in Germany it has been performed in a purpose-built theatre in the city of Bochum since 1988. The show was virtually redesigned and constantly adapts to new technology, including the recent use of drones as lighting sources to create a cosmos effect. "Bochum is probably the perfect production of *Starlight*," claims John Napier.[62]

One of the advantages of bringing in people like Trevor Nunn and John Napier from the subsidized theatre sector was their experience of having worked in a greater experimental atmosphere than mainstream theatre. For John especially there was always this undercurrent attitude of how do we not just do a conventional proscenium production. "Prosceniums were anathema to me. I spent half my career doing away with what I see as a framework of a barrier. Back in my very early days at the Royal Court I did a production called *Big Wolf* and we literally destroyed the proscenium—and we took the stage out, as if a bomb had gone off in the middle of the stage and all the rubble had gone out into the auditorium."[63] It was this kind of thinking that was required for the staging of *Starlight*.

In the end, though, it was decided to go into a conventional theatre, but to radically alter the performing area. Well away from the West End, located close to Victoria station, the Apollo Victoria was one of the country's largest theatres, with a seating capacity of almost twenty-five hundred. To make way for John's ambitious set of a giant racetrack that whipped right round the auditorium, the theatre underwent extensive alterations. That included the removal of a large number of seats, although not too many as to make the show not worth putting on from a financial point of view. "There are always practical things going on as well as the imaginative stuff," says John. "But hundreds of seats were taken out, and that was pretty brave of Andrew."[64]

John's set was the most complex and spectacular that had ever been seen in a British theatre. "It was incredible," recalls Gary Love. "I remember seeing it for the first time and being totally awestruck. It was impossible to get our heads round it and John loved watching the skaters check it out. He had an incredible imagination. He was a genius."[65]

The showpiece elements of the set were a series of racetracks and walkways which extended from the stage out into the stalls, fully enclosing a block of seating, and at a higher level around the edge of the grand circle. There was also a giant skating bowl. In addition, there were mechanical safety barriers which rose around the tracks in the stalls of the auditorium before each race took place. "It was revolutionary," says Arlene, "because what you were bringing, in some sense, was a skate park, almost an arena, into a theatre and bringing the performers right out into the audience. That was a real first."[66]

For a lot of the audience, especially youngsters, the most memorable aspect of the show was the thrill of watching cast members racing past on roller skates at high speed. "They would put their hands out and you would just touch them when you went by," recalls Frances. "It was like a sports event."[67]

The cast of *Starlight Express*, Andrew Lloyd Webber's musical on wheels; critics thought he was crackers to do a musical about trains, but it went on to gross over one billion dollars worldwide.
*Credit*: PA Images / Alamy Stock Photo

The set also included an early example of stage automation, with a large flown bridge which rotated to connect various tracks and parts of the set together. This solved the problem of how to get the skaters up to the different levels. "You need to make something dynamic happen," says John. "Can you imagine what *Starlight* would have been like if it was just on a conventional proscenium stage, with skaters just going round and round."[68] The bridge was a phenomenal piece of equipment, "and quite radical in engineering terms," says John.[69] It was operated manually by a series of joysticks, rather like driving a forklift, and could rotate, rise and fall, or change the angle.

Other ideas couldn't be realized simply because the technology and money weren't available. John wanted cameras attached to the skaters during races and put the live video up onto a giant screen. "We had all kinds of cameras and stuff, but the imagery was just not good enough. We didn't have the budget for the kind of head cameras that we needed. Can you imagine, it would have been a bit like Formula 1."[70]

Walking on the set for the first time, Richard Stilgoe couldn't help but be impressed. "It was absolutely mind-blowing. And straight away I thought, hang on, who is paying for all this and when it all fails are they going to come to me and say, here's the bill. It was thrilling. Just the size of the ambition."[71]

When the cast arrived at the Apollo Victoria theatre to start rehearsing on the track, it had quite an effect on some of them. "Several people in the company burst into tears because it was rather daunting and did look quite dangerous," recalls Jeff Shankley. "I loved it. It was so inspiring."[72] It did mean virtually having to learn how to do the show all over again. "But we did it," says Ray. "That set was overwhelming though. You see a model and then you see the reality and the reality is like, ok, we've got to deal with this because that was the environment John Napier had created for us. We had to act as if we lived in this place and everything that we did was part of that atmosphere and that reality."[73]

It was decided that the very first member of the cast to try out the set would be Frances, since she was considered the worst skater out of everybody, something she only learned later. They also brought in the best skater, too. "I was feeling really confident and went down the bowl and landed on my coccyx and winded myself. I couldn't breathe and started crying for my mum. Trevor Nunn ran up to me and held my hand. It was the most embarrassing thing ever in my life."[74] The whole point of the exercise was if Frances could do it, anyone could do it. As it was, the gradients of the set defeated just about everybody to begin with, and the company had to dig in and master a whole new set of skills. "It took a long time for people to get used to coming down the bowl at high speeds," says Arlene.[75]

For Arlene the biggest challenge once she got everyone inside the auditorium was putting together teams for the races. The leaders, or the engines, were all male, while the coaches were largely female. "You paired up," says Chrissy. "The boys were fearless. And it was which girl could go the fastest hanging on."[76] A lot of the leaders were also street skaters, while the coaches were dancers more rhythmically attuned to working with music. The trick was getting them to work together as a couple that combined speed with rhythm. However, the real difficulty was with the principal players having to roar around on skates while also belting out songs. Take the role of Pearl: she was hardly off stage, singing duets or solos, and bombing around the circuit. "Stamina training was all important," says Arlene. "The power that they built up in their lungs to sing after having done all that running, then coming on and hitting high notes, it was quite remarkable."[77]

What the cast were being asked to do was far more demanding than *Cats*: dancing complicated choreography, counting bars, listening for beats, singing multiple harmonies, all at high speeds on wheels that at the slightest imbalance would bring them crashing to the floor. All the while wearing bulky, oddly weighted costumes and headgear. Very early on Trevor Nunn sent Jeff Shankley and a small group of proficient skaters around the track to see what was safe and what wasn't, where they needed more barriers and more rubber to cover the jagged metal. "One girl fell off the front of the stage, down the concrete steps," recalls Jeff. "She was not a happy lady. More barriers arrived."[78]

At one rehearsal, when the cast hadn't yet received their safety helmets, the bridge was brought in too soon during a race and knocked Jeff's front teeth out and nearly blinded him in one eye. "Thankfully it hit the socket bone so I only got a multicoloured bruise. Unsurprisingly the helmets arrived the next day, while I was having my teeth repaired."[79]

Complementing John Napier's set was David Hersey's lighting that brought the sensation of a rock concert to the West End stage with a ground-breaking high-energy design. This was the early days for computerized moving lights and because of the nature of the show, with the actors covering huge expanses of track in a matter of seconds, David wanted to have some moving lights to follow the action. "I got a quote for something like 10 or 12 moving lights and it was my entire budget. We couldn't do that. So, being young and foolish we decided to build our own and we built a new generation of moving lights. To develop that in a very short period of time and be able to use it in a production was quite a feat, really."[80]

The sheer complexity of installing all the lighting equipment took a full crew many weeks working day and night, and the tech rehearsals were long and arduous. To give a clue as to how big the challenge was, a standard musical back then had between 125 and 175 lighting cues. *Starlight* had close to three hundred. And David only stopped at three hundred because the lighting computer's memory bank was full.

As with *Cats*, only the main principals had designated roles from the beginning, the rest came about as the process evolved. A good example was Chrissy Wickham's character. "I smoked at that point and those were the days when you could smoke at the side of rehearsals, and it was John Napier, he looked at me and said, 'You know what she ought to be, the smoking car, Ashley,' and that was it. My wig was this chimney, and there were nicotine stains on the costume, and I was slightly neurotic, and the part just took off. I loved playing that role."[81] When smoking was banned on trains in the United Kingdom in 2005, and in all workplaces, the character's days were numbered, and it was eventually taken out of all productions.

With the need to give every train or carriage their own style and individual personality, the costumes played a pivotal role. Like most things, it was trial and error getting them right. Jeff Shankley remembers during the workshop being wrapped in black gaffa tape that was supposed to resemble leather, "which looked great but it was too restricting."[82] John Napier designed the costumes and while for *Cats* his job was to combine human with feline, now it was human and machine. "It was slightly more difficult because they were on roller skates and they had to have the bulk of a train."[83] Some of the costumes were even made from the same material that went into the construction of seat covers for British Rail.

Jeff always found John very attentive and sympathetic to the challenges and demands of the artist. "Anything too heavy and restrictive was soon replaced. I found my skates quite stiff and heavy, and they hampered the choreography, so I put them onto a Lonsdale boxing boot, which made them lighter and more pliable. I also asked for a comb to preen my hair, and later we turned it into a spanner, too, so I could tighten my nuts on the codpiece."[84]

Interestingly, because of the metallic, technical look of the costumes and the use of helmets, the sound team could finally move the radio mics from a performer's chest onto the head, a much more preferable location. As a result, *Starlight Express* was the first West End show to feature head mics, and the first time in any production anywhere that all cast members wore them. Before mics were just too big to ask a performer to wear them anywhere on the head. "As luck would have it this sub miniature microphone, called the Sennheiser MKE2, came out just in time for *Starlight*," says Andrew Bruce.[85]

These new mics were road tested by Andrew at his Autograph studio, along with *Starlight*'s sound engineer Martin Levan. Andrew also involved his wife, Siobhan McCarthy. "We put her in the studio for a couple of afternoons and stuck mics all over her head and recorded multi-track while she sang and then compared the various mic positions. The middle of the forehead won hands down. It was a much more natural sound, you could get much more level before feedback, so that clinched it."[86] The practice of using head mics has become the norm ever since for theatrical productions.

It was on a question of sound that the opening night of *Starlight Express* descended into disaster. In the United Kingdom, the use of any radio-transmitting device was required to be licensed. At that time theatres were classified as a "general user," and only four radio frequencies were made available to them. As the musicals typified by Andrew Lloyd Webber grew in size, four frequencies just weren't enough and it became common practice to use, illegally, the frequencies that were assigned to television and radio broadcasters. Andrew Bruce and his fellow sound technicians could hire these radio mics from a local company who manufactured them mainly for the broadcasters, but were happy to rent them to the show's equipment suppliers. "We knew these radio mics were illegal," says Andrew. "But we had no choice. And we used them in the full knowledge that we would not be interfered with nor, due to the extremely low power of the transmitters, would we cause interference to the broadcasters unless they were actually broadcasting in the same building as us, which was very rare."[87] To avoid any mishaps, cooperation existed between theatres, the rental companies supplying the sound systems and broadcasters. If there were due to be any outside broadcasts the television or radio engineers would ask which of their illegal frequencies the theatre show was using and make sure to keep away from them.

This was the case on *Starlight*, and everything was working fine when previews began in March. Then it was announced that Her Majesty Queen Elizabeth and Prince Philip wanted to attend a performance. "That absolutely blew us all away," recalls Chrissy. "It was the ultimate, really."[88] Andrew's shows were now getting the Royal seal of approval, not quite by appointment composer of musicals to Her Majesty Queen Elizabeth, but close. Obviously, the establishment, be it royalty or the political class, can't have failed to notice that the success of these shows, especially abroad, was doing an awful lot for Britain's prestige.

Another repercussion of the queen's visit was to introduce a note of caution into the cast according to Ray. "All of us were very conscious that she was there, so we made sure that we didn't fall. None of us wanted to fall over in front of the queen. We put on a great show, but it was a very careful show."[89]

The presence of Queen Elizabeth turned this particular preview into a gala event, with much attendant fanfare. The royal couple sat alone, along with their bodyguards, in the paddock area, the square in the middle of the stalls that the cast used to skate round. After the performance, everyone assembled on the stage to meet and greet the royal party. "The Queen had a beaming smile when we met her so I think she enjoyed the show," recalls Jeff Shankley. "But I didn't think she'd be rushing out to buy a pair of roller skates any time soon."[90]

Chrissy was standing there on stage, excited, when Sarah Brightman, her old friend from Hot Gossip days, came racing over. Sarah had recently divorced her partner, as had Andrew Lloyd Webber, and the tabloids had been alive for some time with stories about their affair, which began during *Cats*. Sarah wanted to reveal to Chrissy that she and Andrew had got married that afternoon. "I was one of the first people to find out."[91]

Not surprisingly, Queen Elizabeth's visit was covered by every single broadcaster, both independent and the BBC. This necessitated a big meeting where Andrew Bruce and his staff explained the illegal frequencies they were using, and the broadcasters promised to stay off them. The gala went off without a hitch. Opening night was a different story.

*Starlight Express* opened on March 27. As preparations went into overdrive for the big day, Andrew Bruce was told that a reporter from the BBC would be in the lobby at the end of the show doing a live broadcast, apart from that there was no other information. "It didn't occur to us to go looking for him," says Andrew. "We had so many other things to think about."[92] Come opening night, everyone was anxious. Gary Love recalls standing in the wings in the dark with Danny John-Jules, ready to roar out onto the stage for the opening number. "We were so nervous standing there waiting for the music to start, we held hands tightly!"[93]

The first act passed off with no problems, and everyone breathed a huge sigh of relief as the interval was called. Andrew had installed a spectrum analyzer backstage with one of his engineers watching it the whole time making sure all the transmitters for the radio mics were behaving properly. With the second act just about to start, Andrew was made aware that something very big on the spectrum analyzer had just popped up. Andrew checked, and sure enough there was a gigantic spike, as luck would have it, right in among all the principals, not the chorus, but the principals. God, thought Andrew, this is an outside broadcast van, and they haven't got in contact with us. Andrew ran outside and began a desperate search for anything that looked remotely like a radio car or an outside broadcast van. He did a double circuit of the streets around the Apollo; there was nothing to be seen. "Meanwhile I could hear over the walkie talkie they'd started the second act and it was beginning to fall apart, as expected with a high-power transmitter interfering with all those very low power devices on stage."[94]

Andrew was about to go back in the stage door when he looked down a side street and there was a converted ice cream van that had a big aerial sticking out of the roof. Running over he knocked on the glass window. The guy inside looked up from his paper, "Yeah. What?" Andrew asked if he was transmitting. He was. "Is there any chance you can switch your transmitter off," said Andrew, "because right now it's ruining the show."

"It can't be, I'm on a legal frequency."

"Yes, we're on illegal frequencies, but basically you are ruining the show you've come to cover, please switch off."

"I can't do that," said the man.[95] Further pleadings from Andrew and the engineer agreed to phone the control room at Broadcasting House to ask if the transmitter might be switched to low power. This took a while, and the level was reduced but it made no difference. "So, we had a complete disaster during Act 2 of the opening night of *Starlight Express*," confirms Andrew. "And on my birthday."[96] According to Arlene, to combat the sound issues, some of the cast had to skate around with hand mics, "which was not ideal."[97]

This incident perhaps had a bearing on why both Andrew Lloyd Webber and Trevor Nunn wrote letters in support of theatres requiring a special dispensation to use more frequencies; otherwise, they argued, theatre as they were developing it, with bigger and more complex productions, would be dead. It took a couple of years, and more lobbying on behalf of the industry, but things did get changed.

Despite opening night problems, audiences flocked to see the show and loved it. Opening night audiences are not always a good indicator of how the show will actually be received anyway. "They seemed to enjoy it on opening night and made all the right noises," recalls Jeff. "But it was nothing compared to when the general public came. They took the roof off with applause and gave a standing ovation every night."[98]

At that time there were standing areas at the back of the theatre, in the stalls and the circle. "So young students and fans of the show would pack out the theatre," recalls Arlene. "There were queues for standing every night. And it was just so thrilling the screams and shouts coming from the audience."[99] It really was half sporting occasion and half show with people picking sides during the races and cheering them on.

Certainly, the public liked it far more than the critics. *Starlight* was labeled as a triumph of theatrical style over content and symptomatic of a certain type of musical that was all about spectacle, mechanics, and technology. John Napier always resented that kind of criticism. "Yes, theatre is about the voice and the words, but that doesn't mean they're just speaking with a black surround. You've got to give the audience something they can respond to."[100] Things like the bridge in *Starlight*, the barricades in *Les Misérables*, or the helicopter in *Miss Saigon*—these are designed to give the audience, yes something spectacular, but also a meaningful moment.

*Starlight* was never meant to have some great intellectual content anyway. And Andrew and Trevor's hope that it might work as an introduction to a new generation of theatregoers who perhaps never considered going to the theatre before was achieved. "A lot of kids probably got more into theatre because it was something fun," says Frances. "It's really important to take young kids to see something they're going to really love and not something that's going to be too heavy."[101] Back in 1984 that show was *Starlight Express*. "I've got two sources of real pride regarding *Starlight*," says Richard Stilgoe. "The number of children who said it was the first time they went to the theatre and really enjoyed it and wanted to go and see something else. And I'm thrilled to have been part of that. And I'm also thrilled that in 1984 certainly more than half of the black actors who were working in the West End were working in *Starlight*. Now you can colour blind cast almost anything, but back then because they were all trains it didn't matter where anybody came from."[102]

Celebrities flocked to see the show: David Bowie with his son and Stevie Wonder. "He came and sat in the front row," recalled Frances, "and he just moved around to the music the whole time, it was lovely."[103] When Michael Jackson attended a performance, there was a scrum of press and fans outside the theatre. "As soon as the audience realized he was there, the roar was amazing," recalls Ray. "We were standing backstage thinking, 'we've got to follow that?'"[104] After watching the show Jackson asked to meet some of the cast in the wings. "He wore a mask and gloves and spoke in a whisper," recalls Chrissy. "That was incredible meeting him."[105]

Charles and Diana came to see it, the princess blushing and giggling and trying not to laugh at the makeup running down Jeff Shankley's face when the cast met the Royal couple afterwards. "Such a wonderful memory," he says. "Prince Charles found it all a bit silly, although he liked the music. I think Princess Diana would have loved a turn around the track!"[106]

Cliff Richard was a huge fan and according to Chrissy saw it upwards of ten times. "He absolutely loved it. There were rumours that he really wanted to take over from Jeff and be Greaseball."[107] At a special midnight charity show put on to raise money for the Ethiopian famine crisis, Cliff Richard did appear on stage with the cast. "We rode down the bowl, round the bowl and round the paddock with him in the middle," recalls Chrissy. "It was brilliant because he made a speech and everybody there was putting money into buckets. That was a really great night."[108]

With such a physically demanding show accidents were inevitable. Arlene herself had a nasty fall coming down a ramp that left her shaken and in great pain. Chrissy admits to still paying the price today of being in *Starlight*. "I snapped my cartilage. I was 25 at the time, and I had to have that knee replaced. There were a lot of falls. I also broke two fingers and my thumb and my wrist. But I wouldn't change a thing."[109] During the run Jeff had a concussion twice and an x-ray of just about every part of his body. "I displayed them in my dressing room and had regular exhibitions."[110]

It wasn't just the skating that was the issue. Having to dance in such heavy costumes meant that people were breaking down all the time with knee and ankle problems. "Nobody that I have spoken to says their body has ever been the same since," says Gary Love. "I have no cartilage in either knee because of the show! Ouch!"[111] All of this happened in the time before health and safety really got serious with these kinds of things, unlike today where on big productions everything on the set has so many preventative measures. "I think if health and safety had been around when we first did *Starlight Express*, I just wonder whether we could have done the things that we did," claims Arlene.[112] To be fair, there was a lot of after-care given to the performers. Ray Shell recalls that after every ten or fifteen shows trainers would come in to make sure people were okay, check their muscles, and look for any sprains or problems. "The company spent a fortune on physios."[113] Ray thinks he had something like four understudies.

Aside from the daily wear and tear, there were other hazards, too. Discipline was essential. Stopping in the wrong place, a split second's distraction, or a lapse in concentration could result in injury or a fellow skater smashing into you. "It was so important that you knew exactly where you were on that stage all the time," says Arlene.[114] That went for backstage, too, where standing in the wrong place in the semi-darkness could get you floored by someone zooming on or someone hurtling off. "You had to know the set inside out, back to front," says Arlene. "And there was a whole backstage show you had to learn as well. And if there was a crash you had to know exactly who went where and how it was caused, who came too close to whom."[115] In order to reduce accidents, marshals were later brought on stage at the start and end of every race.

Ironically, given all the injuries and technical complexities, the show was only ever canceled once. That was when it rained so badly that water was coming in at the back of the theatre and getting onto the tracks making it too hazardous to perform.

Despite the physical strain of it all, there was a terrific spirit within the company, with some real characters. "It was a great cast," recalls Gary Love. "Jeff Shankley was a wonderful father figure to us all."[116] Ray Shell was another favorite. "He was so committed every night," says Frances. "And so lovely as well."[117] Jeffrey Daniel left perhaps the biggest impression. "We'd all come to the theatre on the tube and he'd have a white limo parked outside," says Chrissy.[118] Daniel was also responsible for arranging for his friend Michael Jackson to see the show. Then, unexpectedly, he walked off the show. "He just disappeared," recalls Frances. "He didn't tell them he was leaving. He just didn't turn up halfway through his contract. And he left without cashing a pay cheque."[119]

Playing the role of Electra, a futuristic engine, it was decided that Jeffrey's song, "AC/DC," be put out as a single. It failed to chart. Indeed, the score from *Starlight Express* failed to have the same kind of impact as either *Evita* or *Cats*. Even so, for Chrissy one of her highlights was recording the cast album. "I'd never sung on an album. I'd never been in a recording studio. There was a huge orchestra and we all had our own microphone and when Ray Shell started to sing the part of Rusty, I just cried all day long. It was something I'll never forget."[120] The royalty checks from the album came in handy, too, for Chrissy. "It helped build a few nurseries."[121]

Andrew was initially reluctant to take *Starlight Express* to New York, fearing a backlash after the success of *Evita* and *Cats* as a "Brit on Broadway." He wanted to tour the show across America, in a huge marquee. Instead, producer Jimmy Nederlander made an offer to put *Starlight* into the Gershwin Theatre where it finally opened in March 1987. Andrew now had a record three shows running on Broadway at the same time. And if he did fear a backlash, that here was this outsider taking over that most American of art forms, the musical, and doing it better in their own backyard, John Napier never sensed it. Indeed, he was personally embraced by the Broadway fraternity. "I can't remember there being any kind of cynicism or jealousy or anything. Maybe it was because they recognised that they were going to make a lot of dough."[122]

The Broadway production of *Starlight* differed extensively from London. The set and costumes were reworked, presenting a race running across a "miniature toy-land America festooned with landmarks, from the Golden Gate Bridge to the New York skyline," reported the *New York Times*, that "lit up like a pinball machine." Changes were also made to some of the songs and choreography. And yet the Broadway version never reached the same imaginative scale of its UK counterpart. "Because nobody on Broadway was willing really to gut a theatre in the same way that we had with the Apollo," says Richard Stilgoe. "And so, the trains didn't venture out into the audience in the same way."[123]

While *Starlight* made money, it came nowhere near the heights of *Evita* nor *Cats* and ran on Broadway just under two years. Back in Britain, the show proved more durable, becoming the ninth longest-running theatrical production in West End history, having been performed over seven thousand times before closing at the Apollo in 2002. Again, there were touring productions all over the world and far from remaining faithful to the original, *Starlight* is a show that has constantly reinvented itself. This is mainly due to the fact that it was very contemporary in 1984 and anything that's very contemporary is in danger of dating. If you write something timeless, like *My Fair Lady*, it shouldn't be touched, but *Starlight* was very much of its time and so every now and again it has been brought up to date. "It was re-written in 1994," says Richard Stilgoe, "and another rewrite quite recently because Andrew's daughter went to see it in Bochum for her 21st birthday and said the attitude to women in this show is just antiquated and disgraceful. So, we sat down and did quite a lot of rewrites and made all the women's roles much stronger and it made the show much better."[124]

Richard has a very good theory as to why the show has endured for so long. "It is the combination of big spectacle and a small human story."[125] *Starlight* began, of course, as something Andrew may have preferred to have done on a smaller scale. Instead, it became this huge gargantuan thing that went on to gross over a billion dollars worldwide. Almost as an antidote, Andrew turned to composing something totally different next, of all things a Requiem Mass.

Audiences loved it, though. And so did the cast, some of whom stayed on with the show for as much as twelve years. "It was an incredible feeling being at the centre of the biggest show in the world at that time," says Ray. "It was a big responsibility."[126] For Chrissy, and many of that original cast, there was something special about that first year. "And I know because I went back four years later and looked after the cast as a production supervisor and it just wasn't the same."[127]

For Arlene it's a particularly special show and one of the toughest things she's ever been through because so much of it was an experiment with nothing quite like this ever having been attempted before. And it's never really gone away, either, with her being asked to choreograph so many of the foreign productions and the updated versions. "In a way, bizarrely, *Starlight* has become my second home because it's been with me for such a long time."

# "I DREAMED A DREAM"

A trip to the theatre as a student in Paris to see a touring production of *West Side Story* changed the course of Alain Boublil's life. It was the first musical he'd ever seen. He didn't sleep that night and couldn't stop talking about the show for weeks, marveling at the genius of updating Shakespeare's *Romeo and Juliet* to 1950s New York. Despite having no musical background to speak of, Alain decided, "This is what I've been wanting to do all my life."[1]

Born in 1941, Alain was the son of a shopkeeper and raised in a French and Jewish community in Tunis, the sprawling capital of Tunisia, then under French rule. As a child he enjoyed writing and staging little sketch shows, bringing in local kids to act in them, and at school excelled at French literature and history. When he turned eighteen, he left for Paris to pursue a business degree.

The American musical really had no heritage in France. Musicals on film were popular, but there was no real tradition of stage musicals coming in from abroad and doing that well; the production of *West Side Story* Alain saw did not last long. Finishing his studies, Alain had no intention of a career in business; he wanted to work in the music industry and got a job at a radio station. A lover of French singers and jazz, along with the emerging musical revolution spearheaded by the Beatles, Alain's knowledge and instinct for picking out hit songs brought him to the attention of a record company. Hired to head up their publishing department, Alain began dabbling in writing song lyrics and one day heard on the radio a song that so intrigued him he had to find out who the composer was. His name was Claude-Michel Schönberg. The year was 1968.

Claude-Michel was born in 1944 in France to Hungarian Jewish émigrés; his father was a piano tuner and a member of the French Resistance during the war. Since childhood, Claude-Michel was attracted to opera; by the time he was seven years old, he knew *Madame Butterfly* by heart. A singer in a local band, Claude-Michel came to Paris and found himself working for a record label as a writer and producer. Like Alain, Claude-Michel admired American musicals and had grown frustrated with the restrictive parameters of the traditional three-minute pop song. Both looked to express themselves in a different way.

In 1972, Alain was invited to the Broadway opening of *Jesus Christ Superstar* and found it to be equally as overwhelming an experience as when he first saw *West Side Story*. "Afterwards I wandered the streets of New York all night in a daze."[2] The thought seized him to create something equally compelling, and he proposed to Claude-Michel that they create a piece of musical theatre revolving around the French Revolution. Borrowing the strategy of Tim Rice and Andrew Lloyd Webber, it was produced first as a concept album, and its success drew the interest of a producer. The rock opera *La Revolution Francaise* opened at the huge Palais des Sports in Paris in October 1973 and to everyone's surprise, not least Alain and Claude-Michel's, it was a big hit. Encouraged, they envisaged their next work together being on an even grander scale.

In 1977, Cameron Mackintosh mounted the first West End revival of *Oliver!* and one of those who came to see it was Alain. As he sat in the stalls watching the Artful Dodger and sundry other Dicken's characters, an image popped into his mind, that of Gavroche, the boy who lives on the streets of early 1800s Paris in Victor Hugo's novel *Les Misérables*. As he continued to watch, more characters from Hugo's literary masterpiece took over the stage, Valjean, Javert, Cosette, the experience was like, he said, "a blow to the solar plexus." The next day he found a copy of Hugo's novel in a secondhand bookstore and began taking rough notes.

Back in Paris, Alain shared his thoughts with Claude-Michel and both decided to set Hugo's most famous work to music. It was a huge risk. People said they were crazy to even attempt it, and maybe they were. Not only was this one of the most cherished works of French literature, it was going to be a gargantuan job. Hugo's tale of injustice, heroism, and love was twelve hundred pages long, so just reading it was something of a feat. It follows the fortunes of Jean Valjean, an escaped convict determined to put his criminal past behind him. But his attempts to become a respected member of the community is put at risk by the dogged pursuit of the police inspector Javert.

Feeling emboldened, both men left their jobs and followed a pattern of working they were not to deviate from for the rest of their careers: Alain would write the book and lyrics, Claude-Michel the music. Again, the strategy was to bring out a concept album first. Casting around for someone to orchestrate the score,

Alain asked a colleague, British record producer Mickie Most, if he could suggest someone that had a background in movie scoring. "We want the sound to be quite cinematic," said Alain. "But we also want someone that has worked in contemporary chart music."³ Most suggested John Cameron, an experienced film composer who had also worked with bands like Hot Chocolate and Heatwave. "I went over to Paris and they sat me down," John recalls. "Claude-Michel doesn't write or read music so essentially, he'd put the whole thing on to tape with him impersonating half of Paris and murdering pianos. It was quite a bewildering several hours trying to get my head round this thing, all in French of course. And I remember sitting on the plane back to London thinking, I've got a headache and I think I said yes."⁴

Over the next few days John listened to the tapes constantly, at home and in the car, "and I thought, this is over the top melodramatic French stuff, but it's great over the top melodramatic French stuff. And it started to grow on me because at that first listen there was so much to take in."⁵ Recorded at CTS Studios in Wembley with British musicians, the album sold well enough for Alain and Claude-Michel to get financial backing to mount a stage production. John was again asked to come in and orchestrate it. "What we tried to do with the show was to create the ambience and the feeling of a movie."⁶

*Les Misérables* opened in September 1980 at the Palais des Sports in Paris. Andrew Bruce had been called in late in the day to sort out a few sound issues and remembers it as a sprawling production. "The set was huge. It was almost 60 metres across. You almost had to run from one side to the other. It was absolutely gigantic."⁷ It was directed by Robert Hossein, a French actor and director. "He was incredibly passionate about the way he directed," says Andrew. "I don't think I've ever worked with anybody so passionate."⁸ It was also very different to the production that eventually landed in London and played around the world. "It had the most stunning finish to it," says John. "Valjean says to Marius and Cosette something like, he who loves his wife, loves God, then throws his arms in the air and dies to the most humongous storm, accompanied by all the rebels on the barricades, and these barricades are basically like stainless steel crucifixes. It's the most nihilistic finale, and the whole place stopped at the end of it, nobody applauded for about 30 seconds. They were so stunned."⁹

John has never forgotten that opening night, nor when he returned a month or so later to see how things were going and there were hundreds of coaches turning up full of people. "Suddenly we thought we've got something here. It was very exciting, and I still look on it as the real birth of *Les Misérables*."¹⁰

Then heartbreak: due to a preexisting booking that the venue had to honor, the show was pulled in mid-December. "The reason we came off was because

**The barricade in *Les Misérables*, like the helicopter in *Miss Saigon*, was criticized as indulgence, but was designed to give the audience, yes, something spectacular, but also a meaningful moment.**
*Credit*: **Donald Cooper / Alamy Stock Photo**

of the Russian State Circus," laments John. "And we were selling out every night."[11] The problem was, having dismantled this huge set, nobody felt like spending the money to put it on anywhere else. So, instead of building on the show's success, momentum was lost. "It just disappeared," says John. "We couldn't get arrested with it."[12] Alain and Claude-Michel had no option but to return to their day job, writing for the French pop market.

As for John and Andrew, they returned to London. John recalls the occasional lunch meeting with a few producers desperate to bring *Les Misérables* over to the United Kingdom, but they could never raise sufficient funds. Andrew went one better. While the show was still running in Paris, he brought the album back with him and contacted Martin McCallum, Cameron Mackintosh's right-hand man. Andrew put the LP on a turntable, "This is the most fantastic musical I've ever worked on," and told him to listen to it. "Martin listened for about five minutes and went, yeah. Whatever. And that was that."[13] Andrew played the album to other people, too, in a bid to raise awareness, but without success.

It took a young Hungarian director called Peter Farago, who had failed to develop an English language version of *Les Misérables* himself, to finally get the ball rolling. In November 1982, he told Cameron Mackintosh to listen to the cast album, and that anyone mad enough to turn T.S. Eliot's cat poems into a musical would surely take on this new challenge. The record lay around Cameron's London flat until one Sunday afternoon, with nothing much better to do, he put it on. Even without a good command of French, Cameron recognized that this was something very special indeed. After listening several more times he tracked Alain and Claude-Michel down. "I think you have written something very exceptional," Cameron told them down a phone line. "You may not realise it, but I need to come to Paris and see you." There was a slight pause on the line. "By the way, I'm the producer of *Cats*."[14] At the time that didn't mean an awful lot. Alain later admitted that he didn't know who Cameron was.

The three men met for the first time in a Parisian restaurant early in 1983. Cameron knew both men had a reputation for being difficult; indeed, he recalls that, "Claude-Michel pretended to speak no English as he sized me up."[15] However, by the end of the meeting they'd all agreed to work together.

From the outset Cameron wanted Trevor Nunn to direct. He'd watched how Trevor created a hit show out of chaos with *Cats* and recalled his Royal Shakespeare Company (RSC) adaptation of *Nicholas Nickleby*, co-directed with John Caird in 1980, that was over eight hours long and shown over two evenings. The Dickens novel shared many similarities with *Les Misérables*: not just its mammoth length, but historical setting and multitude of characters and subplots. Trevor Nunn really was the obvious choice.

Invited to Cameron's flat for a meeting and to listen to the album, Trevor confessed he'd never actually read the novel. That didn't matter, as Cameron explained the main dramatic thrust of the story, about this convict pursued for years by an obsessed policeman, was a nineteenth-century version of the old American television series *The Fugitive*. Trevor was to learn later that Cameron hadn't read the novel either, but his rather simplistic synopsis left a huge impression "of a very simple, theatrical, dramatic motor force. And I suspect that stayed with me longer than the impression of the original recording."[16]

After the meeting Cameron gave Trevor a tape of the album to take with him but then didn't hear anything for several months. Fearing he may have taken on another job, Cameron chased up the director and they held more talks. All this time Cameron sensed a hesitancy on Trevor's part to commit. Then, out of the blue, came a phone call: "I keep listening to the tape in my car and can't get the tunes out of my head," said Trevor. "I'll do it!"[17]

Trevor's acceptance came with two provisos, both non-negotiable. First, that John Caird be brought in as co-director, and secondly, that *Les Misérables* be a co-production with the RSC and put on at the company's home in the Barbican Centre before any West End transfer. In this way Trevor could establish a degree of control over the process which he already knew, having done *Cats* and *Starlight*, he wouldn't have if he went out and just did it in the commercial world. Cameron agreed.

*Les Misérables* was actually a perfect fit for the RSC. While there may have been a few dissenting voices about the company taking on something from the commercial world, along with a feeling that Cameron was using the prestige of the RSC and that Trevor was allowing it to be used, the RSC itself was not averse to doing a whole range of content. For example, some of their more popular shows had recently transferred to Broadway, notably *Nicholas Nickleby* and a production of *All's Well That Ends Well*. Another recent West End hit for the RSC was a production of *Once in a Lifetime*, Moss Hart and George S. Kaufman's comedy about early Hollywood. However, *Les Misérables* was certainly on a scale that the RSC had never attempted before. And so, approaching it as a co-production, with the RSC putting their standard production budget into the show and that being augmented by Cameron's backers, was a very ground-breaking thing to do. Financially the RSC were to do very well out of it, too.

One of the first things Trevor Nunn and John Caird did was a scene-by-scene breakdown of the proposed story elements, a detailed synopsis which the actors later came to call "the bible." Another early decision was that the whole production be mounted on a revolve so the story could be told in a fluid, almost cinematic way, with one scene moving quickly to another. David Hersey's lighting was another tool that was used. "We had to be able to go from one scene to the next scene with a tiny change onstage, and a scene change actually happening but the audience not seeing it, people disappearing into the dark, only coming into light when you need them. The whole flow of all that was a huge challenge."[18]

It was also clear that a literal translation of the original French production just wasn't going to work. The only feasible approach was to go back to the novel and create a new show almost from scratch. This came as something of a shock to Alain and Claude-Michel. "What you did is a draft for French people who know the book," Cameron told them. "If you want this show to be produced in England for international audiences who are not familiar with the book, you have to rework the show."[19] Having gained full confidence in their new collaborators, Alain and Claude-Michel accepted what needed to be done. Often at meetings they would be the first to say to forget about the French version. The next question was: who should do the new adaptation?

Jonathan Miller had just staged an extraordinary version of Verdi's *Rigoletto* at the London Coliseum, transplanting the action from sixteenth-century Italy to the mafia world of Lower Manhattan. It caused a sensation and drew in audiences who had never been to an opera house before. Cameron was especially taken by the fresh, contemporary English lyrics, adapted from the Italian by James Fenton. Cameron had never met Fenton before and wondered, given his reputation as a poet and literary critic, if he'd want to work in musical theatre. In fact, Fenton jumped at the offer. About to embark upon a three-month canoe trip to Borneo, Fenton took along a copy of Hugo's novel, tearing out the pages as he read them and tossing them in the river. "*Les Misérables* must be the first musical begun in a canoe surrounded by crocodiles," joked Cameron.[20]

While Fenton was considered a brilliant poet, the general view was that progress was too slow. The hope had been to open in the autumn of 1984, but without a completed book and lyrics that looked impossible. Everyone tried to hurry things along, regularly sending Fenton to France to liaise with Alain and Claude-Michel, but as "a loner and a perfectionist," in the words of Cameron,[21] Fenton remained determined to work at his own pace. There were other problems too. Cameron felt that his writing was "over-literary" and "un-theatrical," and just wouldn't work in a commercial musical. There were fears, too, of further delays in opening and getting the whole thing finished. Reluctantly, Cameron and Trevor agreed that something had to be done.

Cameron contacted Herbert Kretzmer, a drama critic and lyricist, who had successfully adapted the songs of Charles Aznavour and other French singers into English. The original plan was for Kretzmer and Fenton to work together, but given Fenton's solitary working methods this was never going to be practicable. Besides, Kretzmer voiced a preference to work alone as well. Cameron had no choice but to call Fenton in and fire him. "Contractually, he was within his rights," Fenton recalled. "But it was quite a painful experience just the same."[22] Fenton's work is still there in *Les Misérables*, as Kretzmer was to say, "it remains in the architecture of the whole show."[23]

Kretzmer began work at the beginning of March 1985 and from that moment onwards rarely stepped out of his Basil Street flat, except to attend rehearsals when they began. He later admitted to having never worked so hard in his life. He saw his lyrics as not literal translations, more a re-invention, while at the same time remaining faithful to the mood and sense of the original production. "We already had the structure and narrative of the show," said Cameron. "Now it was Herbert's job to find it a voice."[24]

As the book took shape, the production team was being assembled. Both John Cameron and Andrew Bruce were brought in by Cameron, not least because of their joint experience working on the Paris production. Since Paris, John had gone back into movie and theatre scoring and was working on the Tim Rice rock opera *Blondel* when he was asked to arrange the orchestral score for *Les Misérables* in London. While John had a forty-piece orchestra at his command in Paris, this just wasn't practical for a London theatre, and he had to make do with one a little over half the size. As a result, John's orchestrations for London were less operatic than Paris, and as far away from traditional Broadway as possible, as he made the score sound gritty and powerful—"putting the street into it."[25] In John's view, that's the main difference between the two productions. "The Paris show was more orchestral because it was cinematic in concept. The London show was more street. And although there are huge elements of the epic in the London show and there are huge elements of the street in the Paris show, that was the shift between the two."[26]

For Andrew, the immediate problem he faced was where the hell was the orchestra going to go, as there was no orchestra pit at the Barbican theatre; it had never been finished. The decision was taken to put the orchestra on stage, "which was a real squeeze. They ended up in the wings stage left, unseen. And that was quite difficult to deal with because a lot of the sound of the orchestra came on stage from the left-hand side and we had to overpower it with the PA, otherwise it was very unbalanced."[27] As for head mics, they had become the norm, although it was still a new thing for the performers to get used to. "But most singers took to it readily," says Andrew.[28]

Other key creatives brought in were John Napier and David Hersey, both of whom had worked on the RSC's *Nicholas Nickleby*. It's true to say that the influence of that earlier production on *Les Misérables* was highly significant, with a lot of lessons learned on *Nickleby* being applied. "You could say the *Les Misérables* production was an extension, in some respects, of the development of things we had begun in *Nicholas Nickleby*," says David Hersey. "A lot of the elements grew out of that."[29] Especially the creation in *Nickleby* of a sort of pared down Dickensian feel, without lots of architecture or scenery.

Something else that helped enormously was a weekend visit to Paris undertaken by Trevor Nunn, John Caird, John Napier, and their respective partners. They visited the Victor Hugo Museum and took time to wander the streets where the anti-monarchist uprising of 1832 took place, which forms such a huge part of the story, and where the barricades were set up. It was during this trip that the question was raised of how the barricades were going to be replicated on stage. This couldn't be stylized; it had to be real, and it had to be large. The group were having lunch in a restaurant and there were a couple of condiment pieces on the table. "I've had an idea," said John Napier, as he began moving the salt and pepper pots around and tipping them over. Like watching that skater in Central Park, this was another moment of epiphany and led directly to the idea that the barricade set had to be mobile units.

Peter Polycarpou still remembers the day when John first brought in a model of the set and the cast saw the design for the barricade. "And everybody applauded. That was a special moment. We were all looking at it just in wonder at the design and thinking—how is that going to work."[30]

The implementation of the barricades was overseen, as was pretty much everything else, by production manager Simon Opie. Simon essentially ran the London operation of the RSC at the Barbican. He was someone else that worked on *Nicholas Nickleby*. The job of a production manager, says Simon, is to take the input of the creative team and make it happen on stage. "That means working with the director, the designers, lighting, sound, to understand exactly what the physical show comprises, integrating it all, managing the production budget and making sure it all arrives on time and works, and then seeing it through rehearsals to opening."[31]

The man brought in to turn John Napier's barricade design into reality was Mike Barnett. Something of an unsung hero in the world of theatre and musicals, Mike was an engineering genius who went on to build the revolving and tilting game board for *Chess*, the gondolier and chandelier in *Phantom*, and the helicopter in *Miss Saigon*. A former industrial engineer, Mike worked on diesel engines and diggers. "So, he came from the commercial industrial design world," says Simon. "But he knew a lot about moving weights around and hydraulics, so his involvement was key to a lot of these musical successes."[32]

Mike moved into theatre in the late 1960s, and Simon first worked with him on an RSC show when he was brought in to do some engineering work. "Mike really was the go-to guy for this kind of thing. There were two or three other people that I can recall who were Championship standard, and then there was Mike who was Premiere League, and there was no one else. If Mike wasn't available to do your show you were in serious trouble."[33]

Built in two segments, the barricade units arrived on trucks from opposite ends of the stage and tipped over to join together. Once on the stage, because the barricade was required to turn round on the revolve, there was no way of connecting it to a power source; any wire or cable would come loose. In the end, it was powered by two large car batteries. "The first moment where we tipped them over was a rather stressful event," recalls Simon. "We knew that the mechanism worked but once it had all the cladding and dressing on it, we had to check that it would all mesh together."[34] With so many scenes taking place on the barricade, with actors clambering all over it, there was also a wear and tear issue, along with health and safety concerns. "As these shows got more and more technical," says Simon, "for people in my role safety became a hugely important element and the cause of a lot of sleepless nights."[35]

It was a proud moment for everyone on the team to get that barricade to work. Although there was the occasional technical hiccup, when it appeared on the stage, accompanied by that beautiful music, backlit amid a plume of smoke, audiences hadn't seen anything quite like it before.

Because of the set design challenges John Napier faced, he decided against designing the costumes as well, as he'd done on *Cats* and *Starlight*. "It was kind of out of my realm because I deal a lot with fantasy costumes, and this definitely needed to be period and real."[36] The obvious choice to come in and do them was Andreane Neofitou, who had done acclaimed work at the RSC, including designing the costumes for *Nicholas Nickleby*. There was just one slight problem. Andreane and John had recently gone through a divorce, and she wasn't at all sure about accepting the offer. "But I was persuaded by Cameron and friends that I would be silly not to do it."[37]

The main challenge facing Andreane was the sheer number of costumes that were going to be required, especially with a cast of twenty-seven. Both directors wanted a lot of voices on stage at the same time, which meant most of the ensemble coming in and out of scenes as different characters. One actor had a badge made: "*Les Misérables, more costumes than lines*." All this necessitated some very quick changes, all of which were done in the wings as the dressing rooms at the Barbican were something like three flights up. Fortunately, the wing space was considerable. Things got hectic when the production moved to the Palace Theatre where the wing space was practically zero. "So, you'd have 15 girls trying to get changed in a corridor which is probably the width of a train carriage," recalls Caroline Quentin. "It was bloody hilarious."[38]

In all Andreane recalls over four hundred costume pieces were used for the show. "I didn't have any two costumes identical."[39] The only exception was for the song "Lovely Ladies" featuring the Parisian whores. "And I did that deliberately because as far as the customers were concerned, they were all the same."[40]

In a way, the principles were much easier to design for because Victor Hugo was quite explicit about how they looked. "So, that's what I did, I read and re-read the book and studied the period."[41] That didn't mean Andreane couldn't play around a little bit. The story is fairly grim, and there is only so much an audience can take of grey and grimness, therefore every now and again, either with Trevor and John's direction or Alain and Claude-Michel's music, the atmosphere shifts. "I also changed the atmosphere with the colours that I was presenting," says Andreane. "We started with the greyness of the convicts. Then we go into the farm where I had all those bright reds to try and give some warmth and daylight. Then we go into the factory and I didn't want grey, I wanted blue, to me that's industrial. Then we go into grim again when we enter

Paris. So, you try to keep the piece within a period but also to rest the eye and lighten the piece every now and again visually."[42]

Andreane also employed tricks to get the audience to see what she wanted them to see. For example, the scenes of Éponine in Paris among all the beggars and crowds. Everyone's clothes were dyed from white fabric and then dyed into all various color grades. Éponine's was dyed from beige. "Because she dances all over the stage, I didn't want to lose her. And although she was greyish the same as everybody else, the eye somehow managed to find her wherever she was."[43]

A further advantage to staging *Les Misérables* with the RSC was the casting of some of its repertory players, with the result that a lot of people appeared who would not normally have been cast in West End musicals, like Alun Armstrong and Roger Allam, the original Inspector Javert. "At the time giving these roles to those types of actors was perceived as a massive risk," says Simon Opie.[44] Trevor had tried something similar before when he cast Judi Dench in *Cats*; it was all part of his philosophy about how such shows could be approached. "It was a very integrated company," says Simon, including as it did artists from commercial theatre such as Patti LuPone and Michael Ball. "And I think those people coming in from the commercial world actually quite enjoyed being part of the RSC."[45]

Besides Javert, the other main role was Valjean, and international stars of the stature of Max Von Sydow and Topol flew to London at their own expense to audition. Both were deemed not quite right. Indeed, finding the right Valjean was proving difficult and a real concern. Trevor Nunn turned to Tim Rice for advice, describing what was needed, "Someone who looks like a convict, is very strong, can carry a guy weighing 13 stone on his back around the stage, and still sing beautifully." Without a pause Tim answered, "That's Colm Wilkinson."[46] Tim had worked with Colm on both the *Jesus Christ Superstar* and *Evita* concept albums, but Trevor had never met him. He was brought in, and the moment he began to sing it was obvious they had found their Valjean. Colm had a voice that befitted a rock singer really but just had this phenomenal ability to flick his voice over into a high falsetto which suited so many of the songs in *Les Misérables*.

Trevor had also found his Éponine, the cynical but resourceful street urchin. One day after a performance of *Starlight Express*, he went backstage to see Frances Ruffelle and said, "I've got the perfect role for you." One that suited her cockney roots. There was only one slight problem. She would have to prove that she was the right choice to both Alain and Claude-Michel, and also John Caird. For her private audition, Trevor's idea was for Frances to sing an Edith Piaf song, since Alain and Claude-Michel had based their Éponine on the legendary French singer, who endured a traumatic childhood. "I learnt the song and I went in at six o'clock on a Friday night and on Monday morning at ten they told me I'd got the job. Although Trevor has said to this day it was mine anyway."[47]

Auditions were also held to find other talent. Peter Polycarpou was in a play up in Newcastle when he read about this big upcoming musical, but no matter how hard he tried he couldn't get an audition. At lunch one day his complaints were overheard by someone in the cast, Australian actress Sharon Lee-Hill. She asked what the problem was. "I'm trying to get this audition because I sing a bit," said Peter.

"Well, my boyfriend's directing it," said Sharon, who in just over a year's time would be Mrs. Trevor Nunn. "So, I gave her my picture and CV," says Peter. "And true to her word she put it in Trevor's lap and the following week my agent called saying I had an audition."[48]

As it turned out Trevor wasn't there, instead sitting in the stalls was Cameron and John Caird. "And as I remember Cameron was reading a bloody newspaper, the *Financial Times*, and he was holding it up in front of him and I thought, how bloody rude! I was determined to make him move his bloody newspaper down. So, I started singing Elton John's 'Crocodile Rock' and halfway through this newspaper came down and I thought to myself, I've got you, you bastard."[49] Peter was asked to sing another song and then answer a few questions about himself, and that was that. A week later he was asked to be in the ensemble. It was his first big show, and it had taken just the one audition. Peter later heard horror stories about other people having to go through six or seven.

Caroline Quentin wasn't quite subjected to that, but she remembers going to at least three auditions. Working in the business since the age of sixteen, starting as a dancer and a singer, she'd been doing repertory theatre and bits of television work and even went up for *Starlight Express*. "But I couldn't roller skate. It was so embarrassing. I said, I can't skate, and they said, oh just give it a go, and I went round clutching all the chairs. So, I obviously didn't get it."[50] Caroline's agent sent her up for *Les Misérables* with a little more confidence. "I remember thinking, oh my God, this would be so great, just to be in the West End. I was in my early 20s, it would be really exciting."[51]

At Caroline's second audition, the room was full of hopefuls. Having recently played Edith Piaf in repertory theatre, she sang the Piaf song "L'Accordéoniste," sang it in French, too, and followed that with a number from *Cabaret*. John Caird promptly stood up, said "This is in the wrong key for you," and strode across to the pianist to alter it. Caroline sang it again, "That's the key you should be singing in," he informed. "I said, ok, I'll remember that, left the room and promptly forgot obviously."[52] After one more call Caroline was in the ensemble, playing everything from a whore to a nun, along with a blind beggar woman. She was also second cover for Fantine. And very glad of it, too, with work rather thin on the ground at the time.

Paul Leonard had done a couple of West End musicals and was in the National Theatre's production of *Guys and Dolls* when he heard about the auditions. With *Guys and Dolls* on the verge of a West End transfer, Paul rejected a guaranteed nine-month contract in the hope he might land a role in *Les Misérables*. It was a big risk. "But you have to take these leaps of faith sometimes."[53] It took something like six recalls before he finally got the nod. "I desperately wanted to do it. Everybody wanted desperately to do it. And it was a real badge of honour when you'd got it."[54] Paul found himself in the ensemble and also played a rather nasty factory foreman and Combeferre, an idealistic student, quite a nice little character part. Years later he returned to the production to play Javert.

Sian Reeves had been in London for just over a year, hailing from a small village in Staffordshire, full of dreams of becoming a dancer. Managing to get a grant, she was studying a musical theatre course at ArtsEd, an independent performing arts school; today its president is Andrew Lloyd Webber. Broke, she was working behind the bar at the Prince of Wales Theatre when she saw an ad in the *Stage*, a newspaper aimed at those working in theatre, that was looking for a nineteen-year-old actress. Confident she fit the bill exactly, Sian turned up at the audition only to find herself in a queue with several hundred other girls who felt much the same thing.

Anyway, the audition went well, and word soon got round the Prince of Wales staff that this kid from behind the bar had got a recall for *Les Misérables*, this awful drab sounding musical. "They were very disparaging," says Sian.[55] Word also reached the ears of the theatre's musical director who wandered into the bar one evening and asked Sian if she wanted any help with the song that she had to learn. "Of course, I said, yes please. He then asked if I wanted to stand on the stage and try singing. I'd never stood on a West End stage before. And that helped me so much."[56] Feeling confident, Sian went back and on her fourth recall won a part in the ensemble. It was her first theatre job. Sian was also asked to understudy the role of Cosette.

While Sian was the youngest professional in the show, there were a number of child actors in the cast including Zoe Hart. Attending ballet school where she grew up in Reading, Zoe had appeared at the age of five as one of the von Trapp children in the 1981 West End revival of *The Sound of Music*. Now aged ten, she was sent up for the part of the young Cosette. Her final audition took place at the New London Theatre, "on the middle of that massive stage with the set of *Cats* all around me."[57] Because of the strict laws governing child actors, three girls were cast as the young Cosette for separate performances. Zoe was by far the more experienced. For some it was their first job. "And there were stories of girls waving at dancing teachers as they walked around the Barbican stage in the middle of the show."[58] Because of her experience, especially on *Sound of Music*, Zoe knew how to behave on a large production: you are professional, and you get on and you do your job. It's certainly why Zoe was trusted with playing the young Cosette at both the Barbican and the Palace opening nights.

Trevor and John now had their cast. Vocally they were all very competent, with several standout voices. Characterwise there were some strong personalities in there. And they looked like a cross-section of the proletariat. There were large people, thin people, and people of varying ages and experiences. This was the aim. It wasn't going to be your average chorus line of pretty blokes and beautiful girls. "They wanted the ruddy," says Paul. "They wanted the earthy. They wanted the quirky. They wanted realism. And they ended up with a really good mix."[59]

Rehearsals got underway in late July 1985 at the Barbican, which had a large rehearsal space in the basement. "Rehearsals are always like the first day at school," says Paul. "You're five years old again."[60] Everyone sat in a big semicircle, with Trevor center stage. After introducing himself, the cast all had to stand up individually to say who they were and what characters they were playing. Then Trevor presented a lecture about the history behind Victor Hugo's novel. Everyone was urged to acquaint themselves with the range and depth of the author's concerns and to read the book; not everyone did. Photocopies of key pages from the novel were pinned to the walls of the rehearsal room, and the cast were given separate subjects they had to go away and read up on about the period and about the time. "They also showed us the set and the costume designs," recalls Zoe. "We were included in all of that as kids, which was fantastic. And we all went home on the train signing 'The blood of the martyrs, Will water the meadows of France,' we thought that was so cool."[61]

For much of those opening weeks the focus was on improvisation and working on character, "so we were not to be just an amorphous crowd," says Caroline.[62] This included traditional trust games and exercises. "It was exciting and we all loved it," recalls Paul, "because we had to throw ourselves at doing things we'd never done in improvisation before."[63] In one exercise everyone put on blindfolds and walked around the room in silence. If you bumped into someone you had to identify them by touch only, and if identified that person left the room. An hour later Paul was the only person left. "Trevor had got everybody in the café and they all came back into the room and started shouting at me. I took the blindfold off and realised the buggers had gone off and had a cup of tea."[64]

In another exercise the cast were asked to be cartoon characters. "And that was about liberating a physicality," says Peter Polycarpou. "It was getting people to work outside their own bodies, so they're not embarrassed to challenge themselves or look stupid."[65] It was also a way of trying to find out what the cast could and couldn't do physically. Trevor was judging and working out what other kinds of roles he might be able to put them into. "It was a way of him so to speak auditioning us during the rehearsal process," says Peter. "To see where we best fitted his overall plan."[66]

The cast were sometimes asked to form groups of eight or ten and to take pieces of text from the book and improvise different scenes alternating characters. Caroline got to play Valjean in the moment where he walks into a bar as a stranger in town and everything goes deathly quiet. "It went very well and Trevor came up and 'Trevved' me, put his arm round me and said, well done. Roger Allam came across and said, 'You won't be going back to Pitlochry again will you dear,' meaning my rep days were over because Trevor said I'd done a good job."[67]

For someone like John Cameron, who hadn't worked on an RSC production before, all this improvisation was a little bit head scratching. But then he started to see what the reasoning was behind it all because the cast began to build up trust with each other very quickly. "And I think this was the strength of the show when it opened, the ensemble playing was so strong. There was almost no ensemble or chorus, everybody was a character, everybody had an important role to play and an importance to add to it. This is the thing that Trevor did bring to it."[68]

This inevitably led to a strong sense of family, with no cliques. "It was brilliantly egalitarian, as it should be in that particular musical obviously," says Caroline. "There was no particular delineation between the leads and the chorus."[69] As the youngest Sian felt this the strongest. "There was a family structure. You had the seniors with all that experience right down to the new ones who had done nothing. I learnt so much about how to behave, and how not to behave. And I learnt how to stand up for myself."[70]

A little over a week into rehearsals a new cast member joined, Rebecca Caine. Making her West End debut at nineteen in *Oklahoma!* Rebecca sang the role of Eliza in *My Fair Lady* on the national tour produced by Cameron Mackintosh. Now twenty-five, she was making her debut at Glyndebourne's renowned opera festival. When Trevor Nunn came down to organize a day of improvisation Rebecca stood out, she had a certain look that he liked, and as she was in the chorus at Glyndebourne she could obviously sing. "We broke for lunch and I was 'Trevved,' the arm went round my shoulder."[71] He wanted Rebecca to play Cosette but she wasn't sure about going back into musical theatre—her ambition was to be an opera singer. Trevor's persuasive skills worked, and Rebecca sang for Alain and Claude-Michel. "Actually, it was very clever casting," says Rebecca, "putting somebody who sounded like me against Frances. The class system vocally was clever because I sounded sort of posh and Frances was very street. And it's a very traditional thing in musicals to use the soprano for the virginal character."[72]

Going into *Les Misérables* ended up being an exciting time for Rebecca who had never been part of creating a brand-new musical. Although it gave her pause when a few of the cast members came up to her saying, "It's shit darling, we'll be off by Easter." What Rebecca liked about the company immediately was that there were evidently no "stars," and by implication no divas. "It was very democratic, and no prisoners were taken."[73] It was a big shock later when she joined the original cast of *Phantom of the Opera* to play Christine opposite Michael Crawford, and there was a noticeable power structure in place. "It was very unpleasant."[74]

Following Rebecca's arrival, the final cast member joined rehearsals. Cameron had been keen for Patti LuPone to appear as Fantine and played her the album in New York. She responded to it positively, sure it was going to be a hit just by the "sheer emotionalism of it." The lure of working with Trevor and the RSC was also "irresistible." Patti was going to be in London anyway appearing in the Old Vic's production of the American opera *The Cradle Will Rock*. The day after the opening night Patti showed up for rehearsals at the Barbican.

Patti brought a bit of Broadway oomph to proceedings. "She was wonderful," says Paul Leonard. "She was very dynamic."[75] Frances has never forgotten the very first run through, "and watching Patti doing her death scene in the Barbican rehearsal room and just sobbing my heart out. And realising what a special thing we were in. It was an amazing feeling."[76]

Frances, who turned twenty during rehearsals, had begun them feeling quite self-conscious, especially around the established RSC players who seemed so vastly more experienced and intellectual to a girl who left school at fifteen and never considered herself a good scholar. "I felt really insecure that I wouldn't be good enough, or I wouldn't know enough about the history of the piece. It was quite nerve-wracking. In the end I just found myself watching them and I learnt so much."[77]

It was most unusual to have two directors assigned to the same production; few actors had ever experienced it. Certainly, for Caroline this was the first and only time it happened. But it worked, especially on something like *Les Misérables* with its sprawling narrative and large cast. "They were very much an equal partnership. Trevor was persuasive and kind and detailed and paternal in a good way. John was immensely generous. Both of them had a brilliant quality of allowing actors to explore and I learnt a lot from that process."[78] The two men sometimes worked in tandem or took on separate groups. Trevor perhaps spent more time with the principals. "John is very musical," says Caroline. "He's an incredibly gifted musician, and having him by his side was great for Trevor. It was a perfect combination."[79]

Zoe recalls that the child actors were mainly directed by John. It wasn't until she appeared in the Trevor Nunn–directed *Aspects of Love* in 1989 that she gained a much fuller insight into his way of working. "He would just immerse himself totally into what he was doing. He always started the rehearsal period well dressed, but by the end of it the holes started appearing in the jumpers and the sleeves and the beard would get bigger, the hair would get messier, you saw this progression happening in front of your eyes."[80]

Behind the scenes, there was some controversy about who exactly was calling the shots, Trevor and John or Cameron. It was unusual for the RSC to have outside people coming in with strong decision-making power. And so essentially there were two creative forces in charge. Of course, Trevor and Cameron had worked together on *Cats*, "and there was a very strong mutual respect," says Simon Opie,[81] and so from most people's perspective this unusual state of affairs worked and there was no real friction or disruption between the RSC and Cameron's team; the chain of communication, as Simon recalls, "was very efficient."[82]

This was true of all the core creatives. "We worked very closely together," recalls Andreane. "And I think that's what made the show great. It was a real team effort."[83] They would often meet for long lunches and dinners to discuss how things were going and iron out any problems. "The nice thing about it was we were all friends and we got on so well," says Andreane. "And we all loved the show enough to put our egos aside slightly."[84]

Andreane worked especially close with Trevor and, of course, the actors. Trevor isn't a dictatorial director; he manages to get actors to see a character the way he sees it. As far as Andreane is concerned, the reverse is true, it's how the actors sees their character. "I want the actor to put a costume on and feel that that's their character's clothes."[85] It's a dialogue between the actor and Andreane, and it's a gradual thing, with Andreane giving the actor their costume in stages, "so when they are ready for the full costume the character has developed within them, and they do say to me, the minute I put the clothes on I knew who I was."[86]

As rehearsals continued, they were never frantic and they were never hectic. "But they were always really energised," says Peter Polycarpou. "Everybody was very concentrated, people really worked hard."[87] It was an organic thing, too. The cast contributed significantly to the show during the rehearsal process: Rebecca putting in her high notes, Patti's vocal mannerisms, Frances and Michael Ball doing stuff with their harmonies. "Our DNA is in there," says Rebecca. "It's then written in the score. It became part of the music. And you knew 20 or 25 years later that somebody was still doing your movements that you had improvised on a hot summer's day in a basement at the Barbican and you were still being re-created night after night."[88] Years after Rebecca had left the show, all the Cosettes, no matter their hair color, wore wigs that matched Rebecca's hair. "You then see yourself cloned around the world in different countries and different languages; they're all looking like you."[89]

As rehearsals neared the end, new material and songs were still being added with much of the second act incomplete. At the start of rehearsals, the cast were handed only the script of Act 1. "It wasn't like we started with a finished script and everybody knew what they were doing," says David Hersey. "It developed a lot during rehearsal. And you can only do that with a company like the RSC, who have the resources and the time. To do that commercially was most unlikely."[90] It was a case of, if this doesn't work, change it, or, I've got another idea, or let's try this. "It was a very creative and dynamic time," recalls John Cameron. "I must have lost a lot of weight, rushing from my office to the stage; it was a long bloody way."[91]

Herbert Kretzmer was also around a great deal, on hand for any last-minute tasks that were needed. "He was incredibly diligent," recalls Peter. "Trevor would say to him, we need something there, and he'd say, leave it with me, and two days later he'd come back with this perfect four-line quatrain or whatever it was, to finish off a scene or moment that needed clarification. He was brilliant, and so completely detailed."[92]

Incredibly, the song "Bring Him Home" was a late addition. There had been several discussions about Valjean needing something to sing on the barricade the night before the big battle. "Claude-Michel came in one day, quite late in rehearsal," recalls Peter. "He sat at the piano and started to sing 'Bring Him Home.' Everybody was huddled around the piano, and we all were just completely captivated by this moment, as this beautiful song which has become iconic and hugely important in the show, was played for the very first time. And when we started doing the show it was my privileged position to be no more than three feet behind Colm as he sang this song every night, and I was so moved. For me Colm was the greatest Valjean."[93]

It's one thing to hear these tunes played on a piano, which is the case during rehearsals; it's quite another to hear them with a full orchestra for the very first time. This is known as the Sitzprobe, which is the first complete rehearsal of an opera or musical with the orchestra and the singers together. For Martyn Hayes, who was going to be production manager for any West End transfer, the Sitzprobe for *Les Misérables* remains one of his most memorable theatre experiences. "I think it was on a Saturday morning. I remember going to it and sitting there and just being completely blown away. It was only when you first heard the full orchestra and the vocals that you realised just what a wonderfully constructed musical it was and how moving it was. Of course, we'd heard Colm sing 'Bring Him Home' and Patti sing 'I Dreamed a Dream' in the rehearsal room, but when you heard them with the orchestra, it was goosebumps. Everybody was in tears."[94]

As previews began, it was fairly obvious that the show was too long. This was something that had bedeviled the *Nicholas Nickleby* production. "At that phase, Trevor's shows always tended to be a bit on the long side," states Simon Opie.[95] The first preview clocked in at almost four hours and that was unsustainable; going way past 11 o'clock meant that people coming to see it would miss their trains home, not to mention the Musician's Union costing them a fortune because the orchestra would be on overtime.

It was inevitable that some pretty ruthless decisions had to be made, and the man to make them was Cameron. "It was Cameron who came in with fresh eyes and he did the cuts that were necessary," says Andreane.[96] Cameron looked at it from a purely business, practical point of view of putting bums on seats. He knew it couldn't be that length, especially if they were hoping to go into the West End. Trevor was far from happy. "I do remember there being some fairly forthright exchanges about the length of the show," says Simon Opie. "But it was never confrontational."[97] Others are not so sure; Trevor fought hard against the cuts that Cameron imposed, and it did fracture their relationship.

It was perhaps toughest on the cast, already exhausted from the long rehearsal period only to be faced with wholesale changes. "We sacrificed a lot of really good work," says Paul Leonard.[98] It was added stress, with no one knowing what was going to be sacrificed next. Rebecca recalls hearing Michael Ball through the wall in the next dressing room shouting, "They're going to cut my number." In the end something like thirty minutes was ripped out. "Whole scenes going, half scenes going, sets changing, costumes changing, dialogue cut or changed, it was absolutely terrifying," says Caroline. "And right the way through previews, up until opening night, it was a fairly frenetic wobbly experience."[99] For Sian, she'd never worked so hard in her life. "We were in from ten in the morning until half past eleven or midnight because we'd have notes after the performance."[100]

To be fair, the cast knew it was too long. Although there was a lot of moaning going on, Trevor had brought in leading repertory actors to play in the ensemble, only for many to have their lines taken away. However, when news came that massive cuts were coming it was generally seen as a positive, that there was a potential of it transferring to the West End if Cameron was reworking it and condensing it down. And nothing was really lost. "Because we'd included almost all the core elements of the story in the beginning," says Sian, "when it was stripped down, we still had the authenticity and rawness of who those characters were."[101]

One substantial sequence that was cut involved Valjean and young Cosette being chased through the streets of Paris by Javert and some soldiers. At one point she jumps onto his back, and they climb up the barricades; the only time the barricades became the tenements of Paris in an upright position. Halfway up, Zoe was replaced by a dummy as Valjean continued to climb to the top. "I was absolutely terrified," confesses Zoe, "because I don't like heights and I remember thinking, even halfway up, that was a really long way up."[102]

During the climb up the wall, it was Peter Polycarpou who doubled for Colm, so he was disappointed to see it go. "It was quite a dramatic moment. I used to pretend to fall halfway down the barricades almost to my death as Valjean, it used to get some great reactions. But it taught me a salutary lesson, and that was never to be too in love with the material, always to be ready to compromise, to sublimate your own ego for the good of the piece."[103]

Along with the cuts, other things were being adapted and changed or weren't working at all. In the first previews, the suicide of Javert was not going well. Roger Allam and the choreographer were doing some kind of mime of Javert plunging to his death from a bridge into the river Seine. John Napier felt he had the perfect solution. "I've got an idea," he kept saying to Trevor, only to be waved away. Problems were mounting up, and Trevor hadn't the time to spare, so Javert's suicide continued to disappoint in previews.

Walking down a corridor in the bowels of the Barbican John happened to bump into Trevor. "What was that idea you had John?" he asked.

"Just give me half an hour with Roger and the crew, I'll try and put something together and you can have a look at it."[104]

John's idea was for the bridge to be lowered onto the stage floor in the dark behind Roger Allam who, as he sang, would step onto it. Then when he jumps off, John made him throw his arms up as the bridge shot straight up into the air to give a heightened sensation of falling. "It was as simple as that," says John.

"Trevor saw it and thought it was great. So, we put it in and that night it got an ovation."[105] To complement the effect, David Hersey lit the revolve to give a whirlpool ripple impression. Hersey's brilliance was seen elsewhere, too, such as the sewer scene where a combination of lighting and perspective gave the impression of a vast underground tunnel.

Even with cuts, the production remained long. But something was undeniable, and that was the effect it was having on audiences. "We had standing ovations every night," says Frances. "And that happened from the very first preview."[106] It connected. People found it emotionally compelling. "There were a bunch of American women who were in the dress circle one night at previews," recalls John Napier. "I happened to be going past there as the show closed and they came out and they all had their mascara running down their faces and I said to myself, *I'm going to get the Kleenex concession for this show.* I knew at that moment that it hit a nerve somewhere."[107]

Rebecca Caine's husband, a company manager working in West End musicals, was in the audience at that very first preview and had no doubts about it. "He said to me, 'this is going to be massive.' I said, 'really, do you think so?' Because at that point it just felt incredibly long, and we were all just wondering around and changing one set of grey rags for another set of grey rags. He said, no it's going to be huge."[108]

At another preview, John Cameron was sat at the sound desk, which was situated in the middle of the dress circle, when his sound operator suddenly got out a can of WD-40 and started spraying it on the desk, complaining about a noise in the channels. Neither of them knew what it was or the location of the fault. "Then we both stopped and looked round and the entire dress circle had their handkerchiefs out and were sniffling away. That was the noise. And we thought, hold on, we have got something here."[109]

As opening night approached there was a tremendous sense of momentum among the cast. "The previews had been getting more and more exciting," says Peter.[110] Still, everyone knew the show was a big gamble, and doubts remained about it being too bleak. The general view was that a musical had to be colorful and light-hearted to be really successful; here most of the cast end up dead on stage at the curtain call. On the opening night of October 8, there were a lot of unanswered questions.

The answer arrived soon enough. "The audience stood up and roared and cried," recalls Sian. "They wouldn't let us off the stage."[111] There was an incredible buzz as everyone congregated for the opening night party up in the Barbican Conservatory, a glass-roofed, leafy sanctuary with tropical plants and trees. "That was really exciting," remembers Caroline. "I had my mum there.

We all had relatives or partners there. It was like living in a movie. You're in your early twenties and you simply can't believe you're there. And so many famous people, you turned round and there was somebody off the telly, or someone from a movie or a musical theatre star. Cameron really knows how to throw a party."[112]

It was a memorable night, too, for the young Zoe, who was led around by one of the older child actors, "and we drained any glass of champagne that we could find, which was awesome."[113]

The excitement of the opening night soon gave way to shock and anger when the first batch of reviews came out. Cameron rushed to buy the early morning editions, and the first review he saw was Jack Tinker in the *Daily Mail* christening the production "The Glums." Michael Ratcliffe's review in the *Observer* sported the headline: "Victor Hugo on the garbage dump." Ratcliffe scorned the way the novel had been reduced "to the trivialising and tearful aesthetic of rock opera and the French hit parade of ten years ago."

For Cameron, all this was a dagger in the heart. "I had my usual post-production lunch with the team, and we all felt we'd been to a funeral."[114] Peter Polycarpou remembers Cameron being "very pissed off with the reviews, and literally getting a soap box to stand on and saying, I don't think these reviewers know what they're talking about."[115]

Michael Coveney in the *Financial Times* and Sheridan Morley in *Punch* were the few notable critics who voiced their admiration, but these voices were largely drowned out by a general negative critical tone. "We thought, that's it, all that work, we are not going to transfer," recalls Paul Leonard. "And it was so unfair because we were reading the reviews thinking, you bastards, did you not see the audience's reaction."[116] There was indeed this odd disparity between the public reaction to the show and the critics. "Loads of family and friends came to see it and everybody absolutely loved it," recalls Zoe. "So, it was a real shock when the reviews came out and I remember the atmosphere backstage was very dark."[117]

Was there perhaps an element of snobbery going on? "In some ways we were expecting a bad press," says Andreane, "because we were meddling with Victor Hugo and we were making a very serious book into a musical."[118]

An even bigger question was could the show survive such a critical barrage. While Cameron pondered on its future prospects, for many at the RSC who worked on *Nicholas Nickleby* this was nothing very unusual. That also took a critical pounding. "Bernard Levin was the only critic who gave it a good review," says Simon Opie. "*Nickleby* was different and something that really hadn't been tried before, so I'm not sure people really knew quite what to make of it. And I think that's what happened to *Les Misérables*."[119]

The fact that *Nickleby* had suffered a similar fate gave hope to people like Peter Polycarpou, who believed in the show. "When those reviews came out, I was very angry because I knew they were wrong."[120] Even so, days after opening night the future of *Les Misérables* hung in the balance.

Knocked sideways by the adverse critical response, Cameron had a big decision to make. The plan had always been to transfer the show to the West End after its ten-week run at the Barbican. The Palace Theatre, which had been recently purchased by Andrew Lloyd Webber's Really Useful Group, was available. That plan was now in jeopardy, and rumors and gossip circulated among the cast about what was going to happen. "They were all coming up to me," recalls Andreane, "and saying, have you heard yet. Are we going to go?"[121] Everyone was in the dark. "We didn't expect it to go beyond the Barbican," says Frances. "We were all thinking, what are we going to do next?"[122]

The dilemma facing Cameron was whether to cut his losses, along with those of his backers, or forge ahead. Things looked bleak; the reviews were discouraging, but the advance booking was not looking good either. According to John Napier, "Cameron was seriously thinking about closing it."[123]

Cameron decided to call a meeting at his office. Martin McCallum was one of those present as Cameron talked to the key investors about whether they wanted to spend the last part of their investment in making the move over to the Palace. "At one point Cameron rang up and spoke to the box office and was told there was a queue of people down the street. And I remember one of the investors, a New Zealander, saying, it's a bit like a horse race, you can't stop it at the eighth furlong, you've got to let it run."[124] The overwhelming evidence did suggest that whatever the critics may have made of the show, the audience really enjoyed it and that was starting to have an influence on the box office. After all, audiences sell shows to audiences more than anything else, more than marketing, more than advertising, more than reviews—it's word of mouth. Cameron decided that it was worth the gamble. He would take it into the West End. It was a decision that saved *Les Misérables*.

For the rest of its run at the Barbican, *Les Misérables* played to capacity audiences. The show also began to win positive notices from international critics, the likes of *Newsweek*, the *New York Times*, and the *Washington Post*. Its profile was further raised when Lady Diana attended an early performance. "I was running messages between the sound desk and the orchestra," recalls John Cameron, "and I burst out of a door as she was standing there with all the courtiers and somebody said to me, you could have got shot there."[125] Diana became a huge fan of the show and was to attend numerous performances.

Despite brisk business at the Barbican, it remained a risk taking *Les Misérables* into the West End. There was an underlying feeling: will it work at the Palace? Ironically, Andrew Lloyd Webber was rather banking on it not doing that well as he hoped to open his new show, *Phantom of the Opera*, there within the year. Because of the mixed reviews, Andrew expected Cameron's new show to be just a filler until *Phantom* was ready to move in.

The man organizing the move to the Palace Theatre was Martyn Hayes, who took over from Simon Opie as production manager. He worked at the Production Office with Martin McCallum and Richard Bullimore, and had been asked by Cameron to do a watching brief on the show in preparation for any West End transfer. With the Palace available, it was his job to make sure the show could work there. "That meant a little bit of re-building of the stage floor because it was bigger than the Barbican. It was also a very tight transfer. I think we only had a few days to move everything in."[126]

The cast had something like a weeks' break prior to the opening on December 4. Everyone, that is, except Frances, who was booked to sing on the BBC's Terry Wogan show. "After the performance I was told by the box office at the Palace that there had been queues round the block and the phones hadn't stopped ringing."[127]

Everybody was thrilled about relocating to the Palace. "The Barbican was one thing," says Caroline, "but going into the West End for the first time, being on a West End stage was just brilliant."[128] And there was something special about the Palace itself. "It's one of the most beautiful Victorian theatres," says Caroline. "And going through the stage door there's a plaque above it in stone that says, 'The world's greatest artists have passed and will pass through these doors' and when you're a nobody in the chorus, it's pretty thrilling."[129]

History is one thing, but the Palace was not in the best of states. Paul Leonard had done *Oklahoma!* there in 1980, and it was in a horrendous condition. "Everything was falling apart. And there were cockroaches everywhere, in the girl's wigs, in the dresses. When you went into your dressing room they'd be scurrying about. It should have been condemned."[130] Paul was relieved that at least the cockroach problem was under control. And pretty quickly after they all came in, scaffolding went up as the start of major exterior refurbishment.

Inside, though, it remained grotty for years, and the cast did not appreciate the less than salubrious nature of the dressing rooms, especially after the modern ones they'd enjoyed back at the Barbican. "It was a hole," confirms Rebecca. "I remember Frances pulling Cameron to one side and saying, 'Look at this. It's disgusting. Get it painted.' They didn't."[131] Frances and Rebecca, along with Susan Jane Tanner, who was playing Madame Thénardier, ended up sharing a dressing room. "We literally had to climb over each other to get to the sink," says Frances.[132]

Backstage, things felt a lot more cramped, too, and the cast were told about a couple of ghosts that supposedly haunted the place. There was also a rickety old lift. Andrew's office used to be at the top of the building in those days, and you'd see him occasionally going up and down.

Nestled into the Palace, where the running time was further reduced, *Les Misérables* went on to enjoy an unprecedented run of success for a musical. "I used to swap tickets for the show for Wimbledon tickets," recalls Frances. "We never had one seat empty ever."[133] From very early on it began to attract loyal fans. "They came and saw the show every week and sat in the same seat for years," recalls Paul. "When I went back in 1991 and did Javert those same fans were still in those same seats mouthing the words."[134]

Frances used to regularly get marriage proposals sent to the theatre. Rebecca and Susan used to hang the men's photographs on a wall in their dressing room. Unfortunately, there was an unpleasant side to this: Michael Ball got attacked at the stage door by a fan after a matinee. "This one fan was absolutely obsessed with him, and she lunged at him with a knife," recalls Paul. "Luckily he was unharmed and she was quietly taken away."[135]

For so many working on *Les Misérables*, it was an amazing time and a marvelous adventure. "We still all know each other," says Caroline. "We're still all friends."[136] After the show, especially on Friday and Saturday nights, most of the cast would hang out at the nearby Coach and Horses pub. "We'd take the whole place over," says Caroline.[137] Actors, crew hands, and musicians spilled out into Greek Street. "The Les Mis family sort of owned that quarter of Soho."[138]

Working on the barricade was especially exciting and dangerous; everyone had to find not only a suitable place to die but somewhere that was safe. "There was a great camaraderie about being on the barricade," says Peter. "And it was different every night. We'd find different moments that we'd be able to share with each other. It was a very intense part of the show the barricade because it lasted for most of the second half."[139]

A few of the stage crew dressed in costumes and were on the barricades to make sure all the bits and pieces connected properly and it was all working. Even so, in the early days there was the occasional glitch when it broke down. "And we're all hanging there dead thinking, what do we do, do we get off, do we just stay here and wait for it to be mended," recalls Paul. "Sometimes we'd just have to get off and go into the wings for it to be repaired, which was a terrible anti-climax because then you've got to go back out onto the stage and finish the scene, but of course you've lost the moment."[140]

Most of the cast had to double up as the students and workers that build and man the barricade against the army. At first Patti argued against it, that when she wasn't playing Fantine, she didn't want to be part of the ensemble. In the end she reluctantly agreed. "Patti hated being on the barricade," recalls Sian. "But we all had to do these little parts. And I remember her being upset and crying because she missed her boyfriend who was in New York. She was great, though, can you imagine watching her sing 'I Dreamed a Dream' eight shows a week. What a lesson."[141]

To add to the authenticity, some of the actors fighting on the barricade used real guns. These were decommissioned, but still heavy. During a performance someone dropped their rifle, and it fell on Sian, damaging her neck. Real knives were also used. These were blunt but obviously still quite intimidating and Frances complained about them during rehearsals. "They said not to worry, it would be fine. It wasn't."[142] Sure enough, there was an accident, and she received a nasty cut to the face and her understudy finished the performance. "I was taken to hospital and had to have stitches inside my mouth as well as out."[143] Frances went back on stage the following night. She still carries the scar today.

Despite such traumas, Frances loved performing Eponine every night. "It was a lovely role."[144] And she never got bored of it. "For me, if I'm playing a role, I'm in the moment all the time, I'm in the present, I'm thinking the thoughts and the words for the very first time, so that keeps me from being bored. It also keeps me fresh. And there was so much drama and so much going on in my head, which was Eponine's head, that by the time my role ended in the show it was like a flash going by."[145] One of the most beloved characters in the story, Eponine dies before the end, which left Frances with nothing to do as she waited for the curtain call. Rebecca, too, had plenty of gaps in the show as Cosette and time to kill. "I used to get bored because it was so long. I used to go and hang out on the fly tower and watch the barricade scene. I used to go and stand on the roof and pretend to be a ghost in my costume and bonnet. I used to climb up the scaffolding and pop into someone else's dressing room through the window."[146]

It was a long show for everyone. After a few months, people were feeling the physical and mental strain. Cameron arranged for his doctor to come in and give them B12 jabs. "And he did it on the stairs as we went down for beginners," recalls Paul. "He had his little case open with all the syringes and he said, 'Anyone who wants a B12, I'm here for you.'"[147]

It was particularly tough on the child actors, although Zoe and the other young Cosettes all had to go home at the interval, so never got to do a curtain call, "which I was always gutted about."[148] But her memories of the cast are strong. They all looked after her. Michael Ball used to sweep her up and put her on his shoulders and carry her around. "Alun Armstrong, he was a bugger. The scene where he and Valjean are bargaining for little Cosette, Alun would grab me and because my back was turned to the audience would stick things up my nose. Stage hands would also put things on the set like rubber snakes and spiders. It was really good fun. It was a fantastic company."[149]

Alun was certainly the practical joker, keeping everyone' spirits up. "He was outrageous," says Caroline.[150] He made a surprise appearance at Caroline's final performance. Playing her blind beggar woman, Caroline thought there was someone over there that shouldn't be on stage; she'd never seen this cloaked figure in the scene before. "And as I turned round, he opened the cloak and there was a completely naked Alun Armstrong. My blind beggar woman rapidly regained her sight and rather wished she hadn't."[151] Alun had already left the show by this time and returned specially to say his goodbyes, "which was so kind."[152]

Caroline herself, not averse to mischief, once painted Cosette's face on her left breast and as Roger Allam came over the barricade all was revealed and he corpsed. Then, finishing playing a nun in a scene with Colm, she'd head back to the wings. "And I knew he could see me and I would do all sorts of obscene things with a truncheon trying to make him laugh. To be honest, on stage was fun, off stage was much more fun, all the real fun happened just out of the audience's eyeline."[153]

Another much-loved member of the company was Ian Calvin. Ian was more from the world of variety than traditional theatre, doing summer seasons, panto, and performing in cabaret and on cruise ships. "He came from sparkly sequin jackets into Les Mis and he couldn't believe the shock of having to wear grey rags," says Caroline.[154] Somebody met him under a table during improvisations, and he told them, "Darling, I don't know why I'm here, I'm much more of a Hello Dolly man." Whenever things got too dark and cheerless, Ian was usually around to make things brighter and raise a few laughs. Tragically, Ian was one of the first from the theatrical community to be lost to HIV. He worked right up until a few days before he died in February 1987.

Zoe remembers Colm being an especially protective influence, taking her almost under his wing and looking after her. "He would invite me into his dressing room and make sure I was ok and that things were running smoothly. He was incredibly kind and generous with his time."[155]

Zoe left the production after about a year but returned later to play Gavroche. "I loved playing that part. I was a proper tom boy. One night Alain came in and he stood at the back of the auditorium with Ken Caswell, who was the resident director, and he turned to Ken and said, "This little boy is really good," and Ken had to explain, 'Actually that's the little Cosette that you started out with.' He had no idea."[156]

Peter stayed on for a year and a half before he began to feel things were going stale and left. One of his fondest memories is playing the role of Jean Prouvaire. Like many in the ensemble, Peter took on numerous small roles, and upon reading the book he pointed out to Trevor that Jean was one of the first students to die on the barricade, along with being among the bravest. "Well, you should be the one waving the flag," Trevor announced. "So, I ended up in that iconic moment where everyone is singing 'One Day More' waving the flag at the back, which was very special for me."[157] One day, however, he was otherwise occupied under the stage and missed his cue. "I was seriously reprimanded for that."[158]

John Cameron stayed with the show for something like ten years, going in once a month to check the music was up to scratch. One of the reasons why he thinks the show has endured is the score and the way it pushed the boundaries of musical theatre. "It was probably the first piece of musical theatre that had a Recitative that never stopped in rhythmical propulsion. It was restless if you like, and that's one of its real strengths, the fact that the score never really stops."[159]

Alain and Claude-Michel also regularly came back to make sure the quality was being maintained. "They had notes. They had criticisms," says Paul. "But it was always for the sake of the show. It was their baby, and it had gone further than they ever could have thought."[160]

When news began to filter through that there was going to be a Broadway production, everybody in the cast wanted to go. "But we were told only Colm and that's the end of it," says Frances.[161] Once in New York, though, they couldn't find the right person to play Eponine. The show was already in rehearsals when Cameron managed to persuade American equity to bring Frances over. "He called me up at my flat on a Saturday and said, 'you're going to New York.' I couldn't believe it."[162] Frances caught a flight the next day. The plan was to do a week's rehearsal then return to London for a week to get everything packed before going back. The money on offer was quite low, but Frances didn't care—she just wanted to go to Broadway. "Although I did say to Cameron, can you pay the mortgage on my flat please, because I haven't got time to rent it out."[163] Frances went on to win a Tony Award for her performance.

A delegation from the Shubert Organization had come to London to see an early performance of *Les Misérables* and everyone in the group, save for executive Vice President Philip Smith, didn't care for it at all. "I liked the music, and I thought it was very effective," he told Bernard Jacobs who shot a glance back and said, "Phil, have you lost your mind?" It had become common practice now for the Shubert big wigs to get in touch regarding a Broadway transfer; this time Cameron heard nothing. The silence was so deafening he put a call through himself to their office and got Bernie on the phone. It was obvious that there wasn't a great deal of enthusiasm for it. "So, you didn't like *Les Misérables*."

"Cameron," said Jacobs, "we think it's a pile of shit."[164]

For some reason the decision had been taken to open *Les Misérables* on Broadway in the same week as *Starlight Express* in March 1987. A lot of the same creative people worked on both shows with the result that they found themselves shuttling back and forth between the two. "It was a bit mad," recalls John Napier. "I was burnt out at the end of it."[165]

The transfer from London to Broadway prompted further modifications and tightening. Martin McCallum had always been of the opinion that the show was too lengthy. "I remember sitting there at those early rehearsals thinking, *God, this is just too long, and it needs this and it needs that.* And in fact the piece was worked on for almost two years and the final changes weren't completed until America. And then those changes were brought back and put into the London production. Only then was the show finally set. So, it continued to evolve over quite a long period of time."[166]

In America, *Les Misérables* received fulsome critical praise from the start and arrived with four million dollars' worth of advance bookings. "The reception was fantastic," recalls John Cameron. "I have this vision of being in the hotel lobby with friends, family and God knows who else, with all the newspaper reviews spread out over the floor."[167]

The Broadway production ran until May 2003, closing after 6,680 performances. At the time it was the second longest-running musical in Broadway history. In London it stayed at the Palace for ten years before moving to the smaller Queen's Theatre. So ingrained did it become in the life of London that it was even part of the tourist experience. People visiting the capital for a day or a weekend break saw the usual sights like Big Ben, Buckingham Palace, and in the evening went to see *Les Misérables*.

Internationally, *Les Misérables* was produced in over forty-two countries, becoming a global phenomenon. The question is, why did audiences around the world respond to a storyline that is so unrelentingly grim? Perhaps it's that universal theme of redemption that so many responded to. "Everybody can recognise those characters," says Rebecca. "The man of God who thinks he's right who then has this terrible crisis of faith. Both of those men, Javert and Valjean, think they're acting for God."[168]

The human element is always important, especially in a musical. You can have overblown dance numbers, but you have to connect to it in a human way as well. And that was proven by the amount of correspondence that especially Colm received, things like people talking about a recent bereavement and that coming to see the show had helped them and given them the strength to move forward. "The standing ovations made you want to cry," recalls Paul Leonard, "because you thought, this is having an impact upon people, for all the right reasons."[169] And it lives on with people performing "Do You Hear the People Sing?" in a vigil for the Ukraine conflict to stories of Royal Air Force helicopter pilots returning the wounded from Helmand province during the Afghanistan campaign to the strains of "Bring Him Home."

And there are the anniversaries. The tenth anniversary concert held at the Royal Albert Hall, but more memorably the twenty-fifth anniversary concert at the O2. "That was an incredible experience," recalls Peter Polycarpou. "There were so many people on stage you just couldn't take it in. We all saw each other back stage before we went on and gave each other huge hugs. For many of us it was the first time we'd seen each other for ages, and friendships were rekindled because we lived through a lot of stuff together on that show."[170]

# 5

# "THE MACHINES ARE BEAUTIFUL"

By the mid-1980s, the musical theatre landscape had totally changed. At one point, seventeen musicals were running in the West End, most of them British productions. The bar had been raised by what some might describe as the "event" musical, and a strange sort of hubris was created by other producers eager to jump on the bandwagon in a desperate bid to compete with the likes of Andrew Lloyd Webber and Cameron Mackintosh.

Two musicals that tried but for very different reasons failed to replicate the enormous success of shows like *Cats* or *Starlight Express* were *Time* and *Metropolis*. Although flawed, *Time* must be applauded for ambition alone as being the first eco-musical. As for *Metropolis*, it was an ill-conceived attempt to bring Fritz Lang's science fiction movie classic to the stage. It also ended up a blueprint of how not to put on a musical.

David Soames was in bed one evening in his flat in Highgate when he was awoken by a voice calling him from the street below. Opening the window, he poked his head out to see what was going on. There was his old student friend from the Royal Scottish Academy of Music and Drama, Peter Blake. Standing next to him, David recognized Paul Nicholas. Blake had appeared as Pontius Pilate in *Jesus Christ Superstar* and took over from Tim Curry as Frank-N-Furter during *The Rocky Horror Show*'s original London run. He'd also successfully branched out into television comedy. David told them both to come up.

Blake told David about a friend of his called Jeff Daniels who was looking for someone to write lyrics to some music he was producing. David was interested, and a meeting was arranged. Daniels explained that he had this idea for a song called "The Time Lord." "I want it to be a Doctor Who–type theme and I'd like it narrated like Richard Harris, the way he talks a song." David told Daniels to leave it with him. After a week David had the lyrics in the bag. "But I have an idea for a whole musical," he told Daniels. "I've got all these characters in my head." David went on to explain that it was set in a high court in space. The human race has been put on trial by some high cosmic intelligence for exploiting and polluting the planet. It will be their decision whether Earth will be destroyed or allowed to survive. "And instead of a politician going to defend the earth, this space pirate intervenes and sends a rock star."[1] The musical *Time* had landed.

Since David intended this to be a rock musical, it made sense to have a rock-star defend the earth. "Also, who wants a politician to defend you. I thought, it was a great idea to get a rock star to be the person we send, someone who can actually perform in front of thousands of people and mean something to people's lives a lot more than politicians do."[2]

David and Jeff Daniels began to work together: Daniels taking care of the music, David the lyrics and book. David would send Daniels a lyric, often with a note saying something along the lines of "I'd like this to sound a bit like 'The Long and Winding Road' by the Beatles," just to give him an idea of where his head was at.

As luck would have it, David's agent knew the director of the Overground Theatre in Kingston upon Thames, in southwest London, who responded well to a demo of the music and decided to put it on. The cast was small, just nine people, and there was the innovation of a female rockstar rather than the more obvious male rocker. There was also a five-piece band that included keyboardist Milton Reame-James from the rock band Steve Harley and Cockney Rebel. "Milton was a real rocker," says David. "So that helped with the feel of the music."[3]

Opening in March 1978, *The Time Lord* did moderately well. Someone who saw it was Bob West, who sought David out to tell him how much he enjoyed it and that he was going to recommend it to this then unknown producer he worked for called Cameron Mackintosh. David gave Bob the script and waited to see if anything happened. "I then got a phone call; would you come and meet Cameron. I went to see him and he said, 'I love this idea, but your second act needs work.' I said, 'Leave it with me.' I went away and I worked on the second act, sent it to Cameron and went back to see him. He told me, 'This is really good, it still needs work, like everything needs work, but I'm very sorry David I can't do your show because I've just got this new project called *Cats*.' End of story."[4]

*The Time Lord* sat around for a while and then David's agent gave it to a producer called Danny O'Donovan, who was involved in the music business.

O'Donovan didn't really know what to do with it and sat on the thing for a year. By chance during a Concorde flight to Los Angeles, O'Donovan found himself sat next to Dave Clark, formerly the leader of the 1960s pop group the Dave Clark Five and now a highly proficient businessman. The two knew each other and started chatting. It turned out Clark was looking for a musical to put some money into. "I've got a musical," said Danny.

"What's it about?" asked Dave.

"I'm fucked if I know," said Danny. "It's set in space, there's judges in it, space pirates, I don't really know what it's about Dave."[5]

Clark was intrigued enough to ask O'Donovan to send it to his office when he got back to London. Two weeks later, nothing had arrived. Clark called him. Another two weeks passed, still nothing. Clark chased O'Donovan again, and this time got the package. Undoubtedly what Clark saw in the project was a chance to compete with the likes of Andrew Lloyd Webber and Cameron Mackintosh, to put on a really spectacular show, one that had the potential to play round the world.

It was obvious very early on that Dave Clark intended to take over the project completely. One day he announced to David Soames that he was dropping the word "Lord" from the title, and instead calling it just *Time*. David was fine with that. "And I'm getting a poster done," said Clark. David and Jeff Daniels went up to Clark's apartment to see the poster when it was done, and there emblazoned on the top was the credit: Dave Clark's *Time*. "Dave, it's not your *Time*, really," argued David. "It all came out of my head. You've worked on it with me, you've had things to contribute and all of that, but . . ." Clark was insistent and mentioned that the prolific Tony award–winning American theatrical producer David Merrick had his name above the title of the musical *42nd Street*. "But he was a giant of American theatre," opined David, not unreasonably.[6]

In the end David didn't begrudge Clark having his name above the title. He was to put so much into the show, starting with the inspired casting coup of getting Cliff Richard to star. Instead of bringing in a West End name to act the part of a popstar, Clark reasoned, why not get the real thing. And Cliff was his first choice. The two had known each other for years, and perhaps Clark was aware of Cliff's long-held ambition to star in a West End musical. Cliff read the script and agreed with the environmental philosophy behind the show, that the human race should change its ways and stop polluting the planet. He was also sold on the spirituality of the story, of there being some divine higher intelligence watching over us. "And he loved the score," says David. "He told me, 'This is a real rock score. It's not someone who can't play or write rock music trying to make a rock musical, this is an actual rock n roll score, and that's why I'm doing it.'"[7]

Cliff agreed to commit to the show for a full year, but his diary was booked solid for the next twenty-four months with tour schedules and recording commitments. Agreeing to wait, Clark set his sights on producing the concept album to end all concept albums. For this he relied on his contacts in the music biz. "Dave Clark could pick up the phone and say, is Stevie Wonder there, it's Dave Clark, and get an answer," says David. "That was phenomenal."[8] The talent Clark was able to bring together for the *Time* album was indeed impressive:

Many shows tried to replicate the success of *Cats* or *Starlight Express*, notably *Time*, starring popstar Cliff Richard. Famously, it included the appearance of a holographic Laurence Olivier.
*Credit*: Trinity Mirror / Alamy Stock Photo

Freddie Mercury, Dionne Warwick, Burt Bacharach, Ashford and Simpson, Leo Sayer, Jimmy Helms, Murray Head, and Julian Lennon, on whose song "Time Will Teach Us All" featured Stevie Wonder on backing vocals and keyboard. And there was Cliff Richard, of course, kicking things off with the lead single, "She's So Beautiful," released in September 1985, eight months before the show was due to open. Accompanied by a Ken Russell directed video, "She's So Beautiful" was the only top twenty hit from the show.

With an opening date set for early in April 1986, Clark made a deal for *Time* to go into the Dominion Theatre. Located at the bottom of Tottenham Court Road, a short walk from London's theatre land district, the Dominion was a huge barn of a place, seating a little over two thousand. Clark was nothing if not ambitious. He was a gambler, too, since the Dominion was known predominantly as a cinema.

Rehearsals began in January 1986 in a large studio in Tufnell Park, North London. For David it was a thrill watching his show come together, but also a strange feeling seeing Cliff Richard whose records he used to listen to as a kid. "This was one of my heroes. And there I am, this kid from the back streets of Glasgow, and just eight feet away from me is Cliff Richard singing my songs."[9] It had been a difficult journey for David; thrown out of school at fifteen with no qualifications and working as a laborer, he joined a drama club and went to night classes. Singled out by a teacher who encouraged him to go to drama school, David won a place at the Royal Scottish Academy of Music and Drama. It was here where he learned how a play is constructed and began to write himself, firing his imagination and finding his voice.

Getting to know Cliff, David liked him enormously and admired his approach to the show. "He knew he was against theatrical performers and was learning all the time, asking questions."[10] This is one of the reasons why Cliff had agreed to do the show, it was a challenge. "And it was nothing like anything I'd ever done before."[11] Even something that came so natural to him in his concerts was prohibited, and that was interacting with the audience and his fans. "It was the first time I'd been on stage where you don't need to look at the audience. My concerts are all about looking and smiling at everybody, this was not like that at all, I only looked at the other members of the cast—it was exciting and brand new."[12]

Apart from Cliff, there were no other stars to speak of, but the cast were highly professional and experienced. Jeff Shankley played Lord Melchizedec, the prosecutor presiding over the cosmic court and his three judges. Rosemarie Ford was a dancer and singer who had been on tour with Andrew Lloyd Webber's *Song and Dance* show and had just left the West End hit *Me and My Girl*.

Sent up for an audition by her agent, Rosemarie landed a role as part of a rebellious space gang of four girls and two boys. In the show the gang make their first entrance from the very top of the flies. And in the Dominion Theatre that was very high up indeed. Each wore a harness and descended on ropes to the stage floor. "It was terrifying," recalls Rosemarie.[13] It took at least a couple of weeks to conquer her fear and get used to it. Then once on the ground they burst into a fast, flat-out Arlene Phillips dance routine.

Dave Clark was nothing if not astute and had recruited well. Not just Arlene Phillips as choreographer, but also Larry Fuller from Broadway as director. Not that David Soames had an inkling about Larry coming over to direct. They didn't meet until the first day of rehearsal. "Larry couldn't believe it. He said to me, 'I've been in London for three months, you're the writer who thought this up and I've never met you or spoken to you about your ideas and how you got there and what you were thinking. That's unheard of on Broadway.'"[14]

With an emphasis on spectacle, it was no surprise that Dave Clark sought the services of John Napier as set designer. John was intrigued when Clark approached him to work on the show. He liked him and found him interesting; they were fellow Spurs fans, and John had seen the Dave Clark Five play live in concert as a teenager. "I was kind of seduced, I guess, into doing the show. The potential was there but that potential didn't come to the fore."[15]

Nevertheless, John produced a mechanical marvel of a set with a wall of green lasers, a thirty-eight-foot saucer platform that lifted, tilted, and glowed, and elaborate throne chairs for the judges that hovered in the air and were brought on by hydraulic arms. Such was the array of lasers and lights that notices were placed outside the theatre warning people with epilepsy and heart conditions. "There were some phenomenal bits of engineering in that show," says John. "In regards to the stage craft that went into it, that was absolutely fantastic."[16] The whole thing took around three months to build, and the Dominion had to be completely rewired to accommodate the large power demands of the lighting rig. *Time* still ranks as one of the most spectacular shows ever seen on a British stage. "I remember being in the Dominion one day and Tim Rice was there," recalls David Soames. "I went up and introduced myself. He said, 'I can't believe it. I thought we had the effects in London with *Chess*. You've just wiped the floor with us.'"[17]

The main highlight, and something for which *Time* became renowned, was a holographic performance by none other than Laurence Olivier. It was a stunning coup by Dave Clark. Olivier had agreed to play the God-like character of Akash, who presides over the court, "the final word" of the universe. His "appearance" was prefilmed and directed by Clark himself, and then projected onto a fourteen-foot-high fiberglass sculpture, carved into the shape of Olivier's head. When it emerged hovering within a giant globe, as if in mid-air, the whole thing had the effect of a giant hologram.

Early in the run, Olivier made a personal appearance as part of the audience. "He sat up in the circle," recalls Rosemarie. "At the end somebody in the stalls realised he was in and turned round and looked at him and started applauding. Then others started to turn around, and people were going, it's Olivier, it's Laurence Olivier, and everybody started to slowly stand up and applaud. He half stood up and was waving, because he was quite frail at the time, and blowing kisses, it was wonderful."[18]

Cliff had only agreed to perform matinees for the first six months. The second six months he would only do evening shows and his understudy took over on matinee performances. When Laurence Olivier came to see one of the matinees, it fell in that second six-month period. "I told my understudy, 'John, you can collect your money for this performance, but I'm going on for this one.'"[19]

Unfortunately, there was the odd technical glitch with the effects. Sometimes the giant Olivier head didn't sit correctly on the stage and the projection was slightly askew. Other times it didn't work at all and so just the voice was used. "When it worked, which was most of the time, it was breathtaking," says Jeff Shankley.[20] Cliff recalls the head effect going spectacularly wrong just the once. "I was singing this big dramatic song and the audience started to giggle, then to laugh. I turned around and Laurence Olivier's eyes were on his cheeks. It looked ridiculous! But the crowd loved it. The techs rescued the face, and I continued singing."[21]

Jeff ended up benefiting quite a bit when the management felt that Olivier's long speeches had the effect of slowing down the action. "So, three of Olivier's speeches were given to me so that I could 'move' them more. When Olivier came to see the show, the cast met him backstage and he said something to me I have never forgotten in my darker days. He shook my hand and said: 'Aren't we lucky to have you.' Music to the ears of an aspiring young actor. Words of encouragement to younger actors mean so much to us."[22]

Unsurprisingly the technical rehearsals were long and exhaustive, and going into previews things weren't quite right. But that's always the way with any new show; it's only really when you're working with an audience during the preview period that you can see what's working and what is not. "You don't get in and say, 'right that's it, we're underway,'" states Rosemarie. "Previews are for the tweaking and the changing, all the things that need to be done. And Arlene and Larry would have us in to make sure choreographically we were absolutely bang on, whether we were all in time together or doing a wrong move or not getting a

Pirouette right, they were just cracking the whip all the way along to make sure we were absolutely as perfect as we possible could be."[23]

*Time* opened with much fanfare on April 9. And with Cliff Richard appearing in his first West End musical, the advance box office was phenomenal. Cliff admits that opening night was "nerve-wracking. I didn't relax until the audience gave us a standing ovation at the end."[24] After the curtain came down, everyone's mood was one of excitement and anticipation as they made the short walk down to the Hippodrome nightclub in Leicester Square to celebrate. The mood quickly changed when the reviews came out. It was mostly hostile. The *Sunday Times* called it "a spectacular load of bilge." Sheridan Morley labeled it one of the century's worst musicals. "They thought it was a bit naïve," says David Soames, "which today I can understand in a way. If I was asked to write it now, it would be essentially the same show, but entirely different."[25] John Napier's audacious sets were about the only thing the critics found favor with.

The company rallied themselves in the face of the critical onslaught. "We all talked about it in our dressing rooms," recalls Rosemarie, "and we all went, come on, we're worth more than that, we're better than that."[26] Understandably, Cliff and Dave Clark took it personally, feeling that there was an element of snobbery in the treatment meted out to them, that the theatrical establishment looked down their noses at them. This idea that Clark was no Lloyd Webber or Mackintosh, he was an interloper, and what was the pop world doing gate-crashing the West End.

When Olivier came to the show, he was made aware of the adverse critical reaction when he went to see the cast afterwards. "We all sat around his feet like he was a king on a throne," says Cliff. "When I told him that the press didn't seem to like the show and had been very hard with us, he said, 'My dear boy, they send people who can't dance, can't sing, can't act to criticize people who can.' I loved that response."[27]

Audiences, for the most part, embraced the show. "People first came in not really knowing what to expect and were just blown off their seats," says Rosemarie.[28] The beginning of the show is something of a tour de force as Cliff is taken into space, amid an explosion of lights, effects, dry ice, and blasting rock music. "People sat open mouthed," recalls Rosemarie. "Within the first ten minutes of the show you'd had everything thrown at you, it was quite overwhelming. Audiences couldn't believe what they were seeing within a theatre."[29]

That was the concept, really, to produce a proper rock musical that was as close as possible to the thrill of a live concert. "Dave Clark said that he wanted it to be as rock n roll as it could be while still getting the narrative across," says John Napier. "He was all for it being a colossal mega fest of rock n roll."[30]

The sound of the band was concert-level loud, and the musicians Dave Clark brought in were top class. Underneath the stage, the backing singers were of equal quality.

Inevitably, most of the people that came to see the show comprised of Cliff fans. David Soames recalls talking to a couple that had seen it fifty-nine times. This created a different kind of theatre audience. "At the start we used to get some of the girls in the audience screaming and yelling,' it's Cliff!'" says Rosemarie. "And then they realised they were actually in a theatre show and kind of calmed down a bit."[31]

Despite the criticisms leveled at the show, Cliff continued with incredible enthusiasm and an energy that never wavered. "I have never worked with someone, before or since, that was so genuinely unselfish, unpretentious, and thoroughly professional," states Jeff. "Cliff gave 200% and led the company from the front by example and with humility. His energy was infectious."[32]

Cliff approached the musical in a similar fashion to his concert tours, where he always endeavors to make his band into a team rather than a bunch of individuals. "On *Time*, maybe three times a week we would go out somewhere together. I once booked the Odeon Leicester Square for a midnight showing of the latest blockbuster and we went in secretly carrying pizzas under our jackets and watched it all together. Once you socialise together you do get a closeness."[33] Sometimes the cast played tennis at a nearby sports center after the show until two in the morning. "I don't know what Cliff plugged into," says Jeff. "Probably his faith. Which he never spoke of, preferring to show by example. He was deeply respected for that."[34]

During Cliff's year-long tenure in the show, he never missed a single performance. "Even when he crashed his car on the M4 coming in from Weybridge, he got a lift to the theatre and arrived in time," says David Soames.[35] He felt he owed the audience that much, knowing most of them had come to see him. "Sometimes you could hear that he was physically exhausted," says Rosemarie, "but he never went off and he never half did it."[36]

Neither did he throw his weight around or demand things be changed, except on one occasion. In the moment where his character, in a cacophony of lights and thunderous music, is transported into space, Cliff thought the music should stop, at least for a while, at the moment of his arrival to represent the vast emptiness and silence of space. Instead, the orchestra kept blasting out this music. Cliff felt it wasn't working that way and after a few weeks saw Dave Clark and made his views known. Clark was adamant things stayed the way they were. "One night I said to Dave, if I couldn't have the silence I wouldn't go on," reveals Cliff. "He didn't know I didn't really mean it. So, the music was taken out. It felt like magic. We had echo on our voices. It was just like we thought it should be."[37] And it stayed that way for the rest of Cliff's run in the show. When he left, Clark put it back the way it was.

When it came time for Cliff to bow out after a year, emotions were running high. On his final night he needed a police escort to get him through a throng of four hundred fans waiting for him outside the theatre. "He has such a massive fan base," says Rosemarie, "and they all came and wanted to throw roses on the stage. Cliff found it really emotional because he spent a whole year with us and as a company you bond and become a family, really. He'd had such a great time. He'd absolutely loved doing it."[38]

Within days Cliff flew out of the country for a holiday in the Caribbean, only to spend half of each day exhausted in bed. He hadn't realized how much the show had taken out of him. His adrenalin had powered him through, and now his body was spent like a car battery.

In the weeks leading up to Cliff's departure there were rumors about who was going to take over. Every time a celebrity turned up to watch the show, the cast speculated whether they were going to be taking on the role. One evening David Soames was sitting in the auditorium and a few rows down from him sat John Travolta with Dave Clark. Travolta came to see *Time* on three consecutive nights, and the news David heard was that Travolta had agreed to do it for a limited season on Broadway. Then there was a scheduling conflict, and he withdrew, blowing any chance of a Broadway transfer.

In the end former teen idol David Cassidy was brought in as Cliff's replacement. It made sense to cast another bona fide popstar in the role and Cassidy could act, too; like Cliff, he'd done films and television. He was a good choice and another good company man. Cliff made a promise to himself to go and see him in the show. "I thought he was quite brilliant—but not as good as me!!"[39] But Cassidy wasn't the same draw. When Cliff starred the theatre was around 85 percent capacity every night. With Cassidy, it did only moderate business. The problem was the Dominion was just too big. If you've got twelve hundred people in a two-thousand-seat venue, it looks empty. If there's six hundred in a nine-hundred-seat venue, it looks nearly full. It was also costing a fortune to run such a lavish production, and so it was inevitable that it would have to close, two years after it first opened. However, not before a very special evening.

In April 1988, Dave Clark organized a special gala charity performance of *Time* to raise awareness and money for an AIDS foundation. Cliff Richard returned to join David Cassidy on the Dominion stage, and Freddie Mercury was convinced to perform a couple of songs, too. "When they told me that Freddie Mercury was doing it, I was delighted," says Cliff. "I had to pull out all the stops to keep up with him. I was thrilled to say I'd sung with Freddie Mercury."[40] Sadly, this proved to be Mercury's last ever live performance.

And that was the end of *Time*. With no experience of putting on musicals or contacts in the theatrical world, Dave Clark was unable to drive the show forward, perhaps find new territories in the world to put it on. There were hopes for a scaled down version to be taken on the road, but it never happened.

Dave Clark was his own worst enemy, too. Lots of people working on the show felt it could've done with a rewrite and that cuts needed to be made. Sometimes you have to be brutal and say, this isn't working, out it goes. But Clark was too pedantic. "He wanted everything exactly as it was written in the script," recalls Cliff. "At one of the read throughs with 'the proper actors' as I called them, one said, 'David, I said this sentence three pages ago. Can I change it and make it something else that's similar?' And he said no. He didn't want anything changed. He was very tough with that. I thought too tough, really."[41]

Despite all the difficulties, David Soames is adamant that no one else could've put on *Time* the way Dave Clark did: "Not Cameron Mackintosh. Not Andrew Lloyd Webber. Because Dave put his whole being into it."[42] And it was ahead of its time. "But because saving the planet wasn't a forceful issue back then," says John Napier, "it was ridiculed by the same people that would ridicule something that's not highbrow or has the etiquette of Oxbridge."[43]

David Soames was walking up the aisle after one particular performance, and there were two ladies in front of him. One of them turned to the other and said, "It don't half make you bloody think, don't it?" David had to say something and introduced himself as the author. "That was very nice what you said." The woman looked at him and replied, "Yeah, I really enjoyed it, but it made me think about the whole world and everything."[44] *Job done*, thought David. *Job done*.

The concept to turn Fritz Lang's 1927 Expressionist sci-fi classic *Metropolis* into a full-blown stage musical was on paper an interesting one. Its plot of a futuristic city where a beautiful and cultured utopia exists above a bleak underworld populated by mistreated workers certainly lent itself to the notion of having to go big in order to compete with the Lloyd Webbers and Mackintoshes. Alas the actual contents of the show began to take a secondary level of importance. Going for all out spectacle was a false move that was never going to last, and it crippled any hopes that *Metropolis* might succeed.

The man behind the idea was New York–born Joseph Brooks who'd made a fortune in the advertising business writing jingles for clients including Dr Pepper and American Airlines. At one point in the 1970s, he claimed to have 150 commercials on the air. In 1977 he wrote the song "You Light Up My Life" for the romantic movie of the same name, which he also produced, wrote, and directed. The song won him an Oscar, a Grammy, and a number one hit record.

Brooks got the idea for *Metropolis* in 1986 while living in London and hawked it round various West End producers without success. A lot of the money was being put up by Brooks himself, along with investors of his own, an unusual state of affairs since it was normally the producer that found the finance. In the end renowned theatrical impresario and film producer Michael White took it on. Michael was not really a hands-on type of producer. He would have an assistant that ran the production of the show day to day. He would come in every now and then just to see how it was progressing. In that respect, Michael was the very opposite of Cameron Mackintosh. Particularly, he wouldn't come in and say, "stop, I want this to happen, I want that to happen," which is the way Cameron operates.

A sing through of the show was organized to see what they had. This was a few weeks before Christmas of 1988, with rehearsals planned for January. Joseph Brooks was there, as was Michael White. A group of session singers had been brought in and David Firman, as musical director, was on hand, too. Judy Kuhn, a rising star on Broadway, who had played the role of Cosette there in *Les Misérables*, was flown over to sit in. As yet, no director had been found.

Act 1 was sung through, with piano accompaniment. "Judy paid attention for a bit and then started to read the *Evening Standard* newspaper," recalls David Firman. "It all seemed to be a bit the same."[45] Everyone broke for coffee and then returned for the second act, only thing was there wasn't a second act, just some sketchy ideas for a few songs. It was decided to go ahead with Act 2 anyway, although that didn't occupy anyone's time for very long. "It felt very much like a damp squib," says David.[46] It was obvious there was a real problem here, with rehearsals starting soon and no second act. Everybody looked at everybody else. Joseph Brooks finally piped up. "I've got these great ideas," he said, which didn't go down very well. There was nothing substantial written down on paper.

David Firman was given the task of chasing Brooks and getting the second act out of him. He was reliably informed that Brooks and his wife had flown out of the country to spend New Year's at a fancy ski resort in Switzerland. David flew after them, landing in Zurich where he was met by a concierge from the resort. There was gold braid down his trousers and he wore a fancy cap, and behind him was a limousine. David was driven up into the mountains toward what can only be described as a luxurious hotel. "The crown heads of Europe were there. I had not seen life like that ever. There were people in carriages riding across a frozen lake."[47]

David found Brooks and sat down with him. "There were a few more tunes but they sounded to me exactly like the other tunes."[48] David went back and played them to Michael White's assistant. The reaction was not great. "For Christ's sake, can you write something?" David was asked. Against his better judgment, David took up the challenge, trying to hammer together a score for the second act so at least everyone had something to rehearse with. "But my dad was ill at the time, and I started to get really fed up with the show. There was no feedback coming back. And so, I resigned and went up to see my ailing father in Manchester."[49]

One evening David took a call from Michael White and allowed himself to be talked back into returning, on the strict understanding that he would work on the show until the opening night and then he was gone. "So, I cobbled together a score, and I wrote some lyrics. And in the end, we got through it. And some of it is not too bad. Most of the second act is me, in the sense that it's me either trying to write in the Joe Brooks style or me picking up stuff from the first act and regurgitating it and revising it."[50]

The next hurdle was bringing in the right director. However, no clear candidate presented itself; either everyone was too busy or thought not to be suitable. Simon Opie had been brought on early as production manager and was involved in the director search. He recalls that the name of Jerome Savary suddenly came up in the discussions. Savary was an Argentinian French director and one of the most influential pioneers of the avant-garde theatre in France during the 1960s and onwards. He had staged everything from Shakespeare to a play about comic book hero Asterix and recently put on an acclaimed production of *Cabaret* in Paris. Simon was dispatched, with Brook's wife, to go and see it. "Our job was then to interview Jerome afterwards to see if he'd be interested in doing *Metropolis*. I remember Joe was supposed to come but he discovered his passport had run out."[51] Savary was indeed interested to work in the West End and committed.

While all this was going on, the cast were being assembled. Graham Bickley was a young English actor and singer who had appeared in the ensemble cast of the *Pirates of Penzance* in 1982 at the Theatre Royal, Drury Lane, and was one of the backing singers on *Time*. Then appearing in *Les Misérables*, he heard about the auditions for *Metropolis* and went up for the role of the young romantic lead Steven. This had been offered to Michael Ball only for him to turn it down. A wise move as it turned out, since Ball took a role in Andrew Lloyd Webber's *Aspects of Love* instead, which launched his career.

Graham attended several auditions before landing the role of Steven, including one at the house Joseph Brooks was renting near Harrods. "That was a surreal experience. And it should have warned me of what was to come."[52] Graham met with Brooks; they talked about the show and then began to go through a couple of the songs at the piano. "Joe had a small son," recalls Graham, "about three or four, and he decided in the midst of my trying to perform this song that he would come and stand on the top of the sofa and just wee all over the place. His mum came in and I was like, 'oh my God, should we stop?' And it was like he'd dropped a biscuit, 'Oh dear, never mind,' and I thought, there's a child screaming for attention here."[53]

The show was set to open in March 1989 at the Piccadilly Theatre, not the biggest of West End theatres but well run with a capable backstage team. Rehearsals finally got underway early in February. There was a meet and greet on the first day, and everyone was shown a model of the ambitious sets. Then the real work got underway. "But what became apparent quite early on was that it wasn't complete," says Graham. "It wasn't finished."[54] Graham also got a sense that the company was a strong one and made up of some interesting personalities. "There was Brian Blessed, who is a big personality in a small room, and Judy Kuhn as Maria, who had never been in a London production and she was hoping, like we all were, that this was going to put her on the map. And I think she realised quite early on, what have I walked into. But she gave it her all and was wonderful in it."[55]

It didn't help that the score was still being written. Rumors were rife that Brooks was catching the Concorde and nipping back to the States at the weekends and showing up on the Monday with a brand-new song that was needed to fill a gap somewhere. "The gossip amongst everyone was that he'd gone and got somebody to write a song that he then brought back," says Graham. "He didn't write it. All these rumours were going on."[56]

The cast had difficulties, too, with Jerome Savary's way of working. "He was very strange," admits Graham. "And we soon realised he had no real conception of what he wanted."[57] There were a lot of firsts happening on that production—Graham's first West End lead, Judy's West End debut and being in a new country—and what was absolutely needed was a director to pull it all together. "And Jerome Savary was on a planet of his own," says Graham.[58] It was a struggle. At one point during rehearsals, they were running through a scene and Graham was on stage and had to make an exit. "Where would you like me to leave?" he asked Savary. "Left or right, up or down stage, where do you want me to go?"

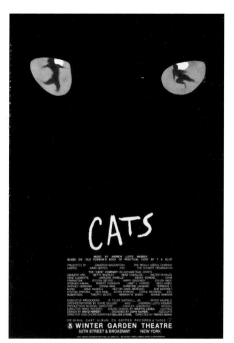

Thanks to the bravery of its staging and sheer innovation, *Evita* set the tone for the musicals of the 1980s and lifted British musical theatre out of the doldrums.
*Credit*: Photofest

This iconic image was seen everywhere and went on to become the second biggest-selling T-shirt in the world during the 1980s, beaten only by the Hard Rock Café.
*Credit*: Photofest

Princess Diana meets the *Starlight Express* cast. Diana was a highly visible patron of these shows, going back to see them time and time again.
*Credit*: Trinity Mirror / Alamy Stock Photo

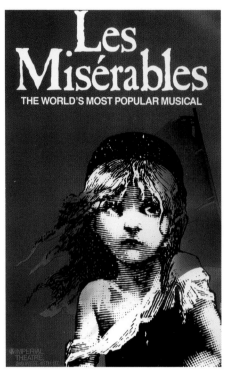

Les Misérables opened to scathing reviews that would have closed lesser shows. The public voted with their feet and turned it into one of the most successful musicals of all time. *Credit*: Photofest

Joining forces with Webber on *Cats* as a young producer, by the end of the decade Cameron Mackintosh was described by the New York Times as "the most successful, influential, and powerful theatrical producer in the world." *Credit*: Photofest

The writer of Evita meets the boys from ABBA—what could possibly go wrong? Their collaboration worked musically, but *Chess* was to skirt from one disaster to another. *Credit*: ilpo musto / Alamy Stock Photo

The London production of *Chess* was radically altered for Broadway, a disastrous decision when it closed after just sixty-eight performances.
*Credit*: Marth Swope / Photofest © Martha Swope

Webber, Sarah Brightman, and Michael Crawford at the opening of *Phantom of the Opera*. The technical demands of the production almost brought it to its knees, but it ended up the longest-running show in Broadway history.
*Credit*: Adam Scull / Alamy Stock Photo

Fresh from their success with *Les Misérables*, Claude-Michel Schönberg and Alan Boublil's Vietnam War set version of Puccini's opera *Madama Butterfly* was another smash hit.
*Credit*: Retro AdArchives / Alamy Stock Photo

With its Vietnam War setting, director Nicholas Hytner wanted *Miss Saigon* to be as truthful and real as possible.
*Credit*: parkerphotography / Alamy Stock Photo

From the stalls came this voice. "Wherever you want to go Graham. It's up to you."[59]

Graham thought, well it's not strictly up to me, is it. You have to tell me. Actors require and like to be directed because there has to be a reason for everything. And they weren't getting much from Savary. Because of the complexities of the futuristic set, there was always going to be an element of discovery that had to happen in situ. "But he wasn't in charge," says Graham. "He wasn't driving it."[60]

David Firman was equally bewildered by Savery's direction. "Jerome had a unique way of working which was without the script."[61] His method was that he didn't want to be encumbered with a script; rather, he wanted to be like a member of the audience understanding what is being shown to him for the first time. David remembers one instance that mirrors Graham's experience. "These five actors came on and Judy was one of them and she said, 'Jerome where do you want me to be?' Jerome said, 'I do not know. How would I know where you are supposed to be? Why should I know? You can go if you want.' Judy said, 'But I'm in the scene!' It was extraordinary."[62]

Brought in to do the lighting design, David Hersey lost his rag during a technical rehearsal when he stormed out of the wings yelling, "Does anybody in the fucking auditorium have a fucking script of this piece!"[63] There was a taped together vocal score which David Firman had put together, and that was about it.

Adding to the general strain were technical rehearsals that seemed neverending due to the complicated set which was built on several levels. It was designed by Ralph Koltai and brilliantly recreated the claustrophobic, nightmarish subterranean industrial city of Fritz Lang's imagination, all pistons, funnels, giant cogs and wheels, walkways, platforms, even a huge engine room. "It was truly spectacular," says Simon Opie, who had worked several times with Koltai. "He was a genius."[64] Berlin born, Koltai was a hugely influential stage designer who created ground-breaking sets for the Royal Shakespeare Company and English National Opera. But he hadn't really had a big commercial success. "So, he was desperate for *Metropolis* to be a hit, and he put everything into that show," says Simon. "There was no element of it that wasn't a huge engineering challenge whether it was the floor that lit up from underneath, or the laboratory that flew down from the skies, never mind the machine elements themselves which were immense. Even the front curtain that spilt in half and said *Metropolis* across it was a huge metallic shield; every single thing was a challenge."[65]

There were also a pair of vertical lifts on the auditorium side of the proscenium arch which started under the stage and went up into the roof. Naturally, they had to be approved by health and safety before they could be used in the show. A man from the local council came to see how they operated and asked for an emergency stop to be performed at the bottom. Each lift had these rings on the outside that were supposed to stop it if they hit an object. Simon had been busy for weeks on technical rehearsals and was close to exhausted and not really thinking straight when he suggested that to prove how safe these lifts were, he'd put his own foot under one. In the end, he thought better of it and decided to use a broom handle which happened to be lying on the stage. "I put this broom handle in position, and we sent the lift down to perform this emergency stop and the lift just chopped the broom handle straight in half. So, we had to go back to the drawing board."[66] The lifts ended up working fine.

Another health and safety stipulation stated that Brian Blessed, who was playing a mad scientist, had to wear a safety harness in the scene where he's flying in on the laboratory set. Only the actor staunchly refused. Simon had to stand next to him and insist for several days until Blessed finally accepted that a safety harness had to be used.

While the technical side was being worked out, the actors were still having to come to terms with the director. "He was taking long liquid lunches," says Graham, "and everything would slow down afterwards."[67] This behavior impacted upon everyone. There was Graham, achieving a long-held ambition to originate a character in a West End musical, only for that to get lost in all the madness around him, along with the work that both he and co-star Judy were trying to achieve. "All because we didn't trust the director. There were no moments where he would say, let's just the three of us go into that room over there and talk about this scene and what we're trying to achieve and what we need to bring to it. We never had that. Everything took second place to the set."[68] The result was that the characters were not as rounded as they needed to be. The cast were let down also by a book that wasn't as good as it should have been. There was nothing for any of the actors to get their teeth into. Dusty Hughes, a playwright, director, and television screenwriter, was trying his best, but again, he was another first, having never written a book for a musical before.

Not helping matters was a huge personality clash that developed between Savary and Brian Blessed. "It was sometimes a dangerous place to be when those two were at it," says Graham. "Brian put his fists through a fair amount of the sets at various times."[69] A lot of that was out of pure frustration that things weren't working. Some people in those kinds of situations go quiet; others, like Blessed, got louder. "I remember one particular time during rehearsal," recalls Graham, "where Brian sang his big number, 'The Machines are Beautiful.' He went slightly off tune and forgot a couple of lyrics but he got through it, we all did the same. And at the end there was a long silence and Jerome was in the audience and said something really sarcastic and very demeaning and Brian just kicked off. He destroyed part of the set. He left the theatre and was gone, down the street. And we all just had to sit and wait quietly for it to resolve itself. So, it was a bit of a tinderbox."[70]

During this time Brooks was usually around, trying to keep the whole thing from falling apart. This was his baby, and he was determined to see it through to the end. "He was the real driving force," claims Simon Opie. "He was the engine of that show. He thought that his music deserved to be up there with the greats."[71]

With the opening date looming, David Firman was still without any orchestrations. In the end he resorted to going into a phone box close to the theatre; armed with a handful of small change, he called as many of his colleagues as he could think of to ask if they could take on this song or that song. These different arrangers would come round to the theatre or to David's house to pick up a vocal score, and he'd talk them through it. David did a couple himself, but all sorts of people came in to do an arrangement. David asked David Lindup to do one. He was a noted composer, arranger, and orchestrator best known for his collaborations with jazz musician John Dankworth. They'd never met before, but David had always admired his work. David was keen for him to handle the denouement of the show. "He arrived at the house and got out of the car and his glasses were like bottle tops and he wobbled up to the front door."[72] David showed him the vocal score and explained what he wanted. All the while David was slightly perturbed since Lindup wasn't taking any notes, and he didn't seem to be able to even see the score. "Then he left, and he walked down the steps towards his car and walked straight into a lamppost. I thought, this is going to be a disaster area, we're not going to see anything. In fact, it turned out to be the best bit of writing in the whole thing."[73]

Problems continued to mount: the set didn't work, and people couldn't find out where to go. At one juncture Blessed reached a point where he'd just had enough. "He marched down to the front of the stage," recalls David, "and fixed a glare at our director Jerome and said, 'I told them not to fucking hire you and they fucking did, you stupid . . .' I mean, he just went berserk. And everybody around me went—yes."[74]

As the show went into previews, it was nowhere near ready; days got longer, and everyone left the theatre later every night and arrived earlier each morning. "Immediately after each performance we held a conference to see what had to be made better," reveals David.[75] It was getting fractious and there wasn't much chance of things actually improving. "Jerome came from a very different world," Simon points out. "He hadn't really appreciated what this new brand of British musical really involved. But where it started to break down was Jerome thought he could fix the show and clearly everybody else had lost confidence in whether he could deliver it."[76]

By the third preview, it was obvious that the only change that had to be made was to fire Jerome Savary. "At that point he was just getting drunker earlier in the day," reveals Graham, "and you can't have, especially on a show that complicated, someone who is not in control of themselves, never mind the company."[77] A meeting was called with Michael White presiding. In attendance was David Firman, Ralph Koltai, and Tom Jobe the choreographer. It was decided that Jerome had to leave. "Security guards were instructed not to allow him into the theatre," says David.[78] The cast were also required to prove who they were to these heavies posted on the stage door. "And we had to sign something not to speak about any of this," says Graham.[79] As for Jerome Savary, the cast never saw him again.

Savary was replaced by the assistant director, who was pleasant enough but really an old-fashioned type of resident director. He wasn't the kind of director they really needed, somebody to parachute into a rescue case like this, grab it by the neck, refocus, and make some sense out of it. "It was a DIY job, really," says Graham. "Do it yourself. We just had to get through it. They were blessed that we had such a great company that everybody just did their absolute best and sung their hearts out."[80]

After opening night, which passed in a blur for most of the cast, the show, with all its faults, settled down into its run. The reviews were scathing, but everyone just battled through. "And actually," says David, "from the cast point of view and from the people backstage, particularly when you know it's a bit of a sick animal, you bond together, because what else can you do."[81]

During the run Graham landed a starring role on the hugely popular BBC television sitcom *Bread*. That meant filming in Liverpool all day, then getting a train back down to London for the show in the evening. After the curtain came down, Graham rushed to catch the midnight train back up to Liverpool to start work again on *Bread* at six in the morning. It was a grueling schedule that did eventually catch up with him. During one *Metropolis* performance, Graham had gone into his dressing room for a quick rest during the interval, only he was so exhausted he fell into a deep sleep. He woke up with a start to someone shaking him, "Mr Bickley. Mr Bickley." The whole company was on stage waiting to start Act 2. "I was due to come down in the lift, and of course the lift had come down with me not in it. I rushed to the stage, and I could hear one of the actors stalling, 'I'm sure that when Steven arrives, he will tell us. Yes, he will tell us what he thinks, because Steven always tells . . .' and I rushed on, wide eyed and breathless. I apologized profusely afterwards and never did that again."[82]

As the months went by, Graham and everyone else could see the houses getting thinner and the inevitability that the show was going to close sooner rather than later. "We knew it wasn't going to survive, but the company worked so hard right to the end. There was no slacking, there was no, 'we'll just walk this because who cares.' We were young, we were keen, and we were ambitious."[83] Before the inevitable happened, Judy left the show to return to America. "I think she was very disheartened," says Graham.[84] So much store had been put on her coming from Broadway, and she'd had to face the realization this wasn't the role that was going to do anything for her. Even so, Judy turned in a wonderful performance and was nominated for an Olivier Award as Best Actress in a Musical. She had a particularly affecting gospel number. "You Are the Light," performed by candlelight which really raised the roof of the theatre when the entire company joined in and provided the show with one of its few highlights. And her transformation into the robot Futura was chilling.

With Judy gone, *Metropolis* lurched on. "Joe used to come with another briefcase full of money every so often," claims David Firman.[85] Finally, no one could keep the thing afloat any longer, and it folded after just six months, longer than it perhaps deserved.

In the final analysis, the book and score of *Metropolis* just weren't good enough, and if those are lacking you've no chance. The set was praised, as was Judy, but you can't have the audience coming out of the theatre whistling the furniture. "It wasn't far off working," admits Simon Opie, "just because of the spectacle and the world that it drew you into."[86]

As for Joseph Brooks, he had a particularly grim final act. In 2009 he was charged with drugging and sexually assaulting thirteen women that he had promised to audition for movie roles. Prior to facing sentencing, he was found dead in his Manhattan apartment in May 2011. The police said his head was wrapped in a plastic bag connected to a tube from a helium tank and that he had left a three-page note. The city medical examiners ruled the death a suicide.[87]

Despite all the problems and things that went wrong, *Time* and *Metropolis* failed for one simple reason. What those hoping to step up to that top level underestimated was the learning curve that people like Cameron Mackintosh and Andrew Lloyd Webber had been through in order to achieve what they did. And even though you get the same creative people in like John Napier, David Hersey, and others, plus you have the same ingredients, all the expertise, and you put it all together like a Meccano kit, success is never guaranteed.

# 6

# "I KNOW HIM SO WELL"

Back in 1972 at the World Chess Championship in Reykjavik, millions of people were captivated by the clash between defending champion Boris Spassky of the Soviet Union and the challenger Bobby Fischer of the United States. Beneath the sporting spectacle, however, something much more important was going on, a battle of wills between the two superpowers. It was this element, along with the drama of the matches themselves, that drew the interest of Tim Rice, and he began to speculate how such a high-powered sporting event could be used to illustrate the drama and tensions of the Cold War.

These ideas slowly took shape over the years, and by 1979 Tim had written the bare bones of a story that involved the defection of a Soviet chess champion to the West. He mentioned the idea to Andrew as a potential follow up to *Evita* but by then *Cats* was very much at the forefront of the composer's mind, and he wasn't interested. Instead, Tim took meetings with several other potential collaborators and investors only for nothing to happen.

The project gained momentum when Tim was in New York meeting with American theatre producer Richard Vos. During their conversation Vos asked, "Have you heard of Arba?"

"No," Rice replied, thinking he was perhaps talking about a type of tree.

"No, no, Arba—'Dancing Queen,' 'Waterloo,' 'Fernando.'"

"You mean ABBA!" said Rice.

"Yes, Arba," Vos continued. "I understand the boys from Arba want to do a stage musical."[1]

Tim was a big admirer of ABBA, and the songwriting talents of Björn Ulvaeus and Benny Andersson, especially the sense of theatre they brought to many of their songs. He began to make some enquiries. As luck would have it, Tim's music publisher in Scandinavia was Stig Anderson, who also looked after ABBA. Tim rang him up, "I understand your chaps are interested in the theatre. I've got a good idea for them."[2] What Tim didn't know at the time was that ABBA was close to splitting up and that Björn and Benny were looking to develop and produce projects outside of the group. One of the things they were interested in doing was a musical, and they were looking for someone with experience to team up with.

In December 1981, Tim flew to Stockholm and met the ABBA boys over dinner. They talked long and hard for hours. Tim had a few sketchy ideas for other musicals, but it was *Chess* that really piqued Benny's interest. With Sweden's close proximity to Russia, they knew all too well those feelings about the Cold War, of what it meant. A musical with that as a background seemed intriguing to them, and more or less everyone agreed that night to work on it together.

Due to other commitments, work couldn't start straightaway. ABBA was winding down, although there was still a greatest hits album to put together and promote, and Tim was busy, too. He'd also hired a new production assistant, Judy Craymer. Judy first met Tim during *Cats* when he popped in a couple of times to the New London Theatre. When Judy heard he was setting up a London production office, she got herself an interview. "Working on *Cats* was life changing but I knew I didn't really want to continue with stage management. I wasn't going to go and do *The Importance of Being Earnest* on tour after the excitement of *Cats*. I wanted to move into production."[3] Tim's office was slap bang in the middle of the West End, and things were hectic: Tim was working on lyrics for the new James Bond theme song and had joined forces with Stephen Oliver, a distinguished composer of classical opera, for a musical called *Blondel*. A comic romp, *Blondel* was based on the legend of a medieval minstrel and opened in London in late 1983. It was only a moderate success.

Judy learned, too, about Tim's plans for *Chess*; one day she was asked to go and pick up Björn at Heathrow airport. A big ABBA fan, Judy got to know both Björn and Benny over the next few months as work on *Chess* began in earnest early in 1983. "They did a lot of the writing here in London. Tim had a beautiful office with a piano, or they'd go to his house in Oxfordshire. Tim would also go and spend time in either Björn or Benny's summer house in Sweden. It was a great creative process. And they all got on incredibly well."[4]

The story and characters of *Chess* began to take shape. With the Cold War remaining as a backdrop, *Chess* concerns a love triangle that arises between two chess grandmasters, one Russian and one American, and Florence Vassey, a

Benny Andersson and Björn Ulvaeus outside the Imperial Theatre on Broadway, unaware of the impending critical onslaught.
*Credit*: Roger Turesson / Expressen / TT News Agency / Alamy Stock Photo

woman who arrives at the international championships as the American's assistant but falls in love with the Russian, who is a married man.

Very early in proceedings it was agreed that the musical should initially take the form of a concept album and that it should be recorded on Björn and Benny's turf, Polar Studios in Stockholm, which had been especially built for ABBA at the height of their mid-1970s success.

Another early development was the involvement of Elaine Paige. Tim and Elaine were in the midst of a not very secret love affair, and the role of Florence was written especially for her. It really came about after Elaine's two disappointments of missing out on Broadway with *Evita* and *Cats*. "Tim wanted to write something for me that he thought might get me to Broadway. He wrote a show called *Blondel*. To be honest it didn't really interest me that much. The subject didn't interest me and neither did the music. So, I passed on it. I'm not sure he was too pleased about that."[5] Something did catch her interest and that was the chess project, especially when she learned that the ABBA boys were going to be involved. "But then again, I thought, chess, that's a bit of a serious subject, not much happening in that, two men with their heads down looking at a board. I can't quite see how this is going to work."[6] Her misgivings were silenced when Tim kept returning from his trips to Sweden with demo tapes that he'd worked on with Björn and Benny. "I can remember thinking, wait a minute, this is amazing. I don't think I'd been so excited about any music that I'd heard since *Evita*."[7] What she loved about it was its classical, almost operatic approach, which harked back to *Evita*, and then there were other songs more pop and rock based.

At one point, Tim took Elaine to the world chess championship in Merano, Italy, where she met Anatoly Karpov. After that they traveled to Hungary since Tim had decided to make Florence Hungarian. Much later on in the process, Elaine began to accompany Tim on weekend visits to Polar Studios. "We'd swap around different ideas on lyrics and songs, whether they would be duets or solos. It was a workshop, a new experience for me to be part of the creative process. And it was a privilege really to be in the room watching it all happen."[8] So committed to the project was Elaine that she later turned down the chance to play Fantine in *Les Misérables*. "I thought, *Chess* is going to knock the spots off of everything else. And for me it is still the most glorious musical score of the 1980s."[9]

Recording on the album began in early November 1983. Michael B. Tretow, the famous engineer who supervised the ABBA recordings, took charge with Benny mixing. Tim, Elaine, and Judy Craymer attended every session. The orchestral and choir elements were recorded later at the CTS Studios in London with the London Symphony Orchestra. "Benny loved working with the orchestra," says Judy.[10] The ABBA boys were certainly taking a different musical route with *Chess*, and the result was a highly melodic score, showing a wide range of influences from Gilbert and Sullivan to Rodgers and Hammerstein, opera to synthesizer-based pop. Swedish singer Tommy Körberg took on the role of the Russian chess master Anatoly Sergievsky. Barbara Dickson sang the role of the Russian's wife.

The American chess master, Freddie Trumper, was sung by the actor and singer Murray Head. Since performing the role of Judas on the *Jesus Christ Superstar* album, Murray had released several solo albums and continued his acting career, notably a leading role in the Oscar-nominated film *Sunday Bloody Sunday* (1971), alongside Peter Finch and Glenda Jackson. Murray enjoyed working on the *Chess* album. "It was the opportunity of doing something utterly unique, which is to create the role in a recording environment, which is so much different from the theatrical world. It allows you much more scope for experimentation and less people putting in their oar."[11] It was after the project moved into a theatrical setting that Murray faced agonizing problems.

Murray had no illusions that he was brought onto the project to lend it something of a rock edge to counter the more traditional Elaine and Tommy Körberg. "Elaine would say to Tim, 'the songs are not covering what I have to say. My character needs more.' Tim would say to the ABBA boys, 'Elaine needs another number,' so they would then champion their singer, Tommy Körberg, and give him another song to keep the balance. While I played piggy in the middle. When you get tired of the ballads you need a rock thing to pump it up a notch, not too much, just enough. So, I was aware of what kind of a cog I was in this machine. And you have to accordingly find your place in all that."[12]

The double LP was released in October 1984, and it was Benny who said, "We should do this as a tour." Thomas Johansson, ABBA's tour promotor, put it together. The idea was to play concert venues with the London Symphony Orchestra, a large choir, and a rock band joined by Björn and Benny and the principals. The first date was at the Barbican Centre in London with subsequent performances in Hamburg, Amsterdam, Paris, and Stockholm. Karin Glenmark, a Swedish pop singer, sang the role of Svetlana as Barbara Dickson was unavailable, except for the final concert in Stockholm. That night, people noticed there was something not quite right about Barbara. When it came to the song "Endgame," Tommy Korberg was singing, but on Barbara's cue there was no sign of her. Unbeknownst to Tommy, Barbara had suddenly taken sick offstage and wasn't coming on. "And there was this moment," recalls Judy, "with the full London symphony orchestra and the choir, and Tommy looked to his left and he looked to his right, and suddenly this voice came in from the back of the choir and it was Karin who realised what was happening. The spotlight found her, and she sang the Svetlana part. And I remember at the end of the song Tommy raised his glass of water to her in thanks."[13]

The album sold well and boasted two hit singles. "One Night in Bangkok" reached number twelve in the United Kingdom and was a top ten hit in the States. But it was the ballad "I Know Him So Well" that became the standout number from *Chess*, reaching the top of the British charts where it stayed for four weeks. Winning an Ivor Novello Award, the song became the United Kingdom's best-selling female duet of all time. Elaine and Barbara didn't know each other at the time, neither did they meet in the recording studio, with Barbara recording her part in London and Elaine in Stockholm; either way, it led to a dear friendship.

Thanks to the success of the album, backers came forward eager to bring *Chess* to the stage. Bernard Jacobs, president of the powerful Shubert Organization in New York, loved the score and wanted to produce *Chess* first on Broadway. Tim, however, wanted its world premiere in London, so Jacobs agreed to wait and work in association with British producer Robert Fox.

Now the search for a director began. Trevor Nunn was approached early in 1985 and while he was positive about the score and the premise, he was committed to his work at the Royal Shakespeare Company and the staging of *Les Misérables* and so passed.

Bernard Jacobs had long been a father figure to Michael Bennett, the brilliant American director behind the smash Broadway hit *A Chorus Line* back in 1975. He followed that three years later with a romantic musical *Ballroom*, which was seen as a disappointment, but bounced back in 1982 with the much more successful *Dreamgirls* about a young female singing trio from Chicago who become music superstars. Jacobs, convinced of the merits of *Chess* and its possibilities, persuaded Bennett to make it his next project.

Tim flew to New York with Benny for a series of meetings with Bennett and they were invited to spend the weekend at his home in East Hampton. A limo was placed at Rice's disposal courtesy of the Shuberts. Close to their destination, and relaxing in the backseat, Rice discovered the driver had no idea where Bennett's home was situated; he was going to have to pull over and phone the office from a pay phone. He stopped the car and got out. It was a lonely stretch of road, and Rice used the time to quickly relieve himself behind some trees. He then noticed a sign displaying some historical points of interest about the area. As he began to read, he heard the limo rev up and speed away, the driver assuming Rice was still in the back. Not only was he stranded, Rice's wallet was in the car and he didn't even have a quarter to make a call. When the limo pulled up outside Bennett's house, the director was standing in the driveway waiting. He opened the back door to see an empty space. A bell rang in the driver's mind. He knew exactly where he'd lost Rice, excused himself, and sped off to pick up his passenger. Bennett and Rice later laughed about the incident.

It was during this weekend that Bennett aired his concept for the show. He likened the piece, he said, to the political intrigue and romantic sacrifice of the 1942 Hollywood classic *Casablanca*. He wanted to heighten the Cold War aspects of the story, rather like a spy film on stage, and focus, too, on the media coverage such events attract, the circus that can build up around sporting personalities.

Everyone knew there was a lot of work to do and not much time. The Prince Edward Theatre had already been earmarked to be the home of *Chess*. *Evita* had been playing there now since 1978 and was no longer making sufficient profits. The decision was made to close the production and launch it on a UK tour. The world premiere of *Chess* was set for May 14, 1986.

Michael Bennett arrived in London with the same creative team he'd worked with on *A Chorus Line* and *Dreamgirls*, including choreographer Bob Avian and designer Robin Wagner. Judy Craymer took an instant shine to Bennett and gravitated toward him, sometimes to the detriment of her relationship with Tim. "Michael was an enormous influence and inspiration to me."[14] Judy was eager to become a fully fledged producer; she would have an executive producer credit on *Chess* but as yet had not produced anything of her own. "And Michael was always so encouraging. I used to hang out with him. He and Bob Avian had a house in Chelsea. It was a great relationship, good fun and quite a lot of vodka. Michael had huge energy, he was incredibly focused but also camp and fun and witty. A real visionary. He always saw *Chess* as being like *Casablanca*. He wanted it to be a heart-breaking love story through all the politics of it."[15]

It had already been agreed that Elaine Paige and Tommy Körberg would reprise their roles from the album; Murray Head, too, and it would be his first West End musical. Barbara Dickson made it known that she did not want to play the Russian's wife Svetlana in the stage version and so Bennett cast Siobhan McCarthy, who had created the original role of the Mistress in *Evita*. For Siobhan, getting to meet Bennett was a huge thrill "because I'd seen *A Chorus Line* and loved it," and in subsequent meetings found him to be "enthusiastic and effervescent, excited and energetic."[16] It was also going to be a return for Siobhan to her *Evita* days, back at the Prince Edward Theatre, where she also played the lead role in subsequent productions, and working again with Elaine and Tim Rice. "It was like being part of the family again."[17]

At an early meeting with the principals, Bennett sat at an enormous table, along with his team, to discuss his approach to the show. Murray knew of Bennett's reputation but had never seen *A Chorus Line*. After Bennett finished his presentation, it was apparent to Murray that this was going to be very much an American musical approach, in other words more song and dance. Murray didn't have an awful lot of faith in dance being able to interpret what was quite a dense and complex narrative. At the end of the meeting Bennett asked if anybody had any questions. "Yes, I have actually," said Murray. "I'm a little concerned. We know that chess to watch is a bit like watching paint dry. I understand the need for physicality as a way of communicating, but it's a highly cerebral thing, can you fill us in on it a bit more?" Murray went on. Well, this was like a red rag to a bull. "Michael Bennet tossed out an answer very quickly and I sensed that I was dead from that moment on. And sure enough I was told, Michael Bennett doesn't like you so I'm afraid that's it."[18] Murray took the news surprisingly calmly. At the time he was recording an album, so he busied himself on that, not expecting to hear anything more about *Chess*.

Elsewhere, the lure of Michael Bennett directing his first proper West End show led to large numbers attending the auditions for the ensemble cast. It was a long and arduous process with Bennett seeking the best dancers in the West End and the best singers, both opera voices and pop and rock. The auditions took place in early December and were run by Alan Hatton, who had been asked to stage manage the show. Alan remembers the very last day well. "It was one of those situations where everybody was on the stage. It was just like *A Chorus Line*. Michael said, 'Will all these numbers step forward,' they did, and then he said, 'Thank you very much ladies and gentlemen, that's all for today,' and sent them away. And then the people who were left on stage he said, 'Ladies and gentlemen congratulations you are now the cast of *Chess*,' and there were lots of squeals of delight."[19]

Leo Andrew was a devotee of Michael Bennett: his production of *A Chorus Line* was one of the reasons why he wanted to get into musical theatre. The opportunity to work with him? Well, that was the chance of a lifetime. "For me, he was a genius."[20] Leo was a former schoolteacher from a small village in Wales. At weekends, he performed his own cabaret show and then went to repertory in Swansea and did a bit of television work. He'd toured the United Kingdom with *Jesus Christ Superstar* playing Jesus and was the narrator in a touring production of *Joseph*, so he was no stranger to Tim or Andrew.

Leo had just finished doing *Sweeney Todd* in Manchester and had already been seen for *Chess* at least twice. He arrived for that very final audition, and the theatre was packed. Separate auditions were taking place throughout the day.

The dancers had been in all morning by the time Leo arrived at midday. He was hoping for a spot in the rock ensemble, out of which covers would be drawn for the role of Anatoly. They sang in groups first, and the numbers were whittled down to who they actually wanted and then made to sing again together. It was five o'clock by the time Leo went out onto the stage to perform on his own, the last man standing. The other candidates for Anatoly had sung and left. His task was to sing "Anthem," Anatoly's big number in the show. And he had to sing it for a panel that numbered at least twelve, including Michael Bennett, Björn, Benny, Elaine, and Tim. No pressure, then. "I finished and I stood there and thought, *what's going on*, because you couldn't see a thing in the auditorium. You knew who was out there but you couldn't see them. And Michael came up on stage and put his arm around me and said, 'Congratulations Leo, you're going to be covering Anatoly.' I can remember bursting into tears immediately because the tension of the whole day was unbelievable."[21]

Julie Armstrong had just come out of *West Side Story* at Her Majesty's Theatre when the *Chess* auditions came up. She was also trying to get into *Time*, "so I was running between stage doors."[22] Julie didn't have an agent then—not everybody did in those days: most people heard of jobs through word of mouth or ads in the *Stage*. She'd heard the *Chess* auditions were quite closed and everyone needed a raffle ticket with a number on to get in. Just seventeen and pretty green, Julie decided to give it a go anyway—what did she have to lose? Turning up at the stage door, Julie saw another girl. "Her name was Aliki and she was very Cockney and cor blimey."[23] They both decided to go in together. "Don't we need a raffle ticket?" asked Julie. "Nah, nah, don't need that," said Aliki. The pair managed to get inside and found themselves in the wings. On the stage were rows and rows of chairs occupied by hopefuls. Somebody was singing down the front. "Hang on a minute," said Aliki. "She's rubbish. That's not good at all." Julie began to think, *who have I got associated with here*, because it didn't sound rubbish, in fact it sounded pretty good.

Bold as brass, Aliki went over to the person in charge, "We're here for the audition."

The man looked at her, "Sorry love, if you haven't got one of these raffle tickets, then you're not going on."

"How much?" said Aliki.

This startled the man. "What are you talking about?"

"How much do you want for a raffle ticket? I'll give you fifty quid, me and her."

This threw him a bit, but the answer was still no.

"Come on mate, fifty quid."

"No, I'm sorry."

"Look, we're not going anywhere. All we want to do is go on there and sing a song and go home. That's all we want to do."[24]

This bartering went on for something like ten minutes. All the while, more singers went up to sing, big opera voices all of them. Julie began to get nervous, hoping that's not what they wanted, "because that's not what I've got."

Aliki was starting to get on the bloke's nerves, so off he went to see Michael Bennett. "I just want to let you know," he said. "I've got a couple of girls out there. They've not got a raffle ticket. They're offering me money to come in and sing. What am I going to do? Should I call somebody?" A smile flashed across Bennett's face. This was like a scene out of *A Chorus Line*. "Let them in," he said. "Let them sing."

The man went back. "Right, you're on next." The nerves for Julie really kicked in then, but Aliki was buzzing and strode out onto the stage to belt out a Tina Turner song. Julie was next, and she sang something from the musical *Pippin*. A voice came from the stalls. Could they both come back for the dance audition?

A few days later, Julie returned to the theatre and quite a sight awaited her: hundreds of dancers massed into different groups. When Julie's group went on, she followed behind. Standing on the stage, a voice rang out; it was Michael Bennett. "Is Julie Armstrong here?" Juile announced herself. "Good," he said, "Let's go." Bennett had made a point of making sure she was there. "It's a complete *Chorus Line* story," says Julie. "We had some story to tell. We had some balls to get ourselves that audition. And he was going to make sure he saw us right through to the end."[25] And he did: both Julie and Aliki won roles in the *Chess* ensemble.

Meanwhile, Murray Head had been working on his album and been approached by Dave Clark to play the second lead alongside Cliff Richard in *Time*. He'd accepted when Judy Craymer called him out of the blue. "Look, we have a problem."

"Yes, you've told me about it, and I'm not involved any longer."

"No, this is something else," stressed Judy. "Michael Bennett wants to see you."

"Look, he's made his decision, let's leave it at that. It's fine. I'm getting on with my life."[26] Murray next mentioned his intention to do the musical *Time* which didn't go down well at all. Judy explained the new situation, that despite a country-wide search they couldn't find anyone that could sing the part of Freddie Trumper, principally the song "Pity the Child," an emotional ballad. During the recording of the track, Murray was asked to sing it in a progressively higher key. "And Benny and Björn, thank god, were not going to drop the key of that song," explains Murray, "and no one could hit it. So, this extraordinary meeting was arranged between myself and Michael Bennett at his flat in Chelsea."[27]

Murray didn't want to hear any apologies—this kind of thing happened all the time—what he wanted to hear was how Bennett was going to make the show work. "Let's take Merano," said Murray. This was an early number that introduces the Tyrolean town of Merano where the World Chess Championship is about to take place. We also get to meet for the first time Freddie Trumper and Florence. The two contemplate the political, financial, and game-oriented elements of the tournament, while the citizens of Merano come in and out praising the virtues of their town. It was a huge number. "And so wordy," says Murray. "I said to Michael Bennett, 'I can't imagine how you're going to do it, how you split it up.' And Michael Bennett split it up, in front of me, to the music, and showed me what he was going to do. It was fantastic. I was suddenly sold on his genius. I felt embarrassed that it had taken this to finally make us understand each other."[28]

Between them, Michael Bennett and his designer Robin Wagner had devised what was going to be one of the most elaborate and complex sets ever seen in the West End. Andrew Bruce had worked before with Bennett on the London production of his Broadway smash *A Chorus Line*. "I found him an amazing director to work with. We had a lot of chats. He was a smashing guy, he really was."[29] Bennett showed Andrew and his wife Siobhan a set model of *Chess* that he'd had made. "And his description of what he was going to do and his concept for the show was amazing," recalls Andrew.[30]

Bennett saw the show in balletic terms, very little scenery, minimalist, abstract. The basis of the design were these huge screens that would fly in from the wings at the beginning of a scene and rest on the floor at different points on the stage. A projected image would then give an indication of a location, be it a hotel bedroom, a street, or up a mountain. There was to be virtually no furniture.

However, the most visually arresting feature was to be a hydraulic floor designed to look like a giant chessboard. It had transparent panels made out of plexiglass that lit up and were capable of being raised and lowered, tilted, or revolved. In addition, there would be huge banks of television screens displaying each chess move during a game, complemented by mock newscasts to convey the world media coverage of the tournament. Leo recalls being told that there were going to be Russian KGB-type spies on gantries with video cameras watching and filming everything taking place on the stage. Some of this footage would also be used on the video wall. "It would have been like watching a spy television drama as the musical was happening."[31]

Bennett's imaginative vision wasn't going to come cheap. In the age of the mega musical, Tim feared that everyone viewed *Chess* in the same league, another goose laying golden eggs. And because it was so certain to be a huge smash, no expenditure was too extravagant, no concept too elaborate.

With rehearsals due to begin early in February 1986, Michael Bennett flew back to the United States for Christmas. He was expected back in London during the first week of January to begin preproduction. The only problem was, he didn't want to come back. The rumors were that he hadn't enjoyed working in London and there had been creative differences and personality clashes. The story buzzing around Fleet Street was that he had fallen out with Elaine and left the production for good.

Elaine meanwhile had decided to take a skiing holiday in France before rehearsals were due to start with her friend Gary Bond. "There I was up a very white mountain when I saw this figure walking towards me. I looked at Gary and said, 'What is that guy doing walking up a mountain?'"[32] It turned out to be the British gossip columnist Baz Bamigboye. "Good God," said Elaine. "What are you doing here?"

"I've found you," he said, almost out of breath.

"How have you managed this," asked Elaine, "on a mountain top?"

"I hear you've fallen out with Michael Bennett, and he's left the production."[33]

This was news to Elaine. "I'd not even heard any rumblings about it. I said to Baz, 'You've come all this way and I have absolutely no idea what you're talking about.' And it was genuine. I really didn't know. That was the spin of course that the press put on it which was a complete and utter lie."[34]

As it turned out, the real reason for Bennett's departure was altogether darker and more devastating.

While holding auditions in London, Bennett was in the theatre climbing up some stairs when suddenly he couldn't breathe. Forcing himself to the top, he collapsed. Something was wrong. There were other warning signs, too, like blotches on his skin. Back in New York, Bennett revealed to his closest colleagues that he had AIDS. In Bernard Jacobs' office, Bennett took his mentor into the bathroom and lifted his shirt to reveal purple lesions and scars on his skin. There was no way Bennett could return to work in London. Jacobs organized letters to be sent out to relieve him of his contract, citing health issues. AIDS was not mentioned. Only a select few working on the show knew the severity or true seriousness of Michael's condition. Siobhan remembers the whole cast being called together where it was explained that Bennett was too ill to do the show. "We were devastated," says Leo.[35] Michael's absence hit Judy Craymer particularly hard "because I adored working with him. I can remember Michael calling me from this medical centre in Arizona kind of saying goodbye. It broke my heart."[36]

Michael Bennett died in July 1987 from an AIDS-related illness. He was only forty-four.

It was not going to be an easy task finding a new director willing to take on a show that was already cast, designed, and scheduled to begin rehearsals in a few weeks' time. Thoughts immediately returned to the original choice, Trevor Nunn. This time, because he would only be required for a short period, he was able to fit it into his schedule. In a way he felt an obligation to come in and help. The Shubert Organization had been huge benefactors to the Royal Shakespeare Company over the years, putting their productions on in New York, and he also felt deeply for Michael Bennett, whom he admired greatly.

Then there was the piece itself. When Trevor listened to the concept album, he liked it immensely, its near symphonic scale in places and the choral ambition of the work. He judged it to be a serious project, with very high-quality musical credentials. Still, he was under no illusions as to the huge difficulties he was facing.

With schedules having to be rearranged, rehearsals were pushed back a month and finally got underway in early March at the Production Village in Cricklewood. The opening date, however, remained fixed. Before starting work, Trevor met the cast individually and asked them to sing. Everyone wondered if this was a new audition. "If Trevor doesn't like my voice, am I out?" This wasn't the case; Trevor just wanted to see what he had and what people could do. It was a large company, and he had to get to know them just as much as they needed to get to know him. Murray Head had an interesting one on one with Nunn and had a question for him. "You wear two hats. You wear one hat for the Royal Shakespeare Company, where you do amazing work with Shakespeare and other things, and then you have musicals. Which hat are you going to wear for this? Because it's an odd one." Nunn paused. "That's a very good question," he said. "And he never answered it," reveals Murray.[37]

He did, however, come to Murray's rescue at a moment when he was floundering in the rehearsals. "They were worried that I wouldn't know it in time and they all surrounded Trevor Nunn and said, 'We don't think he's going to hack it, what do you want to do?' And Trevor Nunn, bless his heart, said, 'No, there's only one person to play this role and that's Murray.' So, he defended me at a time when I really needed that defence."[38]

The majority view was largely positive about Nunn coming in, and not just his valuable experience—*Chess* almost demanded a high-profile director because of the hype surrounding it. And by and large he ingratiated himself well into the company. "The thing with Trevor," says Julie, "he's very clever because he makes you feel, even though you're amongst 30 people, that he's directing you personally."[39] And given the drama already engulfing the show, Trevor's laidback attitude was welcome. As was the calmness of Tim and the ABBA boys. "Benny and Björn and Tim were fabulous," confirms Leo. "They were kind, considerate, and kept their cool."[40]

Trevor faced the tough process of easing himself into a project that was not his and later did admit to sometimes feeling as if he were merely standing in for somebody else. In the final analysis, he was fine with that: he had a job to do, and it certainly didn't stop him imposing his own vision on the piece. His first major decision was a realization that he could never bring Bennett's vision fully to fruition. He explained to Benny, Björn, and Tim how the show had to be less stylized and abstract and placed on a more realistic level. As Leo Andrew saw it, "The costumes didn't change. The set didn't change. It was the concept of the production that changed and how these things were used."[41] A good example of this was Bennet's concept for the song "I Know Him So Well," where Elaine's Florence and Siobhan's Svetlana sing about the man they both love. Andrew Bruce recalls Bennett explaining to him how he was going to stage it. "He was going to have a slowly revolving square with the two girls on opposing corners, and the square was to dip down to the orchestra pit and then steeply rise up at the back. It was a stunning concept."[42] Trevor ditched the pyrotechnics and simply had the two women facing each other throughout the duet. In that one piece of staging, we perhaps see the difference between both director's concepts.

Another casualty were the large screens, which had been built but destined never to be used. "They were just left in the flies," says Alan Hatton.[43] And so instead of projections of locations and sets, a lot more furniture and props were used. "Nunn brought in all these bits and bobs and clutter that the whole thing became a complete nightmare as far as I was concerned," says Alan. "It also meant that the crew had to be visible to bring this stuff on and off stage. So, we had all the stage crew dressed in these hideous green boiler suits and they were just stomping around."[44] Siobhan was on stage when the crew in the flies had to lower in these big doors for the start of a scene. "One night it slipped out of the guy's hand and nearly came crashing down on my head."[45]

Something else that changed was the way the dancers were used. When Bennett pulled out his choreographer, Bob Avian departed too. His replacement was Molly Molloy, a dancer, teacher, and choreographer from America. Molly faced the same difficulty as Trevor: a group of people she hadn't personally chosen. Worse, Bennett had selected dancers with very different styles: ballet, jazz, contemporary. "We were all individual," says Julie. "Michael had chosen us because of our skill set, so when Molly came in and then tried to make us all move the same, her stuff just didn't work on everybody. It was a desperate situation and that element of the show suffered as a consequence."[46]

Molly also insisted that during rehearsals the dancers did a two-and-a-half-hour class every morning. Great for the ballerinas to keep in condition, but Julie considered herself not just a dancer, also a singer and an actress, and this was her idea of a nightmare. "I remember crying in pain and I wasn't the only one."[47] Then when the dancers actually started work on the choreography, it was a big let-down. "It didn't quite justify all that ball ache," says Julie. "She was out of her depth."[48]

As opposed to what Bennett might have had in mind, the dancers found themselves predominately used as crowd extras, banging beer steins together in the Swiss mountain scenes, for example. Or when there were dance routines, the choreography was not up to scratch. "When you look at *Chess*," says Julie, "there's so much instrumental music there that you can only imagine what Michael Bennett would have done with it."[49] On more than one occasion, dancers pleaded with Molly to give them better stuff to do. "The dancers who were doing 'The Arbiter' number almost walked out," claims Julie. "It was that bad."[50]

Over at the Prince Edward, the set was under construction. While the chessboard floor had been scaled back, the technical issues were still considerable. A moving floor of this size was a first for the West End, and it had to be practically built piece by piece in order to be accommodated on the stage. A long process. The original plan was for a computer to control each piece, whether tilting, rotating, lowering, or rising. "However, back in the 80s we weren't very advanced with stage technology," says Alan Hatton. "So, automation, i.e., operating sets with computers, was in its infancy and the guy who was trying to develop the automation could not get the computers to talk to the motors and so we spent weeks trying to get it to work."[51] The result was an awful lot of programming and reprogramming going on night after night, which led to very tired people and tech rehearsals going on much longer than they should have. "The operator was taken to hospital one morning," recalls Andrew Bruce, "because he'd been up all night for God knows how many nights in a row and he collapsed in the morning rehearsal, so that stopped us in our tracks for a while."[52]

By this point, Trevor had brought his cast into the theatre only to be faced with the main piece of the set not working properly. The cast would be on the stage when suddenly something broke or refused to move, and they'd have to stop for the day. Almost at the eleventh hour, it was decided to scrap the computer and bring someone in to develop a manual board to drive the whole thing. This did mean it was more restrictive in what it was able to do, but at least it worked, although Siobhan recalls there was still the odd glitch when either it conked out altogether or went backwards instead of forwards. Murray Head fell off it once during a performance.

At other times, the floor tilted at an incredibly steep angle. "You felt like you were on a ski slope," recalls Elaine. "That's why we had to have rubber put on the soles of our shoes because we kept sliding down the thing. We thought we were going to end up on the trumpeter's lap in the orchestra pit."[53] For one scene, Julie and a few of the other ensemble members were stuck up at the top for quite some time. "The lights at the top of the theatre were right on my head. I actually fainted once and the stage crew behind me dragged me down and then dragged me back up the slope again. It was hilarious."[54] There was a sheer drop behind them. "Health and safety would have had a field day."[55]

One of the most eye-catching elements of the set remained Bennett and Wagner's concept of a giant bank of television screens. This consisted of a series of three video walls that provided a giant multiscreen display. One of these, consisting of sixty-four screens, was the largest of its type ever constructed in the United Kingdom. Weighing 3.8 tons, this was lowered from the flies on steel cables during the performance to display the various moves taking place on the chessboard.

On either side of the stage there were two thirty-two-screen versions of the wall, which showed additional close-ups and news reportage, along with images of the Cuban missile crisis and the Hungarian uprising, all to convey the Cold War tensions. This was eventually reduced since Trevor rightly felt that the huge screens ran the risk of being a distraction for the audience.

The problem for Andrew Bruce was that the sixty-four television screens on both sides of the stage had to be placed where the audience could see them, and that position was usually reserved for the lights and loudspeakers. Andrew was forced to put the speakers in a position that was not ideal, but the team made the sound work. One strange side effect of all those televisions was that whenever one of the actors stood directly next to them, it interfered with their mics and squashed the sound. Andrew had to go to Trevor to ask that members of the cast refrained from going too near them.

As if there weren't enough problems, Trevor twisted his ankle badly one day. Alan Hatton was summoned into the stalls, where the production desk was located, to be told that Trevor wanted him to build a platform across the top of the stalls that linked the production desk to the stage on the same level by a bridge. This was so Trevor didn't have to clamber up and down the steps to get up to the stage every time. "I just looked at him and laughed," says Alan, "and I said, on top of everything else Trevor, with the automation fouling up, with everybody working around the clock and not getting any sleep, 'I don't think that's going to happen.'"[56]

Amid all that was going on, the presence of Björn and Benny had always been a calming influence, although as far as Siobhan can recall it was Benny who was more involved in the actual physical production. "There were no airs and graces about Benny. It was always exciting to have him around, and he gave us a lot of confidence."[57] This was felt most importantly by Andrew Bruce. Right from the start of the project, he knew that as far as Björn and Benny were concerned nothing really mattered so long as the sound was right. "They were very hands on. They were very helpful and interested. Instead of being the poor relation at the back of the auditorium we, the sound guys, were suddenly the drivers. And although Trevor held sway, as far as Björn and Benny were concerned, how it sounded was their primary concern."[58]

The technical issues persisted right up to opening night. But nothing quite prepared the company for what happened during the afternoon dress rehearsal prior to the very first preview. Everything seemed to be going well until word spread like wildfire that Tommy Körberg had collapsed in the wings. No doubt tired and stressed, someone had given him some kind of pill to calm him down. Everyone rushed on stage in a panic. In the aftermath, Leo Andrew heard his name being called out. He was told what had happened, that Tommy had been carried to his dressing room and was going to hospital. Just then Trevor came over. "And he burst into tears," recalls Leo, "because the stress level at this point was unbelievable. This was the very first preview of this musical that everyone had been waiting for."[59]

Leo was asked to sing through the score and was then asked if he knew the blocking and the moves. He did. Leo was then asked to go away and come back in an hour, and they'd let him know what was going on. "I went across the road to Les Mis to see a dear friend of mine called Ken Caswell, and I said, 'I think I'm on tonight.' And I can remember him saying to me, 'Well, that will change your career.'"[60] Several critics and reporters were going to be in that night, and they'd already heard through stage door rumors that something was happening. Leo walked back to the Prince Edward, grabbing a sandwich on the way, and when he arrived it was to the news, "you're on. What do you need?" "So, I went to get my kettle and my hairdryer. And I was so calm, which I couldn't believe because I was thinking, oh my God, this is the opportunity that you've been waiting for, that anybody would be waiting for in their life. And I knew I could do it."[61]

Leo was ensconced in Tommy's dressing room. Because he hadn't been fitted for his costumes yet, Leo had to be put into Tommy's clothes. It was now an hour before curtain up. The company manager came in and told Leo to go back to his room and take the clothes off. "I'll let you know what's happening in a while." Leo took the suit off, grabbed his kettle and hairdryer, and went back to his own dressing room and waited. It was half an hour before curtain up when the company manager arrived with the news that Tommy was going on. "At the hospital Tommy had explained about being given this tablet," says Leo, "and he was so petrified they brought in a Korean lady hypnotist to hypnotise him in his dressing room and he went on that night in a hypnotic trance. Everyone was told, do not speak to him." In an instant, Leo's moment was gone. "And I thought, *nothing like that is going to happen to you again.* And it never did."[62]

The state of Tommy Körberg threw an imbalance on the performance that night. "We were all waiting to see if he could make it to the next scene or not," says Murray Head.[63] Overall, despite a few technical and sound issues, that first preview fared well enough, but there was still a lot of work to be done. Over the next few days, various changes, alterations, and trims were made. The feeling was that audiences were not completely following the various twists and turns of the plot, so extra lyrics were added and others altered to clarify what was happening. "I remember Elaine getting fed up with almost daily rewrites," recalls Siobhan.[64] Some of the changes were rumored not to have been totally embraced by everyone, but Trevor was adamant they were needed, and everyone knuckled down and did what had to be done. "We all wanted it to work because we all knew what we'd gone through to get there," says Julie. "And we were all rooting for Trevor as well to get it right."[65]

*Chess* premiered on May 14, 1986. Opening night was a star-studded event. Björn, Benny, and Tim were there, of course, and there was a special surprise when ABBA's Frida showed up. The audience settled into their seats. "And when it opened on the chess board," says Leo, "with the ensemble all lined up dressed as chess pieces, the applause was unreal."[66]

That whole opening, however, was a cheat. During rehearsals, Tom Jobe, who was playing the Arbiter, was growing anxious about being the first person to vocally open the show. Tom was an American singer, dancer, and actor, extremely talented, but he was really feeling the pressure. A solution was found and that was to record him performing those opening lines only. Then came the realization that the ensemble in their massive chess piece costumes and headgear were going to struggle to be heard anyway. The decision was made to pre-record the vocals for the whole of the opening; only the orchestra played live.

This is nothing very unusual. Often if an actor has to do something strenuous while singing, sometimes elements of a song are recorded. Also, in shows like *Cats* and *Starlight Express*, there were singers behind the stage performing at certain times to create a bigger overall sound.

After the exertions of rehearsals and previews, opening night is often something of a blur. "You're just relieved it's over," says Siobhan. "You hope the reviews are good and then you just want to go out and have fun and party."[67] The job of organizing the after-show celebration fell to Judy Craymer. It took place at the Belvedere Restaurant in Holland Park, a massive sit-down dinner for several hundred guests and then a party. "That was very glamorous and glorious and filled with lots of stars, people like Billy Connolly and Rod Stewart."[68]

The following morning, there was a rush to pick up the papers to see what the reviewers had made of the show. It was mixed, but there were enough good notices to warrant some confidence. *The Times* noted that "it turns out to be a fine piece of work that shows the dinosaur mega-musical evolving into an intelligent form of life." Sheridan Morley in *International Herald Tribune* complimented the show's "remarkably coherent dramatic shape" and "staging of considerable intelligence and invention." And *The Stage* declared, "*Chess* does convincingly prove that the modern musical, which could be said to have started with *Jesus Christ Superstar*, has come of age."

In a way, the reviews didn't matter so much. As we've seen so glaringly with *Les Misérables*, critics can be wrong and it's word of mouth that really matters. And before it had even opened *Chess* was booked out for a year. "People just wanted to see it," says Julie. "And for as long as Elaine was in it, we were packed."[69] It was a hot ticket; the show to see in London. Judy Craymer was given the job of looking after visiting VIPs and celebrities. She recalls Diana Ross coming one evening. "That was incredibly exciting. I took her up to a tiny room at the top of the Prince Edward, and there was somebody collecting for charity and Diana Ross elegantly took a fifty pound note out of her purse, signed it and handed it over."[70]

After all the calamities, *Chess* finally settled into its run. Murray Head enjoyed his time on the show. "What I was hoping to bring to the table, and I think I did to a certain extent, was that singing was merely an extension of script, of talking. That the way I was delivering was just like, maybe out of emotional frustration one resorted to singing to put over one's point. That worked with the angst of Judas and it also worked for Freddie Trumper's angst."[71] Murray, however, never came to terms with the rigidity of doing the same thing exactly the same way every night. "Trevor Nunn allowed you the scope to move as you liked."[72] Once Nunn was gone, soon after opening night, the resident director took over the reins. "I ended up ignoring him when he told me I'd moved to the wrong place or I'd done this and that."[73] Murray seemed to want to battle against the idea that the show was now locked down, "set in aspic," which didn't allow for him to fully express himself. "You are experimenting all the time against a background of restriction."[74]

As for Leo, he did finally get to play Anatoly several times when Tommy was given days off. Tommy, though, was a favorite among many in the cast. "He was just one of us," says Julie. "There were no airs or graces with him. And Tommy and Murray loved us dancers because we were pretty hot looking girls."[75]

Every time Leo stood in for Tommy was a privilege; Anatoly was such a wonderful part to play with a great through journey. "He comes in about 20 minutes in and you literally step on the escalator and it goes very steadily through the entire piece and you finish up with 'Anthem,' dear God, what a gift. Everything he sang I always felt had great depth to it."[76]

Leo was in line to play Anatoly when Tommy's contract expired but narrowly missed out due to backstage politics. He left *Chess* but returned at last to take over as Anatoly during its final months, when everyone knew the show was closing. The cast had noticed audiences were falling off. It didn't help that *Les Misérables* was doing fantastic business just across the street and when *Phantom of the Opera* opened later that year, *Chess* was sandwiched in between two blockbusters and came off worst.

Julie managed eighteen months in *Chess* before leaving to do *Follies* over at the Shaftesbury Theatre, only to return to do pop choir for the final four weeks. "It was nice to be a part of it at the end. But it was an all-new cast, so it had a different feel. There were no friendships there."[77]

The final matinee on the Saturday was a truly surreal experience when ex-cast members, including Elaine, came in to play what were essentially cameos. Murray Head, for instance, just came in and passed through a scene. Leo felt this was self-indulgent, like the last day at school, with the result it disrupted the show. "Myself and the two other principal cast members came off and just went, what the fuck has just gone on on that stage!"[78] At least the evening performance went off normally, and *Chess* came to an end.

For many, it had been a great experience. "Despite all the problems it was a privilege to do that show," says Leo. "I wouldn't have missed a second."[79] *Chess* is especially close to Julie's heart. "There are people I met on that show that I've known all my life."[80] For Siobhan, who took over the role of Florence when Elaine left, it felt satisfying to be involved in something that at least had a bit of ambition. "It felt quite cool to be part of a show that wasn't an old-fashioned musical, but about something serious like the Cold War. It was quite modern in that way."[81]

For Alan Hatton, the whole thing had been something of a nightmare, and he'd been glad to leave soon after opening night to start work on *Phantom*. "*Chess* is probably the worst show I've ever worked on in terms of trying to accomplish too much."[82] Things weren't helped by a less-than-positive relationship with Trevor Nunn. "One of the things that made me crazy working with him was he never once called any of the crew by our names. If he needed you, he'd just shout, 'Stage management!' and hope for the best. I found that very bizarre. When you're working with people, you need to know who you're talking to."[83]

*Chess* ran for three years at the Prince Edward Theatre and so cannot be regarded as having been a failure. Most shows tend to run a couple of years or maybe a bit more. Things like *Cats* and *Les Misérables* are freaks, really. The sense of disappointment that surrounded *Chess* derived from the fact that so many people expected it to achieve blockbuster status. Tim Rice was always wary of the show being spoken about in those terms. Although on a personal level he came to realize that the original album was much closer to what the stage version should have been like. Perhaps it was made too complex. "The book left some audiences a bit baffled," claims Siobhan.[84] Of course, musicals can strive to be intelligent, but *Chess* suffered from the fact that people didn't expect the story of a musical to be that complicated. "I'm not sure whether the story did truly come across," says Julie, "because there was so much else happening. You got whisked up in the amazing music and the set and trying to work out what the hell was happening."[85] Murray Head took just one night off during his eight-month run in the show and took that opportunity to watch his understudy. "And when I went to see it out front the show didn't make anything like the sense that it made doing it."[86]

Elaine felt the production didn't quite gel or achieve the artistic merit of the album or indeed the concert tour, which she loved doing. "That was one of the most exciting things I've ever done. You had to pinch yourself. I did, I used to think, am I really part of this."[87] In the stage version, Elaine never felt her character really worked. "Florence, as it was written, was this Hungarian girl who came to England at the age of two with her mother after the Hungarian uprising. She never knew what happened to her father once the uprising had been crushed because he disappeared. That was all meant to be part of her back story that I thought would be somehow disclosed in the show. But none of it was established, so for me I always felt the character was underwritten and a bit one dimensional."[88] Added to that was a sense that in rehearsals Trevor Nunn paid more attention to the male actors playing the chess masters. "I as a character felt a bit left out, left to my own devices."[89]

Undeniably, the production suffered from some extraordinarily bad luck. In the circumstances, Trevor Nunn did as good a job as anyone could have expected. But there will always be that question of what Michael Bennett might have made of the same material. "I've always said we looked like a very glamorous version of Les Mis," says Leo, "because we walked around chess boards in circles and were far better dressed but didn't have a barricade."[90] And while Tim has admitted to some mistakes with the construction of the piece, there is no denying the quality of the music or the witty and meaningful lyrics. It was a score that was good enough to work, and that deserved to work. "Even though from previews we had a lukewarm reception," says Leo, "people have grown to love *Chess* because of the music. To this day it's the best score I've ever sung. You cannot get bored of it."[91]

Perhaps there could be a resurrection. Perhaps they might have a second chance to get things right on Broadway. And with *Chess* not due to open there until the spring of 1988, they had plenty of time to work things out, with Trevor Nunn taking charge from the beginning this time. His aim was to make the Broadway version an even more serious piece of musical drama. To this end he brought in American playwright Richard Nelson, the author of several well-received political plays.

Over the next eighteen months, the main creative protagonists, Björn, Benny, Tim, Trevor, and Richard Nelson, met to discuss and develop a new version of *Chess*. This involved hundreds of hours of discussion and sometimes heated argument in order to arrive at a collective view of what was the best of the original material and what could be dumped. It was then the job of Trevor and Richard Nelson to structure a new book that was to change *Chess* from a predominantly sung through musical to a traditional book musical, with far more dialogue between the songs. In this way, the hope was to make the plot clearer and some of the characters more rounded.

As the rewriting process advanced, Tim began to develop different ideas of how to move forward and in the end he, Trevor, and Richard Nelson never really managed to find a happy ground on which to finalize the script in complete agreement. For Tim, some of the characters now meant nothing to him. They weren't the ones he had created. For example, in the London version, Florence had been an English woman of Hungarian birth, now she was changed into an American citizen. As the backdrop of the story was the Cold War, Nunn felt that it made more sense to have the two lovers coming from those opposing worlds.

The political context of the show was also greatly heightened, and Robin Wagner designed a radically new set. Neither did the score emerge unscathed with several new versions of music and new songs added. The biggest alteration was the decision to return to the traditional form of the musical play as opposed to the through composed semi-operatic form it had in London.

In retrospect, Tim was to call these changes "a disastrous decision."[92] They had simply gotten out of control. "Instead of going back to the record and saying, 'Let's pretend London didn't happen,' we tried to improve a bit on London and it got worse and worse."[93] Siobhan saw the Broadway version and found it very different. "I enjoyed it, but it was hardly recognizable from the show that we did. It had a much more cinematic quality."[94]

Others were left disappointed, too. Elaine Paige hoped finally to make her bow on Broadway; instead, Florence was played by Judy Kuhn. It was horribly ironic since Tim had written the role for Elaine in the first place in the hope that she would go with it to Broadway. Any hopes Tommy Korberg might have had of playing on Broadway were similarly dashed by American Equity, and Anatoly was played by musical theatre actor David Carroll.

Things seemed to go wrong on Broadway almost from the get go. The first preview overran when the stage crew reportedly had problems with the sets. And then there were the reviews. A few critics praised it highly, especially the score. William A. Henry III wrote in *Time*: "This is an angry, difficult, demanding and rewarding show, one that pushes the boundaries of the form." But most fell on the negative side. Frank Rich of *The New York Times*, who had earned the nickname "Butcher of Broadway" for his supposed power over the prospects of Broadway shows, gave a damning notice, saying, "the evening has the theatrical consistency of quicksand" and described *Chess* as "a suite of temper tantrums, [where] the characters yell at one another to rock music." *Newsweek* were more succinct, calling the show "Broadway's monster."

These reviews, essentially, killed the production. Andrew Bruce was at the opening night party. The evening was buzzing, and he felt going well. "Then the reviews came out at about 11:30 and within minutes the party died on its feet, you could see people walking for the exit. All the smart people who had come to the opening night didn't want to be associated with it."[95]

Both Björn and Benny were extremely hurt by the hostile critical reaction. "I wasn't there for the Broadway launch," says Judy Craymer, "but I know that Björn thought he was having a heart attack. He was hyper ventilating."[96] Björn later didn't mince his words about Frank Rich in particular. "Of course, we didn't have the reputation that *Les Misérables* or *Phantom* had brought from London when they came to Broadway. He couldn't kill those shows off, although he would have wanted to, I'm sure, because I think he thought Broadway was for the American musical, not these bloody European things. So, with *Chess* he rubbed his hands and thought, *Oh good, here comes one I can kill!*"[97]

Despite a healthy box office advance, audiences fell away quickly, and the Shubert Organization had no alternative but to cut their losses and give notice to close. *Chess* ended on Broadway after just sixty-eight performances.

It was a sad fate for a show that Tim has always referred to as his favorite out of everything he's done, and that its reception left him somewhat disillusioned with theatre. Something else, too, might have contributed to its downfall, something that couldn't really have been anticipated: Glasnost. *Chess* appeared just at a time when Cold War tensions were relaxing with the premiership of Gorbachev and the new era of Glasnost. Perestroika made the Russia versus America theme of *Chess* pretty much redundant, certainly by the time it came to Broadway. Less than six months after *Chess* closed, the Berlin Wall fell.

As Judy has said, she never went to Broadway with *Chess*; she'd left Tim's employ by then, determined to strike out on her own. But the experience of *Chess* and working with Björn and Benny had not just been a huge learning curve, but was to shape the rest of her life. "I was so fascinated by meeting them that I sat and studied the ABBA songs much more than I'd ever done before, rather than just dancing to them."[98] Like Tim, Judy recognized the storytelling and theatrical nature of many of them and came up with the kernel of an idea that they might work as the basis for a musical. She approached Björn and Benny and received no encouragement whatsoever; they were moving onto other things, and ABBA was in the past. But she remained on friendly terms, turning up at birthday parties in Sweden, occasionally calling them up on the phone. "I was always there. Then in the mid-1990s Björn gave me a sense of hope, a chink of light. He said, 'ok, maybe there is something here.' I still had to convince Benny because he wasn't completely sure. There was this joke between us of, who will say I told you so. I think their sense of caution was my sense of drive."[99]

The problem was always finding the right story, and that was solved when Judy teamed up with the playwright Catherine Johnson and *Mamma Mia!* was born. It opened in 1999 at the old home of *Chess*, the Prince Edward, and went on to become a global sensation, now seen by over sixty-five million people.

# 7

# "THE MUSIC OF THE NIGHT"

In the summer of 1985, Andrew Lloyd Webber was in New York for the Tony Awards and preparing to attend a dinner for the award nominees at the Plaza Hotel. A strike by city hotel staff meant that an angry mob of picketers had gathered outside, berating and hassling those arriving. Dodging the odd flying egg, Andrew made his way inside. In a corner he spotted Hal Prince and went over. As they chatted, Andrew revealed that he was thinking of doing a musical of *The Phantom of the Opera*, one that emphasized the romantic elements of the story rather than the horrific. "It's the perfect time for a romantic musical," said Hal. "Perfect. There hasn't been a romantic musical in years. That's something I would like to see."[1] That was often Hal's criterion when choosing a project: was it something he would gladly go and pay to watch himself?

Witten by Gaston Leroux and published in 1909, *The Phantom of the Opera*, with its story of a young soprano who becomes the obsession of a disfigured and murderous musical genius who lives beneath the Paris Opéra House, became a gothic horror stable for filmmakers throughout the twentieth century. Given its musical setting, it was something of a mystery why no one had yet turned it into a full-blown musical. Actually, somebody had; well, almost.

Back in 1984 Andrew was leafing through the *Daily Telegraph* one morning when he came across a review of playwright and director Ken Hill's production of *The Phantom of the Opera* playing at the Theatre Royal Stratford East in London. It piqued his interest enough to go and see it. While overall he found the show to be overly pantomimic, he liked its use of opera arias by Verdi, Gounod, and Offenbach that lent the piece the right kind of atmosphere. He contacted

Cameron Mackintosh and raised the idea they might produce it on a bigger scale in the West End, with Andrew writing a new score.

What Andrew had in mind was something along the lines of the *Rocky Horror Show* and so first tried to secure the services of Jim Sharman, the Australian who directed the original stage production and also the film version. Sharman was too busy and declined.

Several months later, Andrew was in New York and passed a secondhand bookstore where he spied a copy of Leroux's novel. He'd never read it before, so he bought it for a dollar and took it back to his hotel room. What surprised him the most after reading it, being mostly familiar with the Lon Chaney and Hammer horror-type films, was how much of a romance it was: a story of unrequited love trying to get out of its horrific trappings. Perhaps Andrew was also seized by its potential as a vehicle for Sarah Brightman. Certainly, there were personal echoes in the story he couldn't fail to recognize and during the entre writing of *Phantom* Sarah was to be his muse. "She was a big motor behind the show," says Richard Stilgoe. "Andrew adored her. She could sing a range that very few people in musical theatre could manage and also there was a wonderful vulnerability about her. It wasn't surprising that Andrew picked that subject because it suited her so well."[2]

*Phantom of the Opera* was Andrew Lloyd Webber's love letter to his new wife, Sarah Brightman. The pair met when she appeared in the original production of *Cats*.
*Credit*: Joan Marcus / Photofest © Joan Marcus

Ditching the idea of working with Ken Hill on his version, Andrew began to piece together a rough storyline of his own, coupled with a search for a new collaborator to write the book. Both Andrew and Cameron approached acclaimed playwright Tom Stoppard, but he politely declined. Next, they tried the American composer, lyricist, and record producer Jim Steinman, best known for his work with Meat Loaf on the album *Bat Out of Hell*. Already committed to recording a Bonnie Tyler album, Steinman turned Andrew down. It was, he later admitted, the worst mistake of his career. Andrew and Steinman were eventually to work together ten years later on the stage musical *Whistle Down the Wind*.

An approach was also made to Tim Rice, but he was busy with *Chess* and ruled himself out. Tim did later admit that although *Phantom* was a brilliant show, "it didn't really interest me desperately."[3] Instead, Andrew turned to his *Starlight Express* collaborator Richard Stilgoe. "I was sent the original Gaston Leroux novel," recalls Richard. "It came by courier and ten minutes later Andrew rang up and said, 'What do you think of it?' I said, 'I've just read the title page.' He called back the next day and of course I said yes. It had all the ingredients you need for a musical."[4]

As he set to work, Richard tried to dismiss from his mind the obvious horror movie connotations of the story. "The first requirement is that the phantom himself must have pathos, which he does in the book, much more than in any of the films. He's a very tragic figure. He kills people left right and centre all the way through but somehow the audience has to be slightly on his side."[5]

It was clear for a show like *Phantom*, taking place as it does in the opulent surroundings of an opera house, that the sets and costume design was paramount. The right person had to be found and brought in at a very early stage. The name of Maria Björnson was quickly identified as the prime candidate. Maria was an acclaimed designer working predominantly in opera. Martyn Hayes, brought in as production manager, knew Maria well, having worked on two shows with her at English National Opera; he both liked and respected her enormously. In discussions with Cameron, Martyn made a point of bringing up her name. As it happened, Cameron was already thinking of Maria, having recalled seeing her work at the Royal Shakespeare Company. "Cameron was very pro Maria," says her assistant Jonathan Allen. "He persuaded Andrew she was a good idea."[6] It would be her first West End musical.

One of the first things Maria and Jonathan did was fly across to Paris to visit the famous opera house. "This guy took us around and was unlocking doors for us to be able to see things the public never gets to see," Jonathan recalls. "It was really quite amazing, certainly going down into the basement and being able to drop a coin through a grate and hearing it hit the water beneath."[7] Famously, the opera house is built over an underground lake. They were also allowed up onto the roof and took hundreds of photographs. The idea was not to faithfully replicate the opera house, but merely to give an impression of it. The design of the famous chandelier, for example, was heavily simplified and abstracted from the one they saw. "The most explicit thing is the masquerade staircase," says Jonathan.[8] The purpose of the visit was really to take in the spirit of the place, and in that respect, the visit was a huge help. "It did give some visual language."[9]

Jonathan first worked for Marie at English National Opera, they seemed to get on well and had a chemistry and started to work together on more shows. "She wasn't easy to work for," admits Jonathan. "We had our fallings out, but you kept returning because you believed in what she did."[10] In many respects *Phantom* was the perfect show for Maria, "because her designs always had an element of fantasy," says Jonathan.[11]

At a very early stage, Maria had a conversation with Hal Prince about *Phantom* where he explained his concept for it. Hal had very clear ideas of what he wanted. He saw the set as being this black box, almost like a conjurer's box, where things arrive and disappear again. This concept of a marvelous box of tricks was Maria's window into the piece, and off she went with the freedom to let her imagination run riot. Martyn Hayes remembers Maria showing him a model of the set she'd made and taking him through it for the very first time. "And everything was there, the mock opera Hannibal with the elephant, the two-way mirror in the dressing room, the gondola, the chandelier rising from the floor. She had a little model of the Phantom and Christine, and moved them around like a toy theatre. It was conceived from soup to nuts. What Maria showed me on that very first model showing was what ended up there on the first night."[12]

Once again, Andrew decided to try out his latest project at his festival in Sydmonton, presenting the first act (the second act had yet to be written) in the summer of 1985. Colm Wilkinson played the Phantom, Sarah Brightman was Christine, Clive Carter played Raoul, a nobleman in love with Christine, and Myra Sands was Carlotta, an opera star. "Colm was fabulous," Myra recalls. "He just sang the hell out of the thing. And when I later heard Michael Crawford sing it, there was no comparison."[13] At the time Colm was contracted to do *Les Misérables* so was never in line for the role.

What the specially invited audience saw that afternoon was a mini version of what *Phantom* became. "We had a very small boat," recalls Martyn Hayes, "or the brow of a boat that was pulled downstage on some string. We had a tiny chandelier. And we had some candelabra."[14] What's interesting to note is that *Phantom* wasn't really at the forefront of Andrew's mind at this time. "The big event that weekend was actually *Café Puccini*," says Martyn. "*Phantom* was the second show on. They had high hopes for *Café Puccini*."[15] This musical, inspired by the work of opera composer, Giacomo Puccini, did not overly trouble the West End. *Phantom* was another story entirely. Its positive reception at Sydmonton was enough to convince Andrew there was something special here. Someone else more than impressed was novelist Jeffrey Archer, who corned Andrew after the performance and said he'd invest five thousand pounds into the show.

Things were looking good, although Andrew and Cameron had begun to harbor misgivings over whether Hal Prince was the right man to take things forward. After all, his last three shows on Broadway had flopped. Had he lost his magic? Thoughts turned to Trevor Nunn. But how to break the news to Hal? It was decided that Andrew and Cameron would fly to New York together and personally meet with him. Cameron duly turned up at Hal's office, but it was a no show from Andrew. Cameron had to face the great man alone. Off they went to a nearby eatery for breakfast where cautiously Cameron explained the situation. Hal was furious, having worked on *Phantom* now for several months. It had also been a long time since he was fired from a show. Hurling a few choice adjectives across the table, Hal got up, left his breakfast untouched, and returned to his office. It took a while to calm down, but once he did Hal instructed his secretary to gather up all the materials on *Phantom* and keep them. He'd a sneaky suspicion Andrew and Cameron would be back. Hal's instinct was right. Andrew wasn't convinced that Trevor was the right man for this particular show, that he would intellectualize the whole thing, demand explanations where there was to be hokum or magic. "Hal is a master showman," said Andrew, "and a showman was what I passionately believed *Phantom* needed."[16] Hal was back in.

With the director now firmly in place, there were issues to be sorted out regarding the book. Richard Stilgoe was floundering, doing rewrite after rewrite after rewrite, not knowing quite where he was going or what was wanted of him. "And the rewrites weren't any better than the first effort."[17] Richard had been working closely with Andrew, dividing the storyline up into scenes and working out where the songs should go and what their purpose should be to drive the narrative along. "And that skeleton of the show is still how the show is," says Richard. "Where I was failing was in writing the right lyrics that Andrew wanted to go with his music."[18] The problem perhaps lay in Andrew's determination to finish the score first. "And that's what I'm least good at," admits Richard, "being handed a finished piece of music and told to put words to it. I would rather do it the Gilbert and Sullivan way and write a complete libretto and hand it to a composer."[19]

At one point, Cameron personally stepped in. "Look, you're struggling with this. Would you like somebody to come in and help you write it?"

Richard flatly refused, feeling quite miffed and insulted.

"Suppose it was Alan Jay Lerner?" teased Cameron. "Would that be alright?"

"Yes, that would be wonderful."[20]

Richard had previously met Alan Jay Lerner at a gala at the American embassy. "And he was a lovely man, absolutely charming."[21] Asked by Cameron to come on board, Lerner took Richard out to lunch. "I've read your stuff," he said. "It's not terrible, but it's not right, and we're going to get it right."[22]

Alan Jay Lerner was one of the great names of musical theatre, the lyricist of such hits as *My Fair Lady*, *Gigi*, and *Camelot*. Alas, it quickly became apparent that he was very ill and everyone's worst fears were realized when he revealed that he had lung cancer, he'd been a heavy smoker all his life, and that it was terminal. "Do you guys mind awfully if I don't spend the last six weeks of my life rewriting somebody else's musical?" he asked. "Which we could all see was a quite reasonable position to take," recalls Richard.[23]

The search began for a new lyricist. Cameron recalled meeting a likely candidate at a recent award show, Charles Hart. He was young, just twenty-five, and inexperienced, not long out of the Guildhall School of Music and Drama, but Cameron had heard good enough things to recommend him to Andrew. A test was devised. Andrew recorded himself playing a tune from the show on a piano, and the tape was sent to Hart for him to provide a suitable lyric. At the time Hart was unemployed so he was able to work on it without any distractions; he sent the tape back with his lyrics and the same evening got a call from Andrew. The next morning, he began work on *Phantom*.

As Charles Hart was brought in, Richard was being told his services were no longer required. "I wasn't terribly surprised. Nor was I terribly thrilled, obviously. Andrew is very single minded about a show, so anything that makes it work, he will do, and anything that doesn't make it work, is history."[24] For Richard, it was a great experience nonetheless, and he particularly savored the chance to work with Hal Prince. "He was brilliant, just the quick and accurate, this might work, this won't work, that's a really useful thing to have. And he had a wonderful calming influence because these things can get quite frenetic and everybody can be jumping up and down too much and Hal was always marvellous at just being ambassadorial."[25]

Despite his departure, Richard was to leave his mark on the show. "I was really pleased with the lyric I wrote for 'Music of the Night,' and I suppose about half of it is still there."[26] Something like a third of the words in *Phantom* remain his, and you can't see the glue. "Which is kind of brilliant of Charles, to use the bits of mine that did work and add his bits without my thinking, *oh, that's a change.*"[27] But even though Richard knew it was the right decision to move him on, it wasn't easy to fully let go. "For a year or two I was really miffed."[28] He sought out other challenges, like writing a couple of musicals for children. And he went to see *Phantom* on its second night and thoroughly enjoyed it; strangely, the healing began then. Today, it's an association that he's extremely proud of, especially in the way that the show has meant so much to so many people. "The number of people who still go and see *Phantom* on anniversaries, on birthdays, on big romantic occasions. You still see in the audience women wearing a flower that their partner has just given them. And if it's played any part in rekindling relationships, that's a nice thing to have been part of."[29]

Originally the idea was for *Phantom* to go into the Palace Theatre. As the new owner, Andrew had already agreed that Cameron could put on his *Les Misérables* there, thinking it wouldn't run very long and that it would almost be a filler until *Phantom* was ready. But with *Les Misérables* going great guns, another theatre had to be found, and the only suitable one available turned out to be Her Majesty's. The only worry with Her Majesty's was there hadn't been any big hits there in recent years, and it had also been the scene of Andrew's disastrous production of *Jeeves* back in 1975.

While a home was being found, the publicity machine was already roaring into life. The plan was to release a single, a duet between Sarah's Christine and the Phantom; just one small problem: they hadn't found their Phantom yet. Singer/songwriter Steve Harley, frontman of the rock group Cockney Rebel, was selected, and the suitably gothic video was directed by Ken Russell. "Phantom of the Opera" was a top ten hit at the beginning of 1986, and Steve Harley made such an impression that he immediately put himself in contention to play the role. At one of the auditions, opera singer James Peterson saw Harley leaving the auditorium, fist pumping and hugging Hal Prince. It seemed he had the role of the Phantom in the bag.

However, Andrew doubted that Harley's rock pedigree could have suitably equipped him for the harsh realities of handling an operatic score eight times a week. Even so, they went ahead with him, and Harley began rehearsing with the orchestra. According to Harley, he was indeed offered the role and negotiations were underway with his agent. After a few weeks, he began to wonder why his casting hadn't been revealed to the press. Andrew said he wanted to pick his moment, but the truth was his doubts hadn't gone away. Cameron, too, thought that Harley wasn't an experienced theatre actor. Put simply, they'd cast him on impulse, and it had been the wrong call. What they needed was a big, experienced star.

It was Ian Adam, Sarah's vocal coach, who suggested Michael Crawford. A boy chorister, Crawford had been going to Adam since the early 1970s and had starred in a couple of West End musicals: *Barnum* and *Billy*. At first, Andrew was slightly taken aback by the idea; like the entire nation, he identified Crawford with one role and one role only, that of the accident-prone, beret-wearing Frank Spencer in the hugely popular 1970s BBC sitcom *Some Mothers Do 'Ave 'Em*. Would he be able to shrug off the baggage of that image, and did he have the singing ability to take on the Phantom?

Crawford happily accepted Andrew's invitation to come and listen to the score at his London flat. *Sod the neighbors*, thought Andrew, as he turned it up full blast. The moment that overture came on, the hairs on Crawford's neck stood up. He was hooked. Andrew called Hal Prince with the news they'd found their Phantom. Hal didn't have much of an idea who Crawford was, so he flew into London for a meeting. Crawford performed the Phantom's theme song for him, which he'd been practicing for weeks.

Steve Harley, of course, was blissfully unaware of any of this going on until his agent called him one morning to say that Cameron had announced that the deal was off. Harley didn't have long to wait to find out why when Crawford's face was on all the front pages of the newspapers. It was casting news that surprised many. Yes, Crawford had done *Barnum*, a show set in a circus where he performed all sorts of acrobatic feats, but playing the Phantom was by far his most challenging project to date, certainly the biggest thing vocally he'd ever had to do. The joke around the production office was how will the audience know it's Michael Crawford under that mask and that make up, and somebody said, "well, you'll see the beret."

While all the machinations behind the casting of the Phantom had been going on, auditions for the other roles and the ensemble were taking place. These were largely overseen by Hal and Gillian Lynne, who Andrew had brought in as choreographer. Lynn Jezzard was in Manchester doing panto when she read in the *Stage* that they were looking for classically trained dancers for *Phantom*. Working with the Northern Ballet for many years, Lynn had never done a musical before but decided to try her luck. These were open auditions and the biggest taking place at the time. Lynn ended up attending seven auditions in total. "I was schlepping up and down every day on the train to get to London and then back to the Northern Ballet for the performance in the evening."[30]

With upwards of a thousand people at that first call, it probably helped that Lynn knew Gillian vaguely. She'd done some adjudicating at Lynn's dance school and, testament to her memory, had remembered her. The dross was got rid of quite quickly and across several more auditions the candidates were whittled down to just nine, out of which six were chosen. The final audition was especially terrifying for Lynn with Hal and Andrew in attendance, especially since she was required to sing as well as dance. "And I'd never sung before in front of anybody, let alone people of that stature. I was very nervous and as I was giving my music to the pianist Andrew arrived, everyone stood up, chairs were moved around, coffee was ordered and I was stuck at the piano warbling away in the background."[31] Due to all the attendant fuss Gillian announced, "That's lovely Lynn, thank you very much," and she left the stage having not really sung to anyone. She got the part.

James Paterson's classical background was with Scottish Opera, and it was an audition for the touring production of *Evita* that landed him a role in *Phantom*. There he was, going up for the part of Magaldi, when an impressed Hal Prince asked if he could come back tomorrow and sing some opera for a few other people. Those people turned out to be Andrew and Cameron. The result was an offer to play two small roles in the *Phantom* ensemble. Coming as he did from the world of opera, James felt a bit adrift in this new environment of musical theatre. He did at least know Maria Björnson from his Scottish Opera days, so there was one familiar face. "I remember on the first day of rehearsal I was having a coffee with Maria at the break and mentioned how excited I was that this was my first musical. And she said, 'I'm excited, too, it's my first musical, as well.'"[32]

Also coming from the world of opera was Claire Moore. Born into a musical family in Bolton, her father was a jazz musician, and there was always music in the house. Studying opera at the Royal Northern College of Music in Manchester, Claire never really gave musical theatre much of a thought until she and a group of friends took a show up to the Edinburgh fringe "and I suddenly realised there was a world out there that I just felt comfortable in."[33] She started doing auditions and got her first West End job in a revival of *Camelot* with Richard Harris at the Apollo. Then she learned about auditions for the West End production of the recent US smash musical *Little Shop of Horrors*, produced by Cameron Mackintosh. American actress and singer Ellen Greene reprised her role as Audrey in London and Claire was her understudy. "And I was on in the first week of previews without a rehearsal."[34] Claire later took over the role. This led to a chance to join the National Theatre for a year, working with the likes of Tom Stoppard and Ian McKellen. "I had the most incredible time, and for me that was my drama training."[35]

It was while she was with the National that Claire got a call to audition for *Phantom* as an alternate for Christine. She went along, impressed the panel, and was handed some sheet music from the show to learn. There was nowhere to practice so Claire shuffled off into a corner, was given a cup of tea, and got on with it. She came back and sang what were early versions of "Think of Me" and "Wishing You Were Somehow Here Again." Cameron was especially surprised by Claire's operatic range, having only heard her belting out *Little Shop of Horrors* "and he was so wonderfully supportive."[36] Claire was asked to join the company. "And that changed my life forever."[37]

One of the more difficult supporting roles to cast was that of Meg, the daughter of the opera's strict ballet mistress Madame Giry. In the story, Meg is the one who suggests to the theatre managers to put Christine in the leading role of the opera Hannibal after Carlotta, their star singer, is spooked by the Phantom. Janet Devenish was then appearing in the ensemble of *42nd Street* over at the Theatre Royal Drury Lane. Despite it being her first West End show, her agent felt confident enough to send her up for Meg. Janet's very first audition was in front of Cameron, Andrew, and Hal. "I remember feeling quite indignant because throughout my performance all three of them never stopped talking. But it turned out to be positive things about me. I always say to students when I'm teaching them now, if people talk in auditions don't presume you know what they're saying because you don't. You always think the worst."[38]

Janet came from a classical ballet background, but also did full drama training, "and that helped enormously because Andrew wanted what he needed vocally, Hal wanted what he needed as an actor and then Gillie wanted what she needed as a dancer, those three things had to come together."[39] After several call backs, including having to be in a room with all the girls in the ballet troupe to make sure she was the smallest, Janet got the part of Meg, her first "acting" role in the West End. Feeling slightly nervous as the youngest member of the cast, it was Mary Millar, playing Madame Giry, who took Janet under her wing and was both motherly and caring throughout the time she was in the show.

Janet has cause to remember the very first day of rehearsals, August 18, 1986, because it was her twenty-first birthday. They took place at Alford House, a community center in Vauxhall. "Everyone called it awful house," says Janet.[40] It wasn't very glamorous but in its own way turned out to be very useful since it had several rooms that could be used for various purposes and one large room that was used for dance rehearsal.

Hal began the first day talking the cast through the show using Maria's model of the set, explaining some of the dramatic moments. He spoke with such eloquence and passion that the whole thing started to come alive for everyone. Hal then suggested it was time they all introduced themselves. Usually that meant sitting in a semi-circle, but there were so many people there that first day, not just the cast but all the technicians, costumiers, and prop makers, that there were rows upon rows of seats.

Rehearsals always began at 10 am. Hal would work on some of the staging and finish before one o'clock, when he'd leave his assistant Ruth Mitchell to review what had been done. Gillian Lynne then took the rest of the time for choreography. Hal wouldn't return until the following morning. After a few weeks an actress raised her hand. "I've been delegated to ask you a question."

"Go ahead," said Hal. "What is it?"

"Where do you go in the afternoons?"[41]

As far as Lynn Jezzard can recall, when rehearsals began there weren't really any ballet sequences in the show, save for the masquerade ball which opens Act 2. "That was something Gillie worked very hard to achieve for us. She talked to Andrew and Hal into doing more bits of ballet here and there, because we'd gone through this massive audition process, most of us had danced to quite a high level in a ballet company, and yet there was very little for us to do."[42] A good example of this is what's known as the Degas scene where we see a group of dancers rehearsing and working in a studio somewhere in the theatre. "It's such a beautiful moment in the show," says Lynn. "But I don't think it was there originally. That was Gillie's vision."[43]

The dancers were to all intents and purposes a separate entity to the rest of the company, doing all their work with Gillian. "And we worked very long hours," confirms Lynn. "The dancers were always the first in and the last to go."[44] It wasn't until they got into the theatre and started staging the big scenes that Hal brought the entire group together. Michael and Sarah, along with Steve Barton, playing Raoul, also tended to rehearse alone with Hal. "We didn't see much of Michael and Sarah till it all started to come together," confirms Janet.[45]

While Andrew was to refer to Crawford as the most consummate theatrical performer he had ever worked with, there were inevitable tensions. One evening Cameron, Andrew, and Crawford were driving to the theatre. Out of the blue, Crawford announced that he wanted his performance of the song "The Point of No Return" prerecorded as he performed it with a hood over his face and feared this might muffle his voice. Cameron took this badly, pointing out that the money Crawford was earning he should be able to sing it live. The car was now stuck in traffic. Inside, the debate was heating up. Cameron accused his star of wanting to phone in his performance. Crawford was incensed, "How dare you." Both men wrestled one another out of the car and started a fist fight, much to the astonishment of fellow drivers and pedestrians. With the traffic easing, Andrew pulled the car away. "May the best man win," he helpfully shouted out of the window. Crawford and Cameron jumped back in, and the rest of the journey was conducted in silence. The issue was never raised again.[46]

As for Andrew and Cameron, they were very accessible during the rehearsal period. "You would see them walking around in the studios," recalls Lynn. "They would sit and chat with people, they were very approachable. There wasn't the hierarchy that you have these days. With Cameron and Andrew there's a respect given to them now when they come into a rehearsal, people don't rush to them and ask them questions. The respect of who they are makes you keep your distance, whereas in the days of the *Phantom* rehearsals they were very much part of the process with all of us. It wasn't just them and us, everybody was part of the process."[47]

One of the most important moments in rehearsals is the sitzprobe, a German term that translated literally means "seated rehearsal." It's where the singers perform for the very first time with the orchestra; it's about focusing attention on integrating the two groups. James Paterson sat there mesmerized, listening to the score for the very first time with a full orchestra. "It was magical, absolutely thrilling."[48] Sat next to him was Mary Millar. "You'll never forget this, Jimmy," she said. And she was right.

Everyone was understandably nervous that producing something like *Phantom* was going to be very expensive. The operating cost was going to be astronomical, too, with its large cast and crew, a big orchestra (with twenty-seven players it was going to be the biggest in the West End), and a legion of dressers. As production manager, Martyn Hayes' biggest challenge was bringing the whole thing in on budget, even though at the start no one knew how much the thing was going to cost. A budget was worked out, in the region of two million pounds, but this was no more than guess work. That didn't stop Cameron constantly badgering Martyn about whether they could do it for the budget. "The problem was," says Martyn, "things like the chandelier, the boat, the candles rising from the floor, these had been conceived by Maria as wonderful effects, but nobody knew how to do them or how much they were going to cost. In the end we just put in a figure and hoped it might be right, and that was even before we'd started to talk to engineers about how do we actually make this work?"[49] As it turned out, Martyn and his team brought the whole thing in on schedule and budget—quite an achievement.

The chandelier was everyone's biggest concern; this big piece of heavy equipment that had to rise up to the ceiling and at one climactic moment fly over the orchestra pit into the audience and crash on the stage floor. From the beginning Martyn kept the local council in the loop, fully aware they were to be the final arbiters of whether the chandelier was safe to use. He sent them concept drawings and told them how it was going to work and how it was going to be made safe. The problem was the council couldn't approve the chandelier until they saw it in operation. "So, we had to install the whole thing, put in all the winches and all the wires, without anybody actually saying, yes this will be ok. And Cameron and Andrew were always saying, 'we're going to be ok with the chandelier, aren't we?' You wanted to say yes but you couldn't before we had the inspection. And I always knew that without the chandelier we were screwed."[50]

When inspection day arrived, Martyn got the impression the health and safety boffins were trigger happy to refuse it, even though all safety precautions had been followed. The demonstration went ahead. A second one was asked for, then another. Finally, it was approved, and there was a huge sigh of relief from everyone on the crew.

Andrew was not happy, though. When he saw the chandelier crash down for the first time, it did so in a fairly unspectacular fashion. "If that's as fast as we can have it, forget it," he said. "It's just not worth it."[51] There began a series of negotiations with the council, a bit of to and froing until eventually the health and safety people allowed the chandelier's drop to speed up a bit more. In later productions, the speed was further increased. For such an impressive effect, the dropping chandelier was fairly simple to achieve, thanks to the use of a cat's cradle of invisible wires and two electric motors.

Things like the chandelier and other technical props fell into the domain of Alan Hatton, the show's stage manager. Alan had trained as a stage manager at the Royal Academy of Dramatic Art with the sole intention of a career in opera. He worked at Glyndebourne, Scottish Opera, and the English National Opera until 1983 when he came to the West End for his first show, a revival of *Fiddler on the Roof* staged by Ruth Mitchell, Hal Prince's assistant. Alan found Ruth "quite a force to be reckoned with, but I was very fond of her."[52] It was Ruth who brought in Alan to stage manage *Phantom*.

A stage manager's job is to support and organize all the different teams involved in the day-to-day running of a theatre production from rehearsals right through to the performances. During rehearsals, as Alan explains, the stage manager is "basically glued to the director's side."[53] It's important to form a good relationship. It's true to say that Alan got on better with Hal than he'd done with Trevor Nunn on *Chess*. "I had the most enormous respect for that man. He treated everybody like a human being. We'd get to the end of a sequence in the rehearsal room and he'd ask me what was happening next, what I required and what was the best thing for us to do. I'd explain and then he'd say, 'Ok, everybody listen, Alan's going to explain to you what happens next.' So, he really worked with me, whereas Trevor Nunn never did, and so Hal got the best out of me. I absolutely adored him."[54]

Alan's biggest headache was the gondola. It was driven by a motor and was radio controlled, which led to issues with it picking up other radio frequencies. There were certain times when the signal was lost completely, and the boat would start moving by itself and then stop. Other times it picked up the local fire station. "We could hear what they were saying over their radios. It was a complete nightmare. Crawford used to go absolutely ballistic when it broke down. There were performances where he actually had to leave the boat because it wouldn't move, grab Christine, and start walking down the stage with his lantern, then suddenly the boat decided to move and nudge him up the bum."[55]

The design of the gondola was interesting since it had to give the impression of a boat but then turn into a bed for Christine. Maria's concept was that it should look like a leaf floating on water. But it was so compact and shallow, the technicians had trouble finding space to put the motor in. This is always a problem when designing for film or theatre: is it art or do you have to consider the practicalities? "It is art," states Jonathan Allen. "And then you compromise."[56] Usually that was Jonathan's job when it came to working with Maria, trying to be the practical person in the relationship. "She used to get awfully annoyed with me."[57]

The gondola and the chandelier mechanism were once again the work of Mike Barnett. "Mike was this design genius," says Martyn. "He lived up in Suffolk and had this tiny little office and if you had a problem, it wouldn't matter what time it was, he'd jump on the train and come down and look at it, get his calculator out, come back and say, 'I know what we can do,' and get the thing working."[58]

Jonathan Allen had worked with Mike before on a number of shows with Maria. "There was usually a point where I would go, 'this isn't going to work,' and we'd phone Mike and he'd come in and say, 'oh no, we can do that, it's fine.' Sometimes you'd find Mike in the theatre looking grumpy. It was because it had all gone well, there was nothing that had gone wrong."[59]

*Phantom* is probably Mike Barnett's pièce de résistance; there were so many different technical effects to get right. Not least the travelator. This was a highly complex piece of machinery and was essentially two towers with a bridge suspended between them. As the towers moved up and down on tracks in the stage floor, one had the ability to move the angle of the bridge. In this way it could represent the Phantom and Christine's journey down three different levels to the Phantom's lair. The whole thing was controlled manually by joysticks. In later years, it was programmed on a computer.

Maria's original concept was that Christine would be led down into the lair on a horse, as in the novel. A life-size model of a horse was built, along with a mannequin of Sarah Brightman, and placed on a wooden base with a mechanism inside that allowed the horse to spin round as it descended, rather like a figure on a music box. Unfortunately, the horse model took just too much time and effort to remove from the platform, holding up the gondola from being moved into position for the scene to continue. In the end, Alan went to Hal to explain that it was physically impossible to do in the time they had. "Either Andrew has got to write more music to cover us or we have to cut the horse."[60] To make his point Alan asked both Hal and Maria to come up on the stage and watch. "Hal only had to see it the one time and he said, 'Absolutely, we have to cut the horse. There's no way we can make this work.' Maria was very upset, but she got over it."[61]

The spinning horse wasn't the only casualty. Running up and down the bridge were radio-controlled rats with red eyes. But they never worked right so were dumped. Hal also came up with the idea of letting live doves loose for the beginning of the rooftop scene to lend it some atmosphere. The crew spent two days doing nothing but flying doves around the theatre. "We had a cage of doves on the floor in the prompt corner," recalls Alan, "and what we did was set another dove high up on a perch with a light shining on it so that the doves on the floor could see it. When we released the doves, they were supposed to flutter straight up into the flies, but they went everywhere else, into the auditorium, sitting on bits of furniture, and then they'd start crapping everywhere."[62] By this point the crew were calling the show "phantom of the menagerie." There was even a bizarre idea, early on, to have a real elephant on stage during the Hannibal opera, instead of the sculptured one that ended up featured. Wisely, the thought of having an elephant in the West End doing eight shows a week just wasn't practical.

There was one effect everyone was eager to keep in the show but they just couldn't make work. In the masquerade ball the Phantom comes down the staircase in an elaborate masked costume holding a staff, and then disappears down a trap door. The original concept was for the Phantom to disappear, but his costume remains standing before crumbling to the floor. It would have been a wonderfully cinematic effect. Days and days were spent trying to get it right only for the team to admit defeat with so many other things left to do.

The great curving staircase for the masquerade was another wonderful Maria design which folded, concertina style, and hung against the back of the stage wall. To look as if there were more people on stage, costumed dummies were brought down on wires to intermingle with the real actors. "We had a rehearsal once with Gillie Lynne," recalls Alan, "and we had all these dummies on the staircase and she said, 'You, the man in green, hello, talk to me, talk to me.' And I said to her, 'Gillie, the man in green that you're pointing to is a dummy.'"[63]

If *Cats* became famous for Gillian's inspired choreography, then *Phantom* is very much remembered for Maria's extraordinary production design. Almost half the budget went on realizing it, "because Andrew and Cameron believed in what she was doing," says Jonathan Allen.[64] There were over two hundred costumes, put together by thirty-five costume makers. And because the story was set in an old opera house, the costumes weren't to look brand spanking new, but have an antique feel. "The design and costumes were absolutely breath-taking," says Janet Devenish. "Maria was one hell of a genius."[65] The attention to detail on the costumes was remarkable. Maria was meticulous on getting the right material, the right colors, the right cut. It wasn't just what the dress looked like; it was how it looked when it was lit and the actor was moving in it.

Maria used to say that a designer's job was to ask what the problems were and solve them. Her designs for *Phantom* were to earn her multiple awards and international recognition. However, her most iconic design for the show was relatively simple: the Phantom's mask. It has become tradition that every actor in the role gets his own mask, made to fit their face. Two in fact are made, in case one of them falls off by accident, which sometimes happens; a mask once fell into the orchestra pit.

As for the facial makeup, the vision of Lon Chaney's monstrous visage is one of cinema's great shock moments. The stage Phantom's makeup had to be effective and believable for those in the front rows but still work for people sat right at the back. Hal approached makeup guru Christopher Tucker, largely on the strength of his work with John Hurt on *The Elephant Man*. Christopher approached the makeup as if it were some deformity or horrendous injury, "something that would indicate a bit of sorrow for the fella, but at the same time being a bit scary."[66] This was achieved using prosthetics and by drawing up the upper lip on one side and making a hole in the side of the head so his skull was showing. It was highly effective.

The first test of the completed makeup was carried out at Christopher's home workshop. Cameron, Andrew, and Sarah were invited. It was handy for Andrew and Sarah, with Christopher living not too far away from Sydmonton. "When Sarah came to do a cast, it took her about 12 minutes to get here," says Christopher. "Mind you she did have a Porsche and she drove like a bat out of hell."[67] While they were waiting for everyone to arrive, Christopher applied the makeup on Crawford. Over the last few weeks Crawford had paid many visits to Christopher's home, and they'd got on really well. Looking at him now,

Christopher joked, "I wonder what Betty would think." For the next seven or eight minutes Crawford performed as Frank Spencer, in his Phantom makeup. "I hadn't laughed so much in years," says Christopher.[68]

According to Christopher, it took something like an hour to put on the makeup, and Crawford would start becoming the character as he sat in the chair. "He would behave normally and speak to you normally but you could see that his mind was fixated on the Phantom."[69]

Crawford spent more time in makeup than he actually did on the stage. But the great thing about the role is that you're talked about the whole night; it's always the Phantom this and the Phantom that, or a brief shadowy figure, and oh my God that must be the Phantom. You dominate the whole evening without being on stage very much. "It's a very intense, concentrated, impactful role," says Janet.[70]

While Christopher did train a makeup artist to apply Crawford's makeup for each performance, he stayed with the show and carried out the prosthetics work for all productions touring round the world. And whenever a new actor arrived to play the Phantom, Christopher would be called in to remold the prosthetics to fit his face. Although for many years the Crawford design remained.

Andrew did plan to open *Phantom* earlier in the year but due to the practicalities of achieving the show, it was put back by several months to allow the set to be built and all the technical side to be worked out. "And even then, it was one of the hairiest fit ups I've ever been on," claims Jonathan Allen.[71] The stage crew were never able to get a clean runthrough of the piece. There was always something playing up, or a technical thing that needed sorting out or practicing. And time was running out. In the end, there was no choice but for a team to come in and work night shifts in the weeks leading up to previews. "I slept in the theatre. I hardly went home," says Martyn. "It was brutal. But that was all the time we had."[72] Nevertheless, there were times, deep into tech rehearsals, when Martyn thought that the show wasn't going to come together or be completed in time. "Hal used to shout at me, 'Martyn, nothing goddamn works here!' I'd say, 'Hal we're doing our best.' You'd have a list as long as your arm of things that needed fixing or weren't working properly."[73]

After the dress rehearsal, there were even more concerns when the chandelier got stuck among numerous other technical foul ups. All through previews, the technical glitches continued, and it was a chore getting the thing to run as a whole. "The show is a sort of moving series of tableau and pulling all that together is like root canal work," said Cameron. "And until it came together it looked ghastly. You thought, we're going to get booed."[74] When the problems persisted, two previews had to be canceled.

CHAPTER 7

After all this trauma, there was a fleeting moment when all the issues seemed like they might resolve themselves and for the first time Martyn began to think, *oh actually maybe this will all work*. Then one evening some of the crew was working on the set when an accident set off all the sprinklers and water began pouring in underneath the stage. "All the motors for the candles that came up and the candelabra were absolutely drenched in water. We had to dry them all out and replace some of the cables. It was a nightmare."[75]

To cap it all, Sarah suddenly fell ill. She'd been fine on the Friday night, but the following morning Claire Moore got a call from Bob West saying Sarah was not well, they were going to cancel both the matinee and the evening performance on Saturday, and she should prepare herself to go on on the Monday. Because Claire was Christine's alternate, she did not feature in any other role or in the ensemble, so had sat out of the rehearsals. No one had even gone through the role with her. The first time she watched rehearsals was when the company went into Her Majesty's for technicals. The plan was to start her rehearsals once the show was up and running. Claire remembers saying, "Yeah, fine, but what happens if anything goes wrong before that?"[76] It's exactly what happened to her on *Little Shop* and because of that experience Claire made sure she had privately learned the role of Christine and was ready for anything. Just as well.

Hearing the news about Sarah, Claire drove to the theatre. When she arrived, the place was in turmoil. Cameron, Hal, Andrew, and Michael were there, and none of them had expected this to happen. The matinee had already been cancelled, and Claire was going to rehearse with the company that afternoon, her first with them; they hadn't even heard her sing. "Look," said Claire, taking matters into her own hands. "If I can get through today, I'll go on tonight."[77] She didn't want to cope with the nerves of having to wait until Monday. It was agreed. "I had to wear Sarah's wig and Sarah's frock because I didn't have any costumes of my own."[78]

Standing in the wings, ready to go on that night, Claire heard the announcement that Sarah would not be performing boom out of the tannoy. There were audible groans from the audience. Ignoring the reaction Claire knew, thanks to her experience at the National Theatre, that she had the stage craft to cope. "And what happens in that situation is that the whole company are so selfless they devote their entire performance to you and that support gets you from A to Z."[79] It was an emotional evening for Claire, "a night I'll never forget."[80] Crawford insisted Claire take the final bow. "I was waiting in the wings, and he shoved me out of the way and went on and then beckoned me to join him. That was a really generous and wonderful gesture."[81]

182

Sarah returned on the Monday but by this time everything was getting to Andrew, whose emotions are close to the surface during a production anyway. "When he's not working on a show Andrew is charming and funny," claims Chris Walker. "And when he is working on a show, he can take on the appearance of a bit of a monster. He was not averse to coming in and stirring things up, just to make people aware of the fact that it was his show and he wanted them to give of their very best all the time. Nothing wrong with that, but the way he did it sometimes was quite confrontational and aggressive."[82]

When things went wrong on *Phantom*, Andrew would sometimes explode in purple-faced rages. At one point he threatened to withdraw his score and went to grab it off the conductor's stand, but it was so heavy he couldn't carry it.[83] Andrew was certainly feeling the pressure. He'd poured his heart into the project as a vehicle for Sarah and he had a lot at stake. By casting Sarah he'd put his professional integrity on the line with calls of nepotism. Sarah, too, faced huge pressure, fully aware that the press was out to get her if she failed.

Previews continued, and the technical problems didn't look like going away. "There was a very low morale right across the board," remembers Alan Hatton. "People were tired, and you could tell that the creative team were not very thrilled with the way things were going. Then the very final preview was a charity gala attended by Diana, Princess of Wales, and it was like we moved from second gear into top gear, something just clicked. Whether it was the fact she was there and everybody was rising to the occasion, but there was a definite mood change and suddenly everything went wild."[84]

As had become the custom, the cast assembled on the stage afterwards to meet the Princess, the main actors out front, the ensemble lined up behind. At the time, Diana was patron of the London City Ballet and two of their dancers were in the *Phantom* company, "and Diana knew them really well," recalls Lynn. "Apparently, she used to go down to the company and do classes with them. When Diana saw them, she came through the row of principals, which of course didn't go down very well. And we were all crowded round her, chatting. She was asking us all sorts of questions about the show. And that was lovely. She made us feel very special."[85] Diana was to become a big fan of the show. "She came back to see it several times after that incognito, not officially, with her sons," recalls Lynn. "She loved *Phantom*."[86]

Finally, the opening night arrived, October 9. "I was very nervous on the first night," recalls Martyn. "You just pray it all goes right. And it did."[87] It was a triumph. Nervous wrecks, Andrew and Cameron stood at the back of the stalls.

For Lynn, opening night was something of an anti-climax. "By the time it arrived we were all quite exhausted. Every time we did a preview, we would be in early next day rehearsing, tweaking, changing, taking things out, moving bits and pieces, so it had been a very long few weeks."[88]

The opening night party took place at the recently opened Limelight night-club, a former chapel on Shaftsbury Avenue just across the road from the Palace Theatre where *Les Misérables* reigned supreme. For many in the cast, the party turned out to be something of a damp squib. "There were so many people there that had nothing, as far as we could see, to do with the show," recalls James Paterson. "I suppose all the investors were there and celebrities, but we could hardly find any of our cast members. It was disappointing because we all felt it was going to be our party and it wasn't."[89] Lynn felt much the same way and left with her friends to go for a Chinese meal.

When the reviews came out, the West End hadn't seen raves like it for years. As the cast and crew arrived at the theatre, readying for that evening's performance, there was an extraordinary feeling of not just being in a hit, but a monster hit. "From very early on we used to have people queuing from the box office, round the corner and well past the stage door," recalls James. "And that went on for years and years."[90] Hal was to recall going in one Sunday and seeing people waiting on the return ticket queue for the next performance, wrapped in sleeping bags or sat in folding chairs with mugs of coffee. "It was extraordinary," says Alan. "We were all completely blown away after everything we'd been through. We were all hoping we might get a good year out of it. Little did we know."[91]

After each performance, crowds regularly gathered outside the stage door to wait for Michael Crawford to emerge and sign autographs. "He was lovely to work with," recalls Lynn, "very friendly. And a very committed actor."[92] He needed to be. The process he went through every day to become the Phantom was quite intensive. A normal day saw him sat in the makeup chair by 5 pm. On a matinee, he would be in the theatre around 12 o'clock. Thanks to false reports that Crawford was unable to eat with all the makeup on, members of the public took to sending him crates of Guinness, thinking he was on a liquid diet. He did, however, keep the makeup on between shows on matinee days, rather than take it off and have it reapplied. It was also his custom, before the doors opened and the public was let in, to walk on stage for a sound check, and always with his mask on. "He never left the dressing room without it, never," recalls James. "And when I covered for him in the role, I would never leave the dressing room without it either. But that practice went after he left the show."[93]

This was a mark of the professionalism Crawford brought to the show, along with his perfectionist nature. Crawford engendered great discipline within the cast. According to James, during the masquerade ball scene, when the Phantom makes his dramatic entrance walking down the stairs, if anybody moved or turned their head or didn't seem to be focused, he would notice them and make his views known. And nobody made a noise in the wings. "We all knew to be very very quiet. It's respectful anyway."[94]

When Claire began to step in for Sarah, doing two shows a week as Christine, she was required to go to Crawford's dressing room for notes. He once scolded her for blinking in the "Music of the Night" scene. "I saw you blink," he said. "You're supposed to be in a trance."[95] Claire did stand up to him on one occasion, "and although it was not pleasant at the time, in a funny kind of way he respected me for it because he knew that I had defended myself."[96]

Crawford's demanding nature became a feature of his run in the show. He would call the resident director and Alan Hatton into his dressing room, and if there were aspects of the show that he thought were wrong, he wanted to know why and he wanted them fixed. This could sometimes happen several times a week. This was often a surreal moment for Alan, with Michael ranting and raving while still in his costume and makeup. "I used to stand there like a naughty schoolboy looking down at the floor."[97] Always, the next day Crawford would apologize to Alan, only for it to happen again. It all got a bit tiresome.

During the *Phantom* run, the company grew very close. "We had great fun," says Lynn.[98] As a bonding exercise, Andrew had the whole company out at Sydmonton for the day. "We had a cricket match, the show versus the village," recalls James Paterson. "There were sideshows and things on the village green, and then we all went up to the house and had a meal on the lawn."[99] Everyone had the freedom of the house. James did a bit of exploring and found himself in the attic where Andrew had set up a huge model railway.

There were also regular parties held right at the top of Her Majesty's Theatre in a large domed room. This was largely used by the dancers to rehearse. "We used to go up there at 6 o'clock every day," says Lynn. "Steve Barton always came to that. He liked being with the dancers."[100] Everyone warmed to him. "Steve was loved, and he was brilliant as Raoul," says Claire Moore. "He had a dignity and a gravitas about him that was perfect for the role."[101]

It was Gillian Lynne who recommended the American actor, singer, and dancer, and Barton brought his young family with him to London. His son was about two years old at the time. "We all used to call him bam-bam," says Lynn, "because he always used to have two cars in his hand and was always going bam bam bam."[102]

In his early thirties, Barton was slightly older than Raoul was meant to be. "But he played it absolutely brilliantly," says Lynn. "I still don't think anyone quite sings the beginning of the show like he did. It was just so beautiful."[103]

Deeply troubled in later life, with alcoholism and an addiction to painkillers, Barton tragically committed suicide in 2001 at the age of forty-seven.

Barton was also understudy to the Phantom, and his services were required a few months into the run when Crawford began to suffer bouts of intolerable pain that was quickly diagnosed as a hernia. The role of the Phantom requires much running and jumping about. There's also a section where Christine faints into his arms, and he carries her back to the bed. As a prop, the gondola/bed was quite unsteady, and Crawford had to put his foot in exactly the right place to steady it and then literally roll Christine into it, all of which was a huge physical strain. All the while he's singing "Music of the Night," the most difficult song of the show. "It's always the hardest thing for any of the Phantoms to do," says Lynn. "Whoever comes in finds it really difficult to do that moment. And in doing it Michael gave himself a hernia and he was unable to perform."[104] Admitted into hospital, Steve Barton took over, but during rehearsals that afternoon landed awkwardly going down the trapdoor, tearing ligaments in both knees.

Christopher Tucker had been alerted to come to the theatre with some makeup pieces for Barton only to see him lying back in the makeup chair looking as white as a sheet. "He was in great pain. But he was determined to go on."[105] To help him with the pain, Barton asked a doctor to give him painkillers. "It really was awful watching him," says Christopher. "I was stood next to the doctor at the back of the balcony. It was just agonising because you could hear these stifled screams as he struggled through it, with the aid of a stick."[106]

Unsure whether Barton could carry on, James Paterson, as third understudy (it's usual for key roles to have two understudies), was asked to come into the theatre early, just in case. Barton did arrive, seemingly willing to perform, and was in the makeup chair when a phone call came through that Crawford had signed himself out of hospital. With Crawford returning, it was decided that Barton should go to the hospital and have his injuries looked at. As a precaution, James was told to sit in the stalls and just watch the performance that night. As far as James could tell, Crawford appeared to be fine.

The following afternoon, James arrived at the theatre to see a crowd of people at the stage door. Pushing past them he made his way inside, only to be confronted by Bob West running down the stairs. "Michael's back in hospital. Steve's had an operation, and you're playing the Phantom tonight." It was that sudden. "The first thing I did was to go up to Bob's office to breathe," recalls James. "And I welled up slightly. I was a little overwhelmed by it all."[107] James put on the makeup and Crawford's costume, "which fitted, except they had to take up the trousers by about two inches."[108]

On doctor's orders, Michael was laid off for around two weeks and James carried on playing the Phantom. "It was really exciting and when I look back, I sometimes still can't believe the privilege that it was to be able to play that role. It really does sometimes feel like it didn't actually happen."[109] When Hal Prince arrived for one of his regular visits to check up on the show, the two of them sat alone on the darkened stage going over some notes. Hal wanted to impress on James how the Phantom sometimes covers his face with his hands, and how spontaneous a reaction it is, comparing the power that he has when he's got the mask on and how debilitated he is and frightened when it's not there. "It sounds as if you're saying it's like blood rushing from a wound," said James. "And so thrilled at that answer, Hal said, 'You've got it.' I'll never forget that. That was one of my most precious moments."[110]

Compassion plays a part, too, Hal wanted to emphasize to James. Christine shows him a great act of compassion when she kisses him at the end. This is when the Phantom decides he has to let both her and Raoul go, revealing that despite his deformity and the fact that he wasn't accepted by society and had to live alone, there was actually a real man behind the hideous visage.

Word of a Broadway move inevitably started quite early, and the hope was that Crawford, Sarah, and Steve Barton might reprise their roles. Again, Andrew came up against the intransigence of the American actor's equity board. There was no issue with Barton as he was American, nor Crawford; it was Sarah that was the problem—she wasn't a big enough star and the board said no. Andrew was incensed. "Fine," he declared, "we're not coming then." Hal was asked to bat on their behalf and spent four months testifying in front of the board. "I kept pointing out the obvious, which is there are almost 40 roles in the show and only one is going to be this English girl who is not a star, and 39 are going to be equity members. We couldn't get anywhere."[111] The board caved in only after it became clear that Andrew wasn't bluffing and meant what he said about not bringing the show to Broadway.

The next problem was trying to find a theatre that could fit the production. Hal wanted the famous Majestic and its owners, the Shubert Organization, helped out by carrying out renovations to the place. "They did an awful lot of work on that theatre to accommodate the show," says Jonathan Allen.[112]

One of the positives for Crawford about doing Broadway was that no one knew his comedy creation Frank Spencer; there were no preconceptions. After performing for the very last time in London, Crawford took the cast, and their partners, for dinner at the Groucho Club. "Then we all ended up in the bar having too much to drink," recalls Lynn. "He was very generous."[113]

Following an avalanche of prepublicity, *Phantom* opened on January 26, 1988. Critical reviews were mostly positive. Howard Kissel from the *New York Daily News* commended the production, calling it "a spectacular entertainment, visually the most impressive of the British musicals." Critical discourse on these shows was now mostly superfluous; the public voted with their feet once again, making *Phantom* an absolute smash and the longest-running show in Broadway history.

Maria and Jonathan also went with the show to Broadway, making sure the London production design was replicated faithfully. "Living in New York for three months was fun," says Jonathan. "And it's a different system, so you're learning how to work in a different way. For example, not being able to just walk on stage and move a prop, you had to go and ask someone to do it for you."[114] The Broadway unions were far stronger than those in London.

One amusing episode on Broadway occurred when Crawford was singing the big duet with Sarah and a mobile phone went off, a rare thing back then. A lady in the front row answered it. Crawford could hear her saying. "Hello. Yes. I'm here. He's singing right now. Listen to this," and proceeded to point the phone at the stage.[115]

Back in London, Dave Willetts took over from Crawford, coming across from the Palace Theatre where he had replaced Colm Wilkinson in *Les Misérables*. James Paterson continued as understudy to the Phantom and was often called to step into the breach. He stopped counting how many times he played the role after around 130. Later, James became resident director on the show in London and on tour for about ten years. He saw his job as maintaining the majesty and style of the original production.

As for Janet, she stayed with the show for two years and loved playing Meg, one of the most important roles in the show. At the very end, we observe the Phantom sit on his throne-like chair and wrap his cloak around himself. This is observed by Meg who enters the Phantom's abandoned underground lair, whips off the cloak, and finds that the Phantom has gone, leaving behind his mask. To do this, Janet was required to climb down a portcullis, wearing a harness. It was quite a daunting task, as quite often Janet was literally at full stretch from fingertip to foot. "There was the odd time when my harness failed and got stuck, and you know you've got to end the show. So, I would climb back up and unhook the harness and climb back down, uninsured, which you would never be allowed to do now. And I did get told off, but the point is, how do you finish the show if you can't do the magic vanishing trick at the end?"[116]

As for Lynn, her story is a remarkable one. In 1989, while pregnant with her first child, she was asked to take over temporarily as the dance captain. "It was a lovely company. Michael Ball was Raoul by then."[117] After three months' maternity leave, Lynn returned, but when she had her second child in 1991 that's when she decided to call it a day. A year later she was contacted again: they needed someone to come in on a ten-week contract. Lynn agreed. That ten weeks ended up being almost thirty years, sixteen of them as a performer, as Lynn took over as dance captain, then ballet mistress, and then resident choreographer. For Lynn, it was always a privilege to stay with the show and to look after Gillian Lynne's work, and never did it become a grind or boring. "For me the excitement was working with different people. Every time you got a cast change, you looked at the show again with a fresh pair of eyes because you were looking at it through their perspective. And they also bring something new to the show. So, you were constantly reinventing your ideas of the show, and for me that's what kept it fresh."[118]

Lynn also had the pleasure of working with Gillian Lynne on the twenty-fifth anniversary shows at the Royal Albert Hall that ran over three nights. "We had over 90 previous cast members."[119] Including four Phantoms! "It was like old times in so many ways," says Janet. "Just such fun seeing everybody again."[120]

Michael Crawford was there, of course. Originally, Crawford was asked to sing a bit of "Music of the Night," but was deeply anxious about doing so. Claire Moore was at home when she got a call from Cameron's office saying Crawford would only appear if she helped him with a bit of vocal work, as she was now also a singing coach. The location was the small piano room at the top of the London Palladium. "And Michael walked in," recalls Claire. "We'd not seen each other for donkey's years. I started doing some work with him and he sang so beautifully. Halfway through I burst out laughing. He asked what the matter was. I said, 'I wish my mum and dad were alive to see me telling you what to do after 25 years.' He had a right laugh."[121] In the end Crawford decided not to sing at the anniversary performances. "It was too emotional for him," says Claire.[122]

It was always the intention that Claire took over as Christine when Sarah left for Broadway, and she played the role until 1989 when she joined the cast of *Miss Saigon*. "I loved that part. I never got bored singing it."[123] As Christine, Claire got to work on a much closer basis with Hal Prince, who visited the production at least once a year to check things were being kept to the right standard. Maria Björnson did much the same thing. "Hal was great," says Claire. "He could say in a sentence what most other people would say in 15 paragraphs. And he'd just give you a little gem, a little nugget of something to get under the skin of what you were trying to do. I had great support from him."[124]

During her time in the show, Claire got to meet numerous stars and dignitaries, the Queen Mother, Margaret Thatcher, and Princess Diana, who was a delight. "Cher used to come quite a lot in a variety of wigs."[125] One night, it was announced that Princess Margaret would be in the audience. This was an unofficial visit. Still, in the interval she would require the services of a private bathroom. Claire was told that Princess Margaret would be using her facilities since she had a private shower and toilet next door to her dressing room. "It was only when second half was about to start that I suddenly had that horrible cold feeling," Claire recalls, "because first off, I realised there was no towel for her to wipe her hands. I always used to come back into my dressing room and wash my hands in that sink rather than the one in the bathroom. So, she must have had to wipe her hands on her frock or the curtains. And furthermore, there was a big 3-D greetings card stuck on the loo door and it was a big caricature of Prince Charles, with big ears and a big nose and it said, 'You've got to kiss a lot of frogs before you get your handsome prince.' Not only that but the nose had fallen off and I'd stuck it back on with blu tack, which didn't look terribly attractive, as you can imagine."[126] Claire was ruminating on all this when it came time to meet Princess Margaret along with the rest of the cast after the show. "And I don't think she was terribly impressed with me and managed to ignore me totally."[127]

As the years passed, *Phantom* began to collect a loyal fanbase. Claire can recall one particular woman who regularly turned up and always dressed as the Phantom, in a black cloak. Michael Jackson was a fan, too, going back to see it at least four times. There was talk of his desire to play the Phantom in a potential film version.

But the widespread popularity of the show has perhaps no modern comparison in musical theatre history. The reasons are simple. It features some of Andrew's best and most popular compositions, and it's timeless. While something like *Starlight Express* has been constantly reinvented in order to keep up with the times, *Phantom* remains resolutely the same, largely due to its period theatrical setting. When Monsieur Firmin, one of the directors of the opera house, rushes onto the stage after a stagehand has been horribly murdered, "Ladies and gentlemen, please remain in your seats. Do not panic. It was an accident . . . simply an accident," he's talking directly to the real people in the auditorium. We are part of the show. "It's the ultimate backstage musical," claims Richard Stilgoe.[128]

For Claire Moore, *Phantom* is simply a magical experience, and whenever she went back to see it, it never failed to give her goosebumps. "It always feels like home going back to *Phantom*. And I see ghosts. I can watch what's on that stage and I see all the people from when we opened that we've lost along the way."[129]

# "THE AMERICAN DREAM"

While thumbing through a magazine one day, Claude-Michel Schönberg came across a photograph showing a Vietnamese mother at an airport handing over her child to her US Army father so that she could have a better life in America. It was a heart-breaking image, one of the many personal tragedies that sprang out of the Vietnam War. Claude-Michel considered this mother's actions "The Ultimate Sacrifice," and it was the springboard for *Miss Saigon*.

Cameron first heard that Alain and Claude-Michel were developing a new project during the after-show party for *Les Misérables* at the Palace Theatre. The writers cornered him, saying that now *Les Misérables* was a hit and their profession of writing musicals appeared secure, they had a new one on the boil. "Having piqued my interest, they then absolutely refused to tell me anything more," said Cameron. "Not even its name. The more I became impatient at their silence, the more they enjoyed teasing me."[1]

A fan of Puccini, Claude-Michel had long dreamed of adapting *Madama Butterfly* into a modern time scenario, just like *West Side Story* was an update of *Romeo and Juliet*. Later, Cameron liked to tell the story of how Claude-Michel visited Puccini's grave and knelt before it, hoping for some inspiration to seep out of the ground. It seemed like an interesting idea to update the story of *Madama Butterfly* to the dying days of the Vietnam War in 1975. Taking the bare bones of that classic story of two individuals from different cultures falling in love, Alain and Claude-Michel shaped a new narrative about Chris, a US marine, who meets Kim, a young Vietnamese orphan who works as a bargirl and prostitute. They fall in love but in the chaos of the American evacuation of Saigon, they are parted. Kim bears Chris' child, a son she hopes one day to take to his father in America. Mother and son end up in Bangkok where Kim comes face to face with Chris' American wife Ellen.

By the spring of 1986, a first draft of Act 1 was ready, and Alain and Claude-Michel flew to London to play Cameron tapes of some of the music at his London flat. The writers recalled that Cameron's reaction bordered on the ambivalent, that he was perhaps unprepared for something so completely different, in both form and content, from *Les Misérables*. Both men left that night crestfallen and flew back to Paris convinced Cameron was going to say no. Just two days later they received a call from Cameron; it was good news. He'd listened to the tapes over and over again and felt there was something really exciting about it and he wanted to produce it, "despite and perhaps because of the extraordinary challenge it represented."[2]

It was a controversial subject to be sure. And like *Les Misérables*, it was rooted in a time of political and social turmoil. The wound of the Vietnam War and its aftershocks still resonated in the United States, and Cameron's underlying intent was not to sugarcoat anything. "If we had tried to make it palatable, I believe it wouldn't have worked."[3] It was going to be a huge balancing act, on the one hand having to deliver what a musical needs to deliver in order to be a musical, while at the same time being utterly truthful to what had happened so as not to betray all the people that were involved in so tragic a piece of recent history. The image that flashed into Cameron's mind was of someone dancing on a razor blade: any misstep and it was all over.

Alain and Claude-Michel approached *Miss Saigon* in much the same way as they did *Les Misérables*, working for months on the dramatic structure of the piece, going through something like three or four versions, before separating to begin their respective contributions. And while Claude-Michel waited for Alain to finish the book before embarking on the score proper, a few melodies were always playing around in his head as the structure was being worked out. Like *Les Misérables*, it was going to be a sung-through musical, its songs and music propelling the drama forward. Claude-Michel also knew that he wanted to hear in the music a clash of cultures. The audience must feel that they are in the Far East, but at the same time the score had to adhere to a Western pop influence.

After eight months of work, there was still no title. It was when Alain came up with the idea of a sleezy version of a Miss America contest in the nightclub that a potential title came to mind. He phoned Claude-Michel and told him the idea and that the show could be called "Miss . . ."; instantly, Claude-Michel jumped in: "Saigon," he said.[4]

Since *Les Misérables*, Alain's command of the English language had advanced to the point where he no longer felt the need for anybody to come in and translate the lyrics. Even so, he did want a collaborator and contacted Herbert Kretzmer. Having enjoyed working on *Les Misérables*, Kretzmer appreciated the approach and thought the new subject matter fascinating, but politically it didn't sit well with him, and he declined. In any case, he said, the project would suit an American writer better, to inject a real understanding of American sensibility into the story.

As it happened, Cameron had already set his sights on the American Richard Maltby Jr., with whom he had worked on Andrew's *Song and Dance* show on Broadway. To Cameron's umbrage and surprise, Maltby turned him down. He gave two reasons: first, he didn't really know who Alain and Claude-Michel were, and secondly, for many Americans the war was still a raw topic and he simply didn't believe audiences would go and see it. "I thought they were crazy to embark on this project," he said.[5]

Over time, Maltby began to change his mind. The unexpected and cathartic success in America of Oliver Stone's Vietnam War film *Platoon* certainly helped, as did repeated listens of the *Miss Saigon* demo tape. The real turning point came when he attended the pre-Broadway run of *Les Misérables* in Washington early in 1987. He came away that evening with an appreciation of what Alain and Claude-Michel were doing: "nothing less than the invention of a new kind of musical story-telling, combining the impulses of grand opera, American and English musicals, and popular music."[6] Maltby contacted Cameron to see if the position was still open. It was.

The original plan was to do a concept album first, and John Cameron was brought in to do the same job he'd done so well on *Les Misérables*. But after listening to the first rough tapes from the recording, Cameron had second thoughts and aborted the project. John Cameron, too, was let go. "I felt very let down," says John. "Alain, Claude-Michel, and myself worked very hard on a concept album and I got a phone call from Cameron saying, 'Do you like what you've written?' And I said, 'It's exactly what they asked for.' He said, 'Ahh, then I've got to find another arranger.' That left a bit of a sour taste."[7] Cameron brought in the American William David Brohn as the show's orchestrator.

Now came the question of director. Alain and Claude-Michel naturally assumed it would be Trevor Nunn. This was also an assumption Nunn was to make. But Cameron had private misgivings about Nunn's suitability and plumbed for Michael Bennett, only to learn that he was gravely ill. Next, Cameron approached Jerome Robbins, the celebrated American choreographer/director, who thought about it for a while before politely declining. When Nunn eventually confronted Cameron about the situation, asking, "So, what's happening with *Miss Saigon*? Am I not directing it?" this put Cameron in a somewhat awkward situation. In the end he told Nunn that he needed to see the finished draft before making up his mind. Later, the two men did have a long frank conversation, during which Cameron expressed his reservation about Nunn taking on *Miss Saigon*. There was no doubting Nunn's supreme talent as a director, Cameron just felt his gifts lay best in tackling classical subjects and giving them a contemporary twist and relevance, as he'd done so well with *Nicholas Nickleby* and *Les Misérables*. Would he be able to bring that same talent to bear on a purely contemporary show?

Muddying the waters was Nunn's intention to direct the new Andrew Lloyd Webber musical *Aspects of Love*, which planned to open in London around the same time. It was Cameron's opinion, Andrew's too, that no director could handle both productions and that Nunn needed to make a choice. Nunn, however, wanted to do both and wrote a letter to the two men expressing that desire. Meanwhile, Andrew was sounding out a young director called Nicholas Hytner who had started his career at Kent Opera and had forged a good reputation in a comparatively short space of time working with the Royal Shakespeare Company and at the National. When this news reached Cameron, and with no obvious candidate to direct *Miss Saigon*, he contacted Nunn's lawyer and formal negotiations began.

As these negotiations continued, Nunn became embroiled in extensive rewrites for the Broadway version of *Chess*. As we know, stories coming out of New York were of fallings out and a tense atmosphere as Nunn pushed the show in a direction some in the production team, including Tim Rice, felt was wrong. Cameron began to fear a similar situation with *Miss Saigon* and broke off negotiations. He even asked Alain and Claude-Michel to make a trip to New York especially to see an early preview of *Chess*. Perhaps stringing Nunn along for so long had been a mistake, and Cameron should have acted upon his initial gut feelings about him. With a sense of guilt, Cameron wrote a letter of apology to Nunn, taking full blame for the situation. Nunn was reportedly furious, and the two men were barely on speaking terms afterwards; their falling out was the talk of London's Theatre Land.

At some point during these struggles, the decision was made to open *Miss Saigon* first on Broadway. Cameron had seen a recent revival of Cole Porter's 1930s musical *Anything Goes*, a big hit on Broadway. The director was Jerry Zaks. Cameron hired him. As it turned out, there were no suitable theatres on Broadway capable of putting on *Miss Saigon* currently available; it didn't help that so much of Broadway was taken up by the British West End hits— *Phantom*, *Les Misérables*, and *Cats*. London was a different story. The Prince Edward Theatre had become free with the closure of *Chess*, and the Theatre

Royal Drury Lane was also available. As well as being one of London's most prestigious theatres, with a huge stage and a seating capacity of over twenty-two hundred, Drury Lane held a personal significance for Cameron, having begun his theatrical career there as a stagehand at the age of eighteen back in 1965.

The choice of Drury Lane presented a huge problem for Simon Opie, *Miss Saigon*'s production manager. Simon had recently gone freelance, after leaving the Royal Shakespeare Company where the Cameron Mackintosh office knew him from his work on *Les Misérables*. Simon rightly identified that the world of the big commercial musical had moved further on, even from *Les Misérables* days. *Miss Saigon* was a culmination of where these musicals were heading. The level of investment and technical aspect of the show was quite different from what had gone before. "Les Mis was tough," says Simon. "But *Miss Saigon* was on a different level."[8]

*Miss Saigon* arrived right at the end of that process of theatres adapting to the more technical challenges of larger productions. The pace of change had been so enormous that inevitably some people were left behind. That was the case with Drury Lane. Unlike some West End theatres where the backstage crew were quite technically adept, Simon felt the team at Drury Lane were a little stuck in the past. The infrastructure, too, wasn't really equipped to deal with the level of technical complication and challenge required of mounting something like *Miss Saigon*. Help was needed.

By then, all big musicals brought in a production team of carpenters and electricians to build the show on stage. The whole infrastructure has to be built first, and then you start to put in the show elements. For *Miss Saigon*, the build period took months. For a start, a full hydraulic installation had to be put in. Simon felt this was all a step too far for Drury Lane. What was required was somebody independent to be brought in and run the show as a sort of head stage technician keeping an absolute handle on things, especially the safety aspect. "That caused a little bit of anxiety, because it hadn't been done before, and Cameron started his career at Drury Lane and so he knew all the crew and quite rightly felt a sense of loyalty to them. So, it was a little bit contentious to persuade him that we needed to bring somebody in because, essentially, they weren't up to the job."[9]

With the decision to launch *Miss Saigon* in the West End rather than Broadway, Jerry Zaks was unwilling to leave his family to come and work in London for perhaps a year or more and dropped out. Meanwhile Nicholas Hytner, once earmarked for *Aspects of Love*, became free when Trevor Nunn was installed as director. In this strange game of musical chairs, Hytner was swiftly brought onto *Miss Saigon*. This was not only to be his first musical, but his first foray into the West End.

One of Hytner's overriding concerns was to avoid those rather stale clichés of the Asian female. In the book, Kim's language was steeped in Far Eastern mysticism, and this just rang false to Hytner. Alain's defense was that young women like Kim, while embracing Western culture, also acknowledged and respected the old values of their ancestors, but did concede that he might have overdone it a bit. This element of Kim's character was slowly eroded until she became much more of a modern young woman. For Hytner, this was not interfering in somebody's personal creative vision, or trying to manipulate a piece into saying something different from what it wanted to say. "But I did work very hard at making it say better what it wanted to say in the first place. Much of a director's job simply consists of saying to the writers: write this better."[10]

When it came to assembling a cast, the biggest challenge was a desire to use as many authentic Asian actors and dancers as possible. Not to mention finding somebody capable enough of playing the demanding role of Kim. At the time, there was a lack of singing and dancing candidates within the Asian community in Britain. When in October 1988 an ad was placed in the *Stage* newspaper announcing two days of auditions, just ten Asian performers turned up on the first day. That number increased to just fifteen on the second day. The irony was that everybody was outnumbered by the amount of press photographers who'd showed up.

A change of plan was called for. Notices began to pop up in Chinese restaurants in Soho and in a Buddhist temple in Wimbledon, ads were taken out in Vietnamese-language magazines in Paris, countless theatrical agencies based in the United Kingdom were contacted, and every Southeast Asian embassy was approached in London. An official from the Vietnamese embassy in London unhelpfully pointed out to the producers that perhaps the show ought to be called "Miss Ho Chi Minh."

It was looking more and more likely recruitment would have to be done largely from abroad. That November, Alain, Claude-Michel, Cameron, and Hytner traveled to America and the Philippines, principally to find their Kim. Auditions began in New York, but these proved a disappointment. Things were marginally better in Los Angeles, where they were able to find a few people but as yet no realistic candidate for their leading role. In Hawaii, they came across Chloe Stewart, an interesting mix of Irish, Chinese, and Korean. Her singing impressed everyone, but at just fifteen years old Cameron knew that British Equity would never allow it; she was just too young. The search continued. Chloe did later perform as Kim on Broadway and on tour.

When the team arrived in Manila, their luck seemed to change, coming across not just one but two perfect candidates. Monique Wilson was an eighteen-year-old student with plenty of local theatre experience. But it was Lea Salonga that took everyone's breath away. A seventeen-year-old student, Lea had been singing professionally since the age of nine, taking the lead in a local production of *Annie*, along with other shows, films, and television. At her first audition she performed "On My Own" from *Les Misérables*. Returning the following day, Claude-Michel took Lea to where there was a piano and began to take her through one of the songs from the show "Sun and Moon." It didn't take her long to pick it up. "She sang it almost like she would be going to do it every night on stage," Claude-Michel recalled. "She didn't need me."[11]

A worldwide search for the right person to play the role of Kim ended with the discovery of seventeen-year-old student Lea Salonga in the Philippines. Her performance turned her into an overnight star.
*Credit*: Courtesy the Everett Collection

So, Lea could sing, no problem. But could she cope with performing in a big London show. They asked her what was the biggest audience she'd ever sung in front of. "I opened for Stevie Wonder," she answered casually. "I think it was 10,000 people, I really don't know, it was dark." Alain looked at her, "I think you answered our question."[12]

It was decided to fly Lea to London and put her on the Drury Lane stage to really see what she was made of. At first it looked as if they'd made a costly mistake. Understandably nervous and perhaps disoriented being in a new and different country, and having never performed in such a grandiose setting, she flopped badly. Told to work with the assistant director on a few things, Lea returned the next day and knocked it out of the park. "It was clear that she would be the one," said Claude-Michel.[13]

Other cast members began to fall into place. Frances Ruffelle had been brought in early in the process to perform demos of the songs meant for Kim. "When I was doing it, I did say to them, 'you know you can't cast me in that role.' Then they searched the world and found Lea and they asked me to play Ellen. I just couldn't do it, I just was so in love with Kim, even though I knew I shouldn't and couldn't play her."[14]

Claire Moore was still in *Phantom* when Cameron asked her to come in and help with a few demos, too. They were also looking for someone to play Chris, and Claire was asked to perform as Ellen alongside suitable candidates. "Eventually after all these workshops my agent finally said, 'By the way, is Claire doing it or what?' And they went, 'Oh yes,' as if it was something I knew all along. That was my audition."[15] The role of Chris was filled by British singer and actor Simon Bowman.

As for the important role of the Engineer, a Eurasian pimp that services the needs of the marines and harbors his own dreams of getting to the United States, it was at a casting conference that Hytner said that what was needed was someone like Jonathan Pryce. If only he could sing. Alain turned to the director and said, "He does." Pryce was contacted and asked to audition. He sang "Willkommen" from *Cabaret* with such verve it elicited prolonged applause from everyone in attendance.

Even though Pryce had already done some singing, *Miss Saigon* represented his first musical and his first major starring role in the West End. As the only "name" in the show, Pryce felt a huge responsibility, and he worked closely with Hytner to get the characterization right. "He was forensic in the way he approached that role," recalls Peter Polycarpou.[16]

Peter was performing with the Royal Shakespeare Company when he got a phone call asking him to audition for the role of John in *Miss Saigon*. An American GI stationed in Saigon, John is Chris' best friend and becomes instrumental in the development of Kim and Chris' relationship as well as their reunion later. Another actor was under consideration for the role, but he'd failed to get to grips with the character's big song, "Bui-Doi." Peter remembers having to learn the song and doubting whether he could sing it either, because it was very high. After enlisting the help of the Royal Shakespeare Company's musical director, Peter went to Drury Lane for the audition and sang it for Claude-Michel and Cameron, both of whom knew him from *Les Misérables*. "I finished the song and there was a bit of a silence and then Claude-Michel came up onto the stage and gave me the most incredible hug and said, 'Thank you so much, thank you.' I don't think he'd ever heard the song sung before in that way."[17] Fortunately for Peter the song sat in his voice in a way he hadn't realized it could. "But during the rehearsal process I did find it very tricky and I said to Claude-Michel, 'Look, if I'm going to sing eight shows a week of this it's going to tear my voice apart, you have to take it down a tiny fraction.' And he did, bless him, for me, and that's why it's in this strange key of a flat as opposed to a natural. And it's stayed in that key in every performance since. And that's down to me."[18]

Long before casting was complete, John Napier had been working on his designs for the audacious sets. Unlike *Les Misérables*, which to a degree was presented in a stylized way, *Miss Saigon* aimed for greater realism. The last thing anyone wanted was for it to look something like *The King and I*. It couldn't have that sort of traditional scenery or any sense of showbiz. There was also a desire for it to be almost filmic in its presentation. As Claire Moore recalls, "It wasn't a set design as such, it was a world created. It was very cinematic."[19] That presents its own problems, of course. Theatre can't compete with film; in theatre, you can only really put the essence of a scene on the stage. "The question you always ask yourself is: to what degree do you go to make it believable?" says John Napier. "Getting the balance right between stylisation and naturalism is the name of the game."[20]

*Miss Saigon*'s stand-out visual highlight, its barricade moment, if you like, is the helicopter. This one single idea changed the show completely. Originally Alain and Claude-Michel saw their show as a small, intimate love story. It was the realization that they would have to recreate in some way the fall of Saigon, and that famous image of a Huey helicopter evacuating people from the roof of the American embassy, that led inevitably to it being a "spectacle" musical.

Unlike *Les Misérables*, the book was almost complete when it was sent to John Napier. "On reading it and listening to the music it was definitely of the opera world. There was this romantic but hard-bitten storyline, and then you get this one incident in the middle of the second act which is a revisiting of the evacuation of the American embassy. And the one thing that Alain and Claude-Michel had underlined was that this has to be the most real moment, everything else can be romanticized, but this has to be hard and real."[21] It was John's task to bring that event to life on stage and to make the audience believe in it.

In the end, it was about creating an illusion. The frame of the helicopter was built out of aluminum by Mike Barnett and then secured to a concealed lift on an articulated hinge-pulley at the back of the stage. It was suspended from a couple of huge cables on a gimbal enabling it to rotate in any direction. The whole thing was manually operated by remote control joysticks. To create the illusion of rotor blades, wound up bungee cord was tied to a motor in opposing directions, with two rubber balls at either end. Then a little bit of silk was tied to the bungee so that when the motor built up speed, because of the centrifugal force, the balls were thrown outwards to create a thirty- to forty-foot circular pattern, which when lit in the correct way gave the impression of whirling rotor blades. "So, it was literally a bit of string, some silk and a couple of rubber balls," says John. "It was as simple as that."[22]

Completing the illusion was the sound provided by Andrew Bruce. Andrew had been brought onto the project earlier than most. He was in Los Angeles with a production of *Les Misérables* when Claude-Michel asked him to record some of the still unfinished score of *Miss Saigon*. At that stage there were no lyrics, just Claude-Michel sort of humming the tunes in his distinctive manner.

Instead of relying on library sounds of a helicopter, Andrew was determined to record the real thing and got permission to go down to the Royal Air Force helicopter training base in Yeovil. "We arrived with a car full of equipment and were given free run of the place."[23] With no clue whatsoever how to go about recording helicopters, Andrew's team set up the equipment in the middle of a field and over a walkie talkie asked the control tower if one of their Sea King helicopters could slowly come in and hover very close to them, almost overhead. There was a slight pause, then a voice said, "Really. Are you sure?" Andrew said, "Yes, yes, absolutely sure." The Sea King duly approached and came overhead, "at which point," recalls Andrew, "everything that we owned, including almost the car, was blown away, all the microphones, the equipment, we were flattened on the ground. And I could hear them laughing in the control tower and this voice said, 'You realise that you're standing in front of five tons of down pressure.'"[24] After that, the helicopter stopped some distance away, and Andrew got everything he wanted.

To create an even more striking effect, the idea was proposed that one of those huge fans used for storm and wind effects in movie studios be placed behind the helicopter as it comes in and lands. It was at one of the technical rehearsals that this fan was used for the first time. "When they turned it on every piece of paper in the stalls, everybody's notes, on every single one of the production desks, ended up on the back wall," says Andrew. "That idea was cut immediately."[25]

The helicopter became very much a talking point of the show. Such was its effect that it was very cleverly integrated into the design of the poster. "But the absolute bollocks that I took for creating the helicopter," complains John. "Not only from the critics, but from within because quite frankly it stole the show. And you're not supposed to do that."[26] For some critics, the helicopter in *Miss Saigon* was symptomatic of this genre of musical, where spectacle was allowed to take over from substance, perhaps forgetting that the story demanded it. "I do what is required for an imaginative audience to follow the narrative of a production and take them on a journey," says John. "That's what I do. I don't do scenery. I'm not interested in scenery. I'm interested in believing in what I'm watching in front of me."[27]

With John taking care of the set design, the costumes were once again the domain of Andreane Neofitou. Most of her research went into acquiring information on military uniforms and daily life after the fall of Saigon. A lot of this data and photographic reference material was in the hands of the Russians. This meant Andreane having to visit the Russian embassy in London several times, leading to certain enquiries about why she was entering such a place. "I felt a little bit paranoid."[28]

Whereas in *Les Misérables* Andreane was allowed a little bit of creative license, here the period and costumes had to be totally authentic. A lot of the army costumes were the real thing. "Some of them had bullet holes in them."[29] Andreane made the actors and dancers wear real flak jackets. "At first, we made a couple ourselves, but they just didn't move correctly, the weight wasn't there. Once the performers had the real ones on and they had the weight of the uniform, then they behaved like soldiers and moved like soldiers."[30] Even the coolie hats had to be authentically Vietnamese.

Andreane was put into contact with someone who could supply uniforms, but they also had ashtrays, bottles, and army uniform insignias from that period in Vietnam. These were bought and used in the show. "One of the top brass in the military came to see it one night," recalls Andreane. "And after the show he came backstage and saw me and he said, 'It broke my heart. It was so real.' That was a wonderful thing to say to me. He had been there. He remembered it."[31]

Working on any production, Andreane always needs a key, something that will unlock how she is going to approach her designs. In *Les Misérables*, it was Valjean, because as a figure he strides through the entire piece. In *Miss Saigon*, her key was the Engineer, everything had to be centered around him. "He was a product of his age, and I knew if I got him right everything else would fall into place. At first the audience see this horrible man that is selling all these girls. It's only as the show develops that you realise that he too was an abused child that had to come up from the gutter. And that's why he had this American dream."[32]

Another important member of the creative team was choreographer Bob Avian, who trained as a dancer and worked with Michael Bennett on his successful Broadway hits *A Chorus Line* and *Dreamgirls*. Hytner and Avian developed a successful way of working. Hytner would stage a scene, and then Avian would come in and add his own touches, not outright choreography—*Miss Saigon* wasn't a dance musical; this was more dramatic choreography, movements for individual players, what Avian called "storytelling beats," which tells the audience where to look. This is the reason Avian insisted his credit on the poster be "musical staging by" rather than "choreography by."

One of the biggest challenges facing Bob Avian was the lack of competent dancers in the ensemble, which was largely made up of people from the Philippines. Most of them required the teaching of basic dance steps, and workouts were held every morning prior to rehearsals. The Philippine ensemble were a mix of people; some came from rich, privileged families, others from more humble backgrounds and they would send their money back home. What all of them brought to the show was huge enthusiasm. At the end of each rehearsal, they would all applaud. "They brought a great deal of humility to the show," says Claire. "A lesson for all of us to learn. They were the heart of the company."[33]

Rehearsals were fun, hard, and engrossing. Claire has always loved the rehearsal process. "You learn to experiment and take risks. That's when you find things in your bubble of safety that a rehearsal room gives you."[34] On the very first day there was the usual meet and greet, and Hytner gave a talk about the Vietnam War, explaining that the task was to be as truthful as they could be within the context of the show and the telling of the story, but to get those elements of the history right. To help them, the cast sometimes watched Vietnam War films, including *The Deer Hunter*. Peter Polycarpou recalls that there were photographs put up around the rehearsal room for reference purposes. "It was all about trying to make this thing as real as possible."[35] In that first week, there were improvisations and group exercises, including getting everyone to pretend to be Western tourists walking along some seedy street, then flipping it around and making them see what it was like to be the exploited locals.

A big problem for many of the girls from the Philippines, most of whom came from staunch Catholic families, was the semi-nudity required for the nightclub scenes and having to dance in skimpy bikinis while being fondled by soldiers.

These were ordinary young girls who had all been in a specially set up school in the Philippines to prepare them for the show. They all knew they were going to play prostitutes in the bar scenes. "But when they came over, they were surprised they had to wear bikinis," says Andreane. "And they were surprised that they had to be touched by the men. That's where I had a problem. A lot of them would cry as I started to dress them: 'no, no, it's too small.' It was a big problem."[36]

Andreane had to come up with a solution. In the end it was simple: just tell them the truth of what they were portraying. Researching into that period, Andreane uncovered so many sad and tragic stories about girls sold into prostitution. She had photographs of girls in bikinis in clubs with numbers on their shoulder straps and the men would come and say, "I want number six or number three." "And the terrible thing is, a lot of their families, who were desperately poor, would sell these girls or send them to these places. The girls would send money back to the family, but they were completely cut off from them because if it was known that one of their daughters was in such a place their other daughters wouldn't be respectably married off."[37] The only chance these bargirls had of a better life was to marry an American and get to the United States. "This is what I explained to them," says Andreane. "What you are doing is, you're not selling yourself, you're representing all those girls, you're showing what really happened. So do it. And that's how I won them over."[38]

Lea Salonga was barely eighteen when rehearsals began, quite innocent, with no world experience, protected and cosseted. In London, her mother acted as chaperone, as well as her business manager. During rehearsals, Lea's mother accepted Hytner's rule that only performers were allowed inside the auditorium, so she positioned herself in the theatre's café. However, whenever there was a break Lea would rush off stage to go to her mother to discuss what had been going on. Hytner's biggest problem during rehearsals was Lea's hesitancy or reluctance to fully commit to being this Vietnamese bargirl intensely involved with a man. "I had to get across to Lea—and, perhaps more important, her mother—the notion that whatever Lea did on stage as Kim had nothing to do with what she was really like as a person."[39]

Perhaps as a concession, Lea was not required to wear a bikini in the bar scene, so Andreane designed a white shift dress for her, which actually worked better by lending her a virginal quality and setting her apart from the other girls.

Deep into rehearsals, a lot of emphasis was placed on those elements in the second half of the show when Saigon falls. "It was really intense work to get that level of hysteria and panic that people were feeling as the Americans were abandoning them and leaving Saigon," says Peter. "There was a lot of intense work around that."[40] Here Peter found Hytner to be helpful, and he enjoyed working with him. "He could be irascible. He was quite funny at times. He was very bright, very in control, and very ordered. He knew exactly what he wanted to get, and he had this fantastic approach which was very broad strokes that he used to start with and then after that he would work on the detail. He was very exacting."[41]

All the while work continued on the lyrics and music. "We had constant changes and rewrites during rehearsals," recalls Peter. At one point, nine music copyists worked round the clock to provide the orchestra with the amended sheet music. By now, Alain and Claude-Michel were used to this kind of thing, that lyrics were changed at the last minute, elements were tweaked, or new songs were asked for and hurriedly written. Take Claire's one solo song as El-len, "Now That I've Seen Her," which comes after meeting Kim for the first time. The lyrics kept changing on a nightly basis during previews. It got so bad that Claire ordered Cameron, Hytner, Alain, and Claude-Michel into her dressing room. "I sat them down, and I perched myself on the dressing table so I could be higher than them, and I just said, 'I can't learn anymore lyrics to this song.'"[42] Even when Claire came to record the cast album, she was asked to perform at least three different versions. On Broadway, too, the song was still being rewritten. In its original form, Claire felt it was too confrontational and didn't take into account that Ellen is just as much a victim of the situation. As it was, Claire got letters from people saying, "why didn't Ellen shoot herself instead of Kim? It would have all been much better."

During rehearsals the decision was also taken that Lea and Peter's two char-acters should share a duet. Alain and Claude-Michel quickly composed what turned out to be the song "Please." The main thing was to leave one's ego at the stage door. If something wasn't working and the criticism was justified, Alain and Claude-Michel were happy to change it. "They were very intent on making it work," says Peter. "And the two of them together always seemed to have that intensity and concentration and level of awareness of what was going on, so they always seemed to know what to do next. There was never any panic or doubt."[43]

That couldn't be said for the technical side of things. The complex nature of the staging, largely computerized, led to numerous breakdowns and glitches. At one point, a giant Ho Chi Minh statue, driven by hydraulic rams, arrives on the stage during a victory parade for the new communist regime. During rehearsals, an actor got their ankle caught underneath, and it was only the quick thinking of Jonathan Pryce, who noticed what was happening and screamed for the prop to be shut down, that prevented serious injury. There were also bomb craters on the stage at certain times, depicting the fall out of battle.

"You can imagine how many sprained ankles that would have caused," says Claire.[44] They were wisely filled in.

It ended up being a huge slog. "The technical elements of the show were horrendous at times," says Peter. "I do remember the technical period as being really long and hard. But I suppose they were breaking new ground."[45] The technical issues got so bad that Hytner ordered the entire company to leave the theatre and rehearse elsewhere for a week while the technical team ironed out the problems.

One late addition was a Cadillac brought onto the stage for "The American Dream" number sung by the Engineer. This idea came from John Napier quite early on, only to be rejected as unfeasible. Then, three weeks before previews, John was asked, "Do you remember that Cadillac idea of yours?" Too late to make a replica, they had to buy a real one, and a garage stripped out the heavy components that weren't needed like the engine and gear box. Even then, it was still a hell of a weight and the only way to fit it in along with the other big props was to suspend it vertically right at the back of the stage.

For Simon Opie, *Miss Saigon* was the most involved show he ever worked on. "Just the scale of it. It was very ambitious. Every single element had its own challenges. It was also following on from *Les Misérables* and was inevitably going to be compared to it, so I sensed there was a lot more anxiety around that creative process, just because the stakes were higher."[46]

No one felt the pressure more than Nicholas Hytner, being relatively inexperienced in the commercial world of musicals. "He was an extremely talented director," says Simon, "but he was learning on the job. He was learning how to put together a show on that scale, with those kinds of resources. I don't think he'd ever had those sorts of resources to work with before."[47] He was also a little bit isolated. Although Claire recalls that he used to join in with the warmups every morning, "even though he was the most uncoordinated human being I've ever seen."[48] Many of the core creative people knew each other and had all worked together before or done other similar shows. This put Hytner in quite a difficult position and at something of a disadvantage. As a result, a number of people working on the show felt there was a tension around the place that just wasn't there on *Les Misérables*.

These big musicals are beasts to put on. With someone like Trevor Nunn, he had learned and understood how to deliver his vision within the constraints of these kinds of shows. And with the sweep and great big dramatic canvas of *Miss Saigon*, Hytner tried hard to still make it a very intimate love story. "You spend so much time getting the bloody helicopter to land on the landing pad that you can lose sight of what's the best way to tell this story and how the main characters interact," says Simon. "But I think Nic did a really good job."⁴⁹

Prior to opening night, a massive publicity blitz had been in operation. It seemed that every red London bus had a *Miss Saigon* poster emblazoned on its side. As a result, Drury Lane saw a massive five million pound advance at the box office. Everyone in the cast were confident they had a big hit on their hands. "I never doubted *Miss Saigon*," says Peter. "The central performances of Lea Salonga and Jonathan Pryce were incredible. They were world beating. When I first heard Lea sing the hairs on the back of my neck stood up."⁵⁰

On the opening night of September 20, 1989, Hytner didn't watch the performance. Instead, he was to be found kicking his heels at the top of the Drury Lane Theatre's grand stairwell. He needn't have worried. "The curtain call lasted I think 20 minutes," says Peter. "They wouldn't let us leave the stage. I remember weeping and being totally overcome with the emotions of that night."⁵¹ Behind the curtain, the reaction of the cast was just as joyous. "We felt we'd achieved something," says Claire. "When you work on a piece and it becomes so special to you, you really invest in it, you just want people to love it."⁵²

There is pressure of an altogether different kind when a show opens, not whether it will succeed, but of personal failure, of blowing lines, and letting the side down. "Just remember, don't fuck it up," was Jonathan Pryce's advice to Peter. But it went brilliantly. "You could sense that the audience were with us almost from the opening number," says Peter. "It was a very special night."⁵³

After the performance, the cast and invited guests boarded a boat that took them up the Thames to a riverside warehouse where Cameron had organized his customary lavish party. Outside the building, a huge flag with the show's iconic poster logo greeted them, while inside there was Asian food and show-themed cocktails. "You forget at that point that you've got to do a show the next day," says Claire.⁵⁴

The next day, the critical response was largely positive. Milton Shulman in the *Evening Standard* said, "The roar of approval was the most spontaneous acclaim I have heard at a first night since the opening of *My Fair Lady*." There were a few dissenters, though, but not enough to deter the inevitable. *Miss Saigon* was another smash hit. As the hottest ticket in town, celebrities flocked to it. George Michael came one night, as did Mandy Patinkin, Diana, Princess of Wales, and Steven Spielberg, who at the end of the show met the cast in the stage manager's office.

In December 1994, *Miss Saigon* became Drury Lane's longest-running musical, eclipsing the record previously set by *My Fair Lady*. It finally closed after 4,264 performances in 1999.

Peter stayed with the show for a year and a half. It was a wonderful experience, and a moving one. "I got letters from Vietnam veterans saying how powerful they thought the piece was and how the music had intensely brought back memories that they would never forget. Also, how the song 'Bui-Doi' made them think about all the kids that were left behind."[55] Bui-Doi were Amerasian children (one American and one Asian parent) who were often shunned and left in Vietnam after the war. With such a backstory to the song, Peter's performance of it was emotionally charged every night. "I didn't really have to sing the song; the song was sung for me by the images of those Amerasian kids that were projected behind me. The melodic line was also so moving and powerful that I really just had to be in the song and let it happen, and it did move me every night and I was transported by it. It wasn't like I was doing a song. It was like I was doing a speech and that's how I approached it. I suppose all I wanted to do was be this honest broker between the words and the audience."[56]

Two remarkable incidents took place during Peter's run in the show. One of the crew actually turned out to be a bank robber. He was using one of the prop guns to do a series of robberies and was traced back to the theatre and arrested. There was also a terrible accident when one of the backstage team up in the flies stumbled and fell sixty feet down onto the stage. "I heard it on the tannoy," recalls Peter. "There was this terrible scream. He was very severely injured."[57]

For Peter, *Miss Saigon* was a personal triumph. This was his first major role in a West End show, and it marked a big change in his career, with offers of more work notably in the long-running BBC sitcom *Birds of a Feather*. Before he moved on, everybody played a delicious trick on him. During the interval, Peter always used to chat to Jane Salberg, the company manager, then leave it to the last minute to change into his costume for "Bui-Doi," which opened Act 2. On this occasion they were chatting away when suddenly over the tannoy came the intro for his song and there was Peter still in his underpants. "I couldn't believe it. I'd been distracted for so long I hadn't realised the time. I started rushing down the stairs, putting my shirt on, a tie, my trousers and literally arriving at the stage just as the final bar of the intro had finished. And then I realised the safety curtain was still in place. I looked around and saw the whole cast assembled on stage looking at me and laughing their heads off. What Jane had done was record the overture and played it over the tannoy five minutes early. It was just a way of saying goodbye to me. It was a brilliant gag, and I fell for it hook line and sinker."[58]

*Miss Saigon* arrived on Broadway in April 1991 surrounded by a whirlwind of hype, and with the largest advance that Broadway had ever seen. It was virtually critic proof. Some queried why it took two French men and a British producer to make a musical based on one of the most important American events of contemporary history. However, this concern paled into insignificance when a row erupted over whether Jonathan Pryce should reprise his role of the Engineer. Foreign actors appearing on Broadway needed to be approved by American Equity. There was no question that Lea Salonga would be welcomed. And as Pryce was a recognized star, his involvement was allowed without the role requiring an American casting call. This led to protests from the American Asian acting community. In London, there had been little or no outcry over Pryce's appearance, but in New York the production faced a much bigger theatrical community of ethnic diversity. The argument was plain and simple: allowing a white actor to play an Asian role was comparable to allowing a white actor to portray blackface. It had also blocked the opportunity for an Asian actor to compete for the role.

The opposition to Pryce's casting soon gained momentum, becoming seen as a moment for the Asian American acting community to stand in the way of such discrimination. Alain and Claude-Michel had perhaps foreseen such a controversy by making the Engineer a half caste in the story. However, in London Pryce had still used prosthetics on his eyes and a Clinique bronzing lotion.

After persistent pressure, American Equity accepted that the casting of Pryce was insensitive and formally turned down his application to appear on Broadway. Cameron was furious. By this time, the storm had reached the media, and most commentators fell on the side of Cameron and the show, perhaps mindful that Broadway was going to lose out on a lot of money. The office of American Equity was deluged with letters of complaint and phone calls from their own members asking for them to think again. In the midst of all this Cameron placed a full-page ad in the *New York Times* featuring the *Miss Saigon* logo along with huge black capital letters spelling out the word: CANCELLED. "It was very striking," remembers Andrew Bruce. "I think American Equity capitulated soon after that."[59] Was it a bluff? Cameron certainly had a strong hand with the amounts of money involved. So, if it was a bluff, he called it and won. The bottom line almost always takes precedence over artistic and ethical considerations.

This did little to calm the situation, and the show saw picketing outside the theatre. And the controversy surrounding *Miss Saigon* has never really gone away, with groups continuing to claim the production is racist and misogynistic and bemoaning its stereotypical treatment of Asians and Asian women in general. But the show has remained popular, and it has changed with the times. The extraordinary story of Jon Jon Briones is a case in point. Briones was twenty-two years old and an engineering student in the Philippines when Cameron and Nicholas Hytner first arrived to carry out auditions. Briones had a friend who was a local producer that was helping facilitate the auditions and was asked to lend a hand. At that time, Briones was involved in theatre and had been singing since he was a child. But he'd no idea who Cameron Mackintosh was. Helping organize all the auditionees, Briones decided to throw his own hat into the ring. Handing out headshot and résumés, he finished by handing Cameron his own. "He looked at me, and I think he thought I was kidding."[60]

Briones won a role in the ensemble and flew over to London, his first time outside of the Philippines. From appearing in the original production, Briones went on to understudy the role of the Engineer and perform it on various tours. In 2014, he played the Engineer in the West End revival of *Miss Saigon* and when the production transferred to Broadway, making the part truly his own.

*Miss Saigon* was really Alain and Claude-Michel's achievement, to produce a second show of such quality and one that was so very different to *Les Misérables*. Many people much prefer *Miss Saigon*; its music is less operatic, much more of a musical, and it's less stylized, too. Because there was so much story to tell in a relatively short space of time, *Les Misérables* employed stylization. *Miss Saigon* tells its story in a far more realistic way. And the music brings that whole world to life in a beautifully crafted way. The sounds are authentic, and yet also have that beefy American feel.

For Claude-Michel, the *Miss Saigon* connection is a very personal one indeed. He later adopted a daughter from the Philippines and also opened an orphanage there named Sun and Moon after one of the show's musical numbers.

# THE CURTAIN FALLS

The success of *Miss Saigon* on Broadway followed in the wake of Alain and Claude-Michel's *Les Misérables*, as well as the Andrew Lloyd Webber hits *Cats* and *Phantom*. In much the same way as these shows changed musical theatre in Britain, their effect on Broadway was just as spectacular. In the early 1990s, Michael Eisner, head of the Walt Disney Company, bumped into Andrew at an industry function. They chatted, during which Eisner was genuinely astounded to learn how much money *Cats* and *Phantom* were making on Broadway. Eisner decided to create a stage version of *Beauty and the Beast*, Disney's most successful animated feature for many years. With lyrics by Tim Rice, it opened on Broadway in 1994. This was followed by *The Lion King* in 1997, again with lyrics by Tim Rice. Both of these shows were massive hits and had the effect of changing the makeup of Broadway, turning it even more into a destination for tourists and families.

It's interesting to learn that even detractors of the Andrew and Cameron juggernaut ended up having a positive effect. Jonathan Larson was a struggling songwriter and a critic of a Broadway ruled by *Cats* and *Phantom*—it did not speak to his generation. His response was to write the musical *Rent*.

It wasn't just Broadway, of course. Andrew and Cameron did much to "internationalize" the musical after completely revolutionizing it back home. "Up until Andrew music theatre had been completely dominated by the Americans," says Richard Stilgoe. "Here in the UK we were already known for Shakespeare, Shaw, we produced terrific theatre, but our musicals were never up to the standard of the Americans. And Andrew changed that completely."[1]

In Britain during the 1980s the likes of Andrew, Tim Rice, and Cameron, along with a whole team of brilliant creative talent, rediscovered the musical and pushed it in new directions, took risks, just the way they did back in the heyday of Broadway in the 1940s and 1950s. The sheer originality of these shows made them stand out and created a formula that's still pretty much followed today.

The nature of theatre was changing, too, and these musicals were right at the forefront of that change, bringing in new technical content, engineering, automation, and computers. There was the inevitable backlash, of course, along with a large chunk of jealousy, people stuck in their own time frame, or stuck in a mindset of how shows should be done. A lot of this criticism was leveled at the increase of spectacle and effects, those big moments like the helicopter in *Miss Saigon* or the chandelier in *Phantom*. Martyn Hayes recalls Hal Prince telling him that a musical is a set of heartbeats, it goes up and it comes down, and the audience leave the theatre remembering the high points of the heartbeat and the trick is not to let the low beats go on for too long. Shows like *Phantom* or *Cats* were just new forms of the musical. Yes, they were spectacles and events, but as John Napier asserts, "The music was still the driving force. I could do as many spectacular bits and pieces as you like, if the performers don't cut the mustard, along with the music and the narrative, it'll close."[2]

It was all about the storytelling, really. Andrew knew that, and it was the reason why he brought in someone like Trevor Nunn from the world of classical theatre. "The thing about Andrew is the story is very important," says Arlene Phillips. "The heart of a show is the story you tell. And Trever, being a great storyteller, was very much what Andrew wanted. The story is an integral part of anything Andrew does."[3]

The contribution of Trevor Nunn cannot be underestimated. Out of the seven big shows in this book, he directed four of them. "He had a really strong vision," says Simon Opie. "And his way of telling a story was a step above nearly everybody else that I worked with. He's a tremendously good leader, by any standards, in any industry. He had a very strong ability to get the best out of other people and that is a key quality of leadership. You believed in him and also, he had a way of making you believe in yourself, and that's not that common."[4]

Nunn made for a brilliant addition to Andrew and Cameron's ranks, as did the likes of Hal Prince, John Napier, Alain and Claude-Michel, Andreane Neofitou, David Hersey, and Andrew Bruce. It was their talent, along with all the actors and backstage crew, many of which we have heard from in this book, whose contribution to those shows was so important. Those great shows of the 1980s, whether it's *Cats* or *Starlight Express* or *Les Misérables*, was a huge collaboration. Sometimes, there's an alchemy that happens. You get shows where you think, the set's doing one thing, the costumes are doing something else, the music's doing something different; it all seems a bit disparate. Then there are shows where everybody's singing from the same song sheet, the lighting, the sound, the effects, the costumes, the choreography—it's all focused; there's nothing fighting against anything. And that's what happened with so many of those 1980s shows discussed in this book. There was an incredible consistency running through them, which certainly had never happened before in British musical theatre and hasn't happened since.

What made those productions so special, so unique, was in a way their Britishness. It was taking the odd or unconventional idea that is almost undoable, going off into the realms of French literature or T. S. Eliot, and not doing it in a traditional British way, that kind of *Half a Sixpence*, *Oliver!*-type music hall approach. Or to try and replicate that *42nd Street/A Chorus Line* Broadway formula. "We kind of came at it from a naive kind of perspective," admits John Napier. "Knowing that we didn't want to do the conventional, because that way, disaster lies."[5]

That was so indicative of how Andrew in particular approached those shows, choosing subjects that nobody else in their right mind would make a musical about and then do it in a quite challenging way. The extraordinary thing is, it worked, and it launched a British invasion of America that rivaled the Beatles. It all had to end, of course. *Miss Saigon* was the last of the British pop-operas to succeed on Broadway for many, many years. But the impact of those shows has left its mark. As the famous ad line on the poster for *Cats* declared: Now and Forever.

# BIBLIOGRAPHY

*The Complete Phantom of the Opera*, by Jane Rice and Clive Barda, Henry Holt & Co, 1987

*Harold Prince and the American Musical Theatre*, by Foster Hirsch, Cambridge University Press, 1989

*The Complete Book of* Les Misérables, by Edward Behr, Little Brown, 1989

*One Singular Sensation: The Michael Bennett Story*, by Kevin Kelly, Zebra Books, 1991

*The Story of* Miss Saigon, by Edward Behr and Mark Steyn, Arcade Publishing, 1991

*Oh, What A Circus*, by Tim Rice, Hodder and Stoughton, 1999

*The Musical World of Boubil & Schonberg*, by Margaret Vermette, Applause Books, 2006

*Razzle Dazzle: The Battle for Broadway*, by Michael Riedel, Simon & Schuster, 2015

*Unmasked: A Memoir*, by Andrew Lloyd Webber, HarperCollins, 2018

# NOTES

**CHAPTER 1: "DON'T CRY FOR ME ARGENTINA"**

1. *Unmasked: A Memoir*, by Andrew Lloyd Webber, HarperCollins, 2018
2. Guardian, September 2014
3. Guardian, January 2021
4. Chris Walker: Author interview
5. Plays and Players, June 1978
6. David Firman: Author interview
7. *Evita: The Making of a Superstar*, BBC 2018
8. *Oh What A Circus*, by Time Rice, Hodder 1999
9. Larry Fuller: Author interview
10. *Evita: The Making of a Superstar*, BBC 2018
11. *Oh What A Circus*, by Time Rice, Hodder 1999
12. Siobhan McCarthy: Author interview
13. Siobhan McCarthy: Author interview
14. Mark Ryan: Author interview
15. Mark Ryan: Author interview
16. Mark Ryan: Author interview
17. Elaine Paige: Author interview
18. Elaine Paige: Author interview
19. Elaine Paige: Author interview
20. Elaine Paige: Author interview
21. Elaine Paige: Author interview
22. Elaine Paige: Author interview
23. Elaine Paige: Author interview
24. Larry Fuller: Author interview

25. Larry Fuller: Author interview
26. Larry Fuller: Author interview
27. Elaine Paige: Author interview
28. Elaine Paige: Author interview
29. Elaine Paige: Author interview
30. Elaine Paige: Author interview
31. Elaine Paige: Author interview
32. Elaine Paige: Author interview
33. Elaine Paige: Author interview
34. Larry Fuller: Author interview
35. Larry Fuller: Author interview
36. Larry Fuller: Author interview
37. Larry Fuller: Author interview
38. Martin McCallum: Author interview
39. David Firman: Author interview
40. David Firman: Author interview
41. David Firman: Author interview
42. Larry Fuller: Author interview
43. David Firman: Author interview
44. *Unmasked: A Memoir*, by Andrew Lloyd Webber, HarperCollins, 2018
45. David Firman: Author interview
46. Larry Fuller: Author interview
47. Robin Merrill: Author interview
48. Robin Merrill: Author interview
49. Robin Merrill: Author interview
50. Susannah Fellows: Author interview
51. Susannah Fellows: Author interview
52. Robin Merrill: Author interview
53. Robin Merrill: Author interview
54. *Evita: The Making of a Superstar*, BBC 2018
55. Elaine Paige: Author interview
56. Elaine Paige: Author interview
57. Elaine Paige: Author interview
58. David Firman: Author interview
59. Susannah Fellows: Author interview
60. Susannah Fellows: Author interview
61. Siobhan McCarthy: Author interview
62. Siobhan McCarthy: Author interview
63. Siobhan McCarthy: Author interview
64. David Firman: Author interview
65. Timothy O'Brien: Author interview
66. David Firman: Author interview

67. Susannah Fellows: Author interview
68. Larry Fuller: Author interview
69. Robin Merrill: Author interview
70. Mark Ryan: Author interview
71. Michelle Breeze: Author interview
72. Susannah Fellows: Author interview
73. Mark Ryan: Author interview
74. Mark Ryan: Author interview
75. Elaine Paige: Author interview
76. Elaine Paige: Author interview
77. Larry Fuller: Author interview
78. Elaine Paige: Author interview
79. Martin McCallum: Author interview
80. Robin Merrill: Author interview
81. Timothy O'Brien: Author interview
82. Timothy O'Brien: Author interview
83. Timothy O'Brien: Author interview
84. Timothy O'Brien: Author interview
85. Myra Sands: Author interview
86. Michelle Breeze: Author interview
87. Timothy O'Brien: Author interview
88. *Oh What A Circus*, by Time Rice, Hodder 1999
89. David Hersey: Author interview
90. David Hersey: Author interview
91. David Hersey: Author interview
92. Martin McCallum: Author interview
93. Martin McCallum: Author interview
94. Larry Fuller: Author interview
95. Myra Sands: Author interview
96. Susannah Fellows: Author interview
97. Siobhan McCarthy: Author interview
98. Andrew Bruce: Author interview
99. Andrew Bruce: Author interview
100. Andrew Bruce: Author interview
101. Robin Merrill: Author interview
102. Mark Ryan: Author interview
103. Larry Fuller: Author interview
104. Myra Sands: Author interview
105. Elaine Paige: Author interview
106. Myra Sands: Author interview
107. Myra Sands: Author interview
108. Larry Fuller: Author interview

109. Mark Ryan: Author interview
110. Martin McCallum: Author interview
111. *Evita: The Making of a Superstar*, BBC 2018
112. David Firman: Author interview
113. Siobhan McCarthy: Author interview
114. David Firman: Author interview
115. Susannah Fellows: Author interview
116. David Firman: Author interview
117. Siobhan McCarthy: Author interview
118. Siobhan McCarthy: Author interview
119. Robin Merrill: Author interview
120. *Evita: The Making of a Superstar*, BBC 2018
121. Mark Ryan: Author interview
122. Elaine Paige: Author interview
123. Elaine Paige: Author interview
124. Elaine Paige: Author interview
125. Susannah Fellows: Author interview
126. Susannah Fellows: Author interview
127. Mark Ryan: Author interview
128. Mark Ryan: Author interview
129. Mark Ryan: Author interview
130. *Oh What A Circus*, by Time Rice, Hodder 1999
131. Larry Fuller: Author interview
132. Susannah Fellows: Author interview
133. Elaine Paige: Author interview
134. Mark Ryan: Author interview
135. *Oh What A Circus*, by Time Rice, Hodder 1999
136. Mark Ryan: Author interview
137. David Hersey: Author interview

## CHAPTER 2: "MEMORY"

1. *Unmasked: A Memoir*, by Andrew Lloyd Webber, HarperCollins, 2018
2. BBC Radio 2 documentary, 2019
3. BBC Radio 2 documentary, 2019
4. David Firman: Author interview
5. Bonnie Langford: Author interview
6. Richard Stilgoe: Author interview
7. Janet Devenish: Author interview
8. Paul Nicholas: Author interview
9. Paul Nicholas: Author interview

10. Judy Craymer: Author interview
11. BBC Radio 2 documentary, 2019
12. David Firman: Author interview
13. BBC Radio 2 documentary, 2019
14. Vulture.com, December 2019
15. Finola Hughes: Author interview
16. Finola Hughes: Author interview
17. Finola Hughes: Author interview
18. Finola Hughes: Author interview
19. Bonnie Langford: Author interview
20. Bonnie Langford: Author interview
21. Finola Hughes: Author interview
22. Jeff Shankley: Author interview
23. Jeff Shankley: Author interview
24. Bonnie Langford: Author interview
25. Bonnie Langford: Author interview
26. BBC Radio 2 documentary, 2019
27. Bonnie Langford: Author interview
28. Finola Hughes: Author interview
29. Jeff Shankley: Author interview
30. Jeff Shankley: Author interview
31. Seeta Indrani: Author interview
32. Finola Hughes: Author interview
33. Bonnie Langford: Author interview
34. Myra Sands: Author interview
35. Myra Sands: Author interview
36. Jeff Shankley: Author interview
37. Paul Nicholas: Author interview
38. *Chicago Tribune*, September 1981
39. BBC Radio 2 documentary, 2019
40. John Napier: Author interview
41. John Napier: Author interview
42. John Napier: Author interview
43. John Napier: Author interview
44. John Napier: Author interview
45. Finola Hughes: Author interview
46. Jeff Shankley: Author interview
47. Paul Nicholas: Author interview
48. John Napier: Author interview
49. John Napier: Author interview
50. John Napier: Author interview
51. John Napier: Author interview

52. Myra Sands: Author interview
53. Bonnie Langford: Author interview
54. Bonnie Langford: Author interview
55. Bonnie Langford: Author interview
56. John Napier: Author interview
57. Judy Craymer: Author interview
58. Paul Nicholas: Author interview
59. Vulture.com, December 2019
60. Paul Nicholas: Author interview
61. BBC Radio 2 documentary, 2019
62. David Hersey: Author interview
63. David Hersey: Author interview
64. Martin McCallum: Author interview
65. Chris Walker: Author interview
66. Chris Walker: Author interview
67. Chris Walker: Author interview
68. Andrew Bruce: Author interview
69. Andrew Bruce: Author interview
70. Andrew Bruce: Author interview
71. Bonnie Langford: Author interview
72. *Unmasked: A Memoir*, by Andrew Lloyd Webber, HarperCollins, 2018
73. BBC Radio 2 documentary, 2019
74. *Unmasked: A Memoir*, by Andrew Lloyd Webber, HarperCollins, 2018
75. Paul Nicholas: Author interview
76. BBC Radio 2 documentary, 2019
77. Bonnie Langford: Author interview
78. Finola Hughes: Author interview
79. Judy Craymer: Author interview
80. Finola Hughes: Author interview
81. Chris Walker: Author interview
82. Chris Walker: Author interview
83. Chris Walker: Author interview
84. Chris Walker: Author interview
85. David Firman: Author interview
86. Bonnie Langford: Author interview
87. David Firman: Author interview
88. John Napier: Author interview
89. John Napier: Author interview
90. John Napier: Author interview
91. John Napier: Author interview
92. John Napier: Author interview
93. John Napier: Author interview

94. John Napier: Author interview
95. Jeff Shankley: Author interview
96. Jeff Shankley: Author interview
97. Jeff Shankley: Author interview
98. Myra Sands: Author interview
99. Myra Sands: Author interview
100. Myra Sands: Author interview
101. Seeta Indrani: Author interview
102. Elaine Paige: Author interview
103. Elaine Paige: Author interview
104. Elaine Paige: Author interview
105. Bonnie Langford: Author interview
106. David Firman: Author interview
107. Myra Sands: Author interview
108. *Unmasked: A Memoir*, by Andrew Lloyd Webber, HarperCollins, 2018
109. *Unmasked: A Memoir*, by Andrew Lloyd Webber, HarperCollins, 2018
110. John Napier: Author interview
111. Martin McCallum: Author interview
112. Bonnie Langford: Author interview
113. Bonnie Langford: Author interview
114. David Firman: Author interview
115. *Unmasked: A Memoir*, by Andrew Lloyd Webber, HarperCollins, 2018
116. Martin McCallum: Author interview
117. Elaine Paige: Author interview
118. David Firman: Author interview
119. Elaine Paige: Author interview
120. Elaine Paige: Author interview
121. Chris Walker: Author interview
122. David Firman: Author interview
123. David Firman: Author interview
124. Finola Hughes: Author interview
125. Bonnie Langford: Author interview
126. Bonnie Langford: Author interview
127. Myra Sands: Author interview
128. Jeff Shankley: Author interview
129. Finola Hughes: Author interview
130. Myra Sands: Author interview
131. Finola Hughes: Author interview
132. Myra Sands: Author interview
133. Chris Walker: Author interview
134. Caroline Quentin: Author interview
135. Bonnie Langford: Author interview

136. John Napier: Author interview
137. Bonnie Langford: Author interview
138. David Firman: Author interview
139. Finola Hughes: Author interview
140. Finola Hughes: Author interview
141. BBC Radio 2 documentary, 2019
142. BBC Radio 2 documentary, 2019
143. Myra Sands: Author interview
144. Seeta Indrani: Author interview
145. Paul Nicholas: Author interview
146. Bonnie Langford: Author interview
147. *Judi Dench: And Furthermore*, by Judi Dench, Weidenfeld and Nicolson 2010
148. Jeff Shankley: Author interview
149. Jeff Shankley: Author interview
150. Seeta Indrani: Author interview
151. Finola Hughes: Author interview
152. John Napier: Author interview
153. *Razzle Dazzle: The Battle for Broadway*, by Michael Riedel, Simon & Schuster, 2015
154. David Hersey: Author interview
155. David Hersey: Author interview
156. Seeta Indrani: Author interview
157. Finola Hughes: Author interview
158. Martin McCallum: Author interview
159. Martin McCallum: Author interview
160. Martin McCallum: Author interview
161. Daily Telegraph, August 2019
162. Seeta Indrani: Author interview
163. Judy Craymer: Author interview

## CHAPTER 3: "THERE'S A LIGHT AT THE END OF THE TUNNEL"

1. Richard Stilgoe: Author interview
2. Richard Stilgoe: Author interview
3. Richard Stilgoe: Author interview
4. Richard Stilgoe: Author interview
5. Richard Stilgoe: Author interview
6. Richard Stilgoe: Author interview
7. Richard Stilgoe: Author interview
8. Richard Stilgoe: Author interview

9. John Napier: Author interview
10. Richard Stilgoe: Author interview
11. *Unmasked: A Memoir*, by Andrew Lloyd Webber, HarperCollins, 2018
12. Richard Stilgoe: Author interview
13. *Starlight Express* theatre program
14. *Starlight Express* theatre program
15. Richard Stilgoe: Author interview
16. Richard Stilgoe: Author interview
17. John Napier: Author interview
18. John Napier: Author interview
19. Arlene Phillips: Author interview
20. Arlene Phillips: Author interview
21. *Starlight Express* theatre program
22. Richard Stilgoe: Author interview
23. Arlene Phillips: Author interview
24. Richard Stilgoe: Author interview
25. Richard Stilgoe: Author interview
26. Frances Ruffelle: Author interview
27. Frances Ruffelle: Author interview
28. Frances Ruffelle: Author interview
29. Frances Ruffelle: Author interview
30. Frances Ruffelle: Author interview
31. Jeff Shankley: Author interview
32. Jeff Shankley: Author interview
33. Ray Shell: Author interview
34. Ray Shell: Author interview
35. Frances Ruffelle: Author interview
36. Arlene Phillips: Author interview
37. Arlene Phillips: Author interview
38. Arlene Phillips: Author interview
39. Chrissy Wickham: Author interview
40. Arlene Phillips: Author interview
41. John Napier: Author interview
42. Chrissy Wickham: Author interview
43. Chrissy Wickham: Author interview
44. Arlene Phillips: Author interview
45. Arlene Phillips: Author interview
46. Frances Ruffelle: Author interview
47. Gary Love: Author interview
48. Ray Shell: Author interview
49. Ray Shell: Author interview
50. Frances Ruffelle: Author interview

51. Chrissy Wickham: Author interview
52. Chrissy Wickham: Author interview
53. Ray Shell: Author interview
54. Frances Ruffelle: Author interview
55. Frances Ruffelle: Author interview
56. Frances Ruffelle: Author interview
57. Arlene Phillips: Author interview
58. Arlene Phillips: Author interview
59. Arlene Phillips: Author interview
60. Richard Stilgoe: Author interview
61. Richard Stilgoe: Author interview
62. John Napier: Author interview
63. John Napier: Author interview
64. John Napier: Author interview
65. Gary Love: Author interview
66. Arlene Phillips: Author interview
67. Frances Ruffelle: Author interview
68. John Napier: Author interview
69. John Napier: Author interview
70. John Napier: Author interview
71. Richard Stilgoe: Author interview
72. Jeff Shankley: Author interview
73. Ray Shell: Author interview
74. Frances Ruffelle: Author interview
75. Arlene Phillips: Author interview
76. Chrissy Wickham: Author interview
77. Arlene Phillips: Author interview
78. Jeff Shankley: Author interview
79. Jeff Shankley: Author interview
80. David Hersey: Author interview
81. Chrissy Wickham: Author interview
82. Jeff Shankley: Author interview
83. John Napier: Author interview
84. Jeff Shankley: Author interview
85. Andrew Bruce: Author interview
86. Andrew Bruce: Author interview
87. Andrew Bruce: Author interview
88. Chrissy Wickham: Author interview
89. Ray Shell: Author interview
90. Jeff Shankley: Author interview
91. Chrissy Wickham: Author interview
92. Andrew Bruce: Author interview

93. Gary Love: Author interview
94. Andrew Bruce: Author interview
95. Andrew Bruce: Author interview
96. Andrew Bruce: Author interview
97. Arlene Phillips: Author interview
98. Jeff Shankley: Author interview
99. Arlene Phillips: Author interview
100. John Napier: Author interview
101. Frances Ruffelle: Author interview
102. Richard Stilgoe: Author interview
103. Frances Ruffelle: Author interview
104. Ray Shell: Author interview
105. Chrissy Wickham: Author interview
106. Jeff Shankley: Author interview
107. Chrissy Wickham: Author interview
108. Chrissy Wickham: Author interview
109. Chrissy Wickham: Author interview
110. Jeff Shankley: Author interview
111. Gary Love: Author interview
112. Arlene Phillips: Author interview
113. Ray Shell: Author interview
114. Arlene Phillips: Author interview
115. Arlene Phillips: Author interview
116. Gary Love: Author interview
117. Frances Ruffelle: Author interview
118. Chrissy Wickham: Author interview
119. Frances Ruffelle: Author interview
120. Chrissy Wickham: Author interview
121. Chrissy Wickham: Author interview
122. John Napier: Author interview
123. Richard Stilgoe: Author interview
124. Richard Stilgoe: Author interview
125. Richard Stilgoe: Author interview
126. Ray Shell: Author interview
127. Chrissy Wickham: Author interview

## CHAPTER 4: "I DREAMED A DREAM"

1. *Los Angeles Times*, May 2019
2. *The Complete Book of Les Misérables*, by Edward Behr, Little Brown, 1989
3. John Cameron: Author interview

4. John Cameron: Author interview
5. John Cameron: Author interview
6. John Cameron: Author interview
7. Andrew Bruce: Author interview
8. Andrew Bruce: Author interview
9. John Cameron: Author interview
10. John Cameron: Author interview
11. John Cameron: Author interview
12. John Cameron: Author interview
13. Andrew Bruce: Author interview
14. *Los Angeles Times*, May 2019
15. *The Complete Book of Les Misérables*, by Edward Behr, Little Brown, 1989
16. *The Complete Book of Les Misérables*, by Edward Behr, Little Brown, 1989
17. *The Complete Book of Les Misérables*, by Edward Behr, Little Brown, 1989
18. David Hersey: Author interview
19. *Playbill*, January 1998
20. *Guardian*, February 2013
21. *The Complete Book of Les Misérables*, by Edward Behr, Little Brown, 1989
22. *The Complete Book of Les Misérables*, by Edward Behr, Little Brown, 1989
23. *Guardian*, February 2013
24. *Guardian*, February 2013
25. John Cameron: Author interview
26. John Cameron: Author interview
27. Andrew Bruce: Author interview
28. Andrew Bruce: Author interview
29. David Hersey: Author interview
30. Peter Polycarpou: Author interview
31. Simon Opie: Author interview
32. Simon Opie: Author interview
33. Simon Opie: Author interview
34. Simon Opie: Author interview
35. Simon Opie: Author interview
36. John Napier: Author interview
37. Andreane Neofitou: Author interview
38. Caroline Quentin: Author interview
39. Andreane Neofitou: Author interview
40. Andreane Neofitou: Author interview
41. Andreane Neofitou: Author interview
42. Andreane Neofitou: Author interview
43. Andreane Neofitou: Author interview
44. Simon Opie: Author interview
45. Simon Opie: Author interview

46. *The Complete Book of Les Misérables*, by Edward Behr, Little Brown, 1989
47. Frances Ruffelle: Author interview
48. Peter Polycarpou: Author interview
49. Peter Polycarpou: Author interview
50. Caroline Quentin: Author interview
51. Caroline Quentin: Author interview
52. Caroline Quentin: Author interview
53. Paul Leonard: Author interview
54. Paul Leonard: Author interview
55. Sian Reeves: Author interview
56. Sian Reeves: Author interview
57. Zoe Hart: Author interview
58. Zoe Hart: Author interview
59. Paul Leonard: Author interview
60. Paul Leonard: Author interview
61. Zoe Hart: Author interview
62. Caroline Quentin: Author interview
63. Paul Leonard: Author interview
64. Paul Leonard: Author interview
65. Peter Polycarpou: Author interview
66. Peter Polycarpou: Author interview
67. Caroline Quentin: Author interview
68. John Cameron: Author interview
69. Caroline Quentin: Author interview
70. Sian Reeves: Author interview
71. Rebecca Caine: Author interview
72. Rebecca Caine: Author interview
73. Rebecca Caine: Author interview
74. Rebecca Caine: Author interview
75. Paul Leonard: Author interview
76. Frances Ruffelle: Author interview
77. Frances Ruffelle: Author interview
78. Caroline Quentin: Author interview
79. Caroline Quentin: Author interview
80. Zoe Hart: Author interview
81. Simon Opie: Author interview
82. Simon Opie: Author interview
83. Andreane Neofitou: Author interview
84. Andreane Neofitou: Author interview
85. Andreane Neofitou: Author interview
86. Andreane Neofitou: Author interview
87. Peter Polycarpou: Author interview

88. Rebecca Caine: Author interview
89. Rebecca Caine: Author interview
90. David Hersey: Author interview
91. John Cameron: Author interview
92. Peter Polycarpou: Author interview
93. Peter Polycarpou: Author interview
94. Martyn Hayes: Author interview
95. Simon Opie: Author interview
96. Andreane Neofitou: Author interview
97. Simon Opie: Author interview
98. Paul Leonard: Author interview
99. Caroline Quentin: Author interview
100. Sian Reeves: Author interview
101. Sian Reeves: Author interview
102. Zoe Hart: Author interview
103. Peter Polycarpou: Author interview
104. John Napier: Author interview
105. John Napier: Author interview
106. Frances Ruffelle: Author interview
107. John Napier: Author interview
108. Rebecca Caine: Author interview
109. John Cameron: Author interview
110. Peter Polycarpou: Author interview
111. Sian Reeves: Author interview
112. Caroline Quentin: Author interview
113. Zoe Hart: Author interview
114. *Guardian*, February 2013
115. Peter Polycarpou: Author interview
116. Paul Leonard: Author interview
117. Zoe Hart: Author interview
118. Andreane Neofitou: Author interview
119. Simon Opie: Author interview
120. Peter Polycarpou: Author interview
121. Andreane Neofitou: Author interview
122. Frances Ruffelle: Author interview
123. John Napier: Author interview
124. Martin McCallum: Author interview
125. John Cameron: Author interview
126. Martyn Hayes: Author interview
127. Frances Ruffelle: Author interview
128. Caroline Quentin: Author interview
129. Caroline Quentin: Author interview

130. Paul Leonard: Author interview
131. Rebecca Caine: Author interview
132. Frances Ruffelle: Author interview
133. Frances Ruffelle: Author interview
134. Paul Leonard: Author interview
135. Paul Leonard: Author interview
136. Caroline Quentin: Author interview
137. Caroline Quentin: Author interview
138. Caroline Quentin: Author interview
139. Peter Polycarpou: Author interview
140. Paul Leonard: Author interview
141. Sian Reeves: Author interview
142. Frances Ruffelle: Author interview
143. Frances Ruffelle: Author interview
144. Frances Ruffelle: Author interview
145. Frances Ruffelle: Author interview
146. Rebecca Caine: Author interview
147. Paul Leonard: Author interview
148. Zoe Hart: Author interview
149. Zoe Hart: Author interview
150. Caroline Quentin: Author interview
151. Caroline Quentin: Author interview
152. Caroline Quentin: Author interview
153. Caroline Quentin: Author interview
154. Caroline Quentin: Author interview
155. Zoe Hart: Author interview
156. Zoe Hart: Author interview
157. Peter Polycarpou: Author interview
158. Peter Polycarpou: Author interview
159. John Cameron: Author interview
160. Paul Leonard: Author interview
161. Frances Ruffelle: Author interview
162. Frances Ruffelle: Author interview
163. Frances Ruffelle: Author interview
164. *Razzle Dazzle: The Battle for Broadway*, by Michael Riedel, Simon & Schuster, 2015
165. John Napier: Author interview
166. Martin McCallum: Author interview
167. John Cameron: Author interview
168. Rebecca Caine: Author interview
169. Paul Leonard: Author interview
170. Peter Polycarpou: Author interview

## CHAPTER 5: "THE MACHINES ARE BEAUTIFUL"

1. David Soames: Author interview
2. David Soames: Author interview
3. David Soames: Author interview
4. David Soames: Author interview
5. David Soames: Author interview
6. David Soames: Author interview
7. David Soames: Author interview
8. David Soames: Author interview
9. David Soames: Author interview
10. David Soames: Author interview
11. Sir Cliff Richard: Author interview
12. Sir Cliff Richard: Author interview
13. Rosemarie Ford: Author interview
14. David Soames: Author interview
15. John Napier: Author interview
16. John Napier: Author interview
17. David Soames: Author interview
18. Rosemarie Ford: Author interview
19. Sir Cliff Richard: Author interview
20. Jeff Shankley: Author interview
21. Sir Cliff Richard: Author interview
22. Jeff Shankley: Author interview
23. Rosemarie Ford: Author interview
24. Sir Cliff Richard: Author interview
25. David Soames: Author interview
26. Rosemarie Ford: Author interview
27. Sir Cliff Richard: Author interview
28. Rosemarie Ford: Author interview
29. Rosemarie Ford: Author interview
30. John Napier: Author interview
31. Rosemarie Ford: Author interview
32. Jeff Shankley: Author interview
33. Sir Cliff Richard: Author interview
34. Jeff Shankley: Author interview
35. David Soames: Author interview
36. Rosemarie Ford: Author interview
37. Sir Cliff Richard: Author interview
38. Rosemarie Ford: Author interview
39. Sir Cliff Richard: Author interview
40. Sir Cliff Richard: Author interview

41. Sir Cliff Richard: Author interview
42. David Soames: Author interview
43. John Napier: Author interview
44. David Soames: Author interview
45. David Firman: Author interview
46. David Firman: Author interview
47. David Firman: Author interview
48. David Firman: Author interview
49. David Firman: Author interview
50. David Firman: Author interview
51. Simon Opie: Author interview
52. Graham Bickley: Author interview
53. Graham Bickley: Author interview
54. Graham Bickley: Author interview
55. Graham Bickley: Author interview
56. Graham Bickley: Author interview
57. Graham Bickley: Author interview
58. Graham Bickley: Author interview
59. Graham Bickley: Author interview
60. Graham Bickley: Author interview
61. David Firman: Author interview
62. David Firman: Author interview
63. David Firman: Author interview
64. Simon Opie: Author interview
65. Simon Opie: Author interview
66. Simon Opie: Author interview
67. Graham Bickley: Author interview
68. Graham Bickley: Author interview
69. Graham Bickley: Author interview
70. Graham Bickley: Author interview
71. Simon Opie: Author interview
72. David Firman: Author interview
73. David Firman: Author interview
74. David Firman: Author interview
75. David Firman: Author interview
76. Simon Opie: Author interview
77. Graham Bickley: Author interview
78. David Firman: Author interview
79. Graham Bickley: Author interview
80. Graham Bickley: Author interview
81. David Firman: Author interview
82. Graham Bickley: Author interview

83. Graham Bickley: Author interview
84. Graham Bickley: Author interview
85. David Firman: Author interview
86. Simon Opie: Author interview
87. *New York Times*, May 2011

## CHAPTER 6: "I KNOW HIM SO WELL"

1. Theartsdesk.com, September 2009
2. Theartsdesk.com, September 2009
3. Judy Craymer: Author interview
4. Judy Craymer: Author interview
5. Elaine Paige: Author interview
6. Elaine Paige: Author interview
7. Elaine Paige: Author interview
8. Elaine Paige: Author interview
9. Elaine Paige: Author interview
10. Judy Craymer: Author interview
11. Murray Head: Author interview
12. Murray Head: Author interview
13. Judy Craymer: Author interview
14. Judy Craymer: Author interview
15. Judy Craymer: Author interview
16. Siobhan McCarthy: Author interview
17. Siobhan McCarthy: Author interview
18. Murray Head: Author interview
19. Alan Hatton: Author interview
20. Leo Andrew: Author interview
21. Leo Andrew: Author interview
22. Julie Armstrong: Author interview
23. Julie Armstrong: Author interview
24. Julie Armstrong: Author interview
25. Julie Armstrong: Author interview
26. Murray Head: Author interview
27. Murray Head: Author interview
28. Murray Head: Author interview
29. Andrew Bruce: Author interview
30. Andrew Bruce: Author interview
31. Leo Andrew: Author interview
32. Elaine Paige: Author interview
33. Elaine Paige: Author interview

34. Elaine Paige: Author interview
35. Leo Andrew: Author interview
36. Judy Craymer: Author interview
37. Murray Head: Author interview
38. Murray Head: Author interview
39. Julie Armstrong: Author interview
40. Leo Andrew: Author interview
41. Leo Andrew: Author interview
42. Andrew Bruce: Author interview
43. Alan Hatton: Author interview
44. Alan Hatton: Author interview
45. Siobhan McCarthy: Author interview
46. Julie Armstrong: Author interview
47. Julie Armstrong: Author interview
48. Julie Armstrong: Author interview
49. Julie Armstrong: Author interview
50. Julie Armstrong: Author interview
51. Alan Hatton: Author interview
52. Andrew Bruce: Author interview
53. Elaine Paige: Author interview
54. Julie Armstrong: Author interview
55. Julie Armstrong: Author interview
56. Alan Hatton: Author interview
57. Siobhan McCarthy: Author interview
58. Andrew Bruce: Author interview
59. Leo Andrew: Author interview
60. Leo Andrew: Author interview
61. Leo Andrew: Author interview
62. Leo Andrew: Author interview
63. Murray Head: Author interview
64. Siobhan McCarthy: Author interview
65. Julie Armstrong: Author interview
66. Leo Andrew: Author interview
67. Siobhan McCarthy: Author interview
68. Judy Craymer: Author interview
69. Julie Armstrong: Author interview
70. Judy Craymer: Author interview
71. Murray Head: Author interview
72. Murray Head: Author interview
73. Murray Head: Author interview
74. Murray Head: Author interview
75. Julie Armstrong: Author interview

76. Leo Andrew: Author interview
77. Julie Armstrong: Author interview
78. Leo Andrew: Author interview
79. Leo Andrew: Author interview
80. Julie Armstrong: Author interview
81. Siobhan McCarthy: Author interview
82. Alan Hatton: Author interview
83. Alan Hatton: Author interview
84. Siobhan McCarthy: Author interview
85. Julie Armstrong: Author interview
86. Murray Head: Author interview
87. Elaine Paige: Author interview
88. Elaine Paige: Author interview
89. Elaine Paige: Author interview
90. Leo Andrew: Author interview
91. Leo Andrew: Author interview
92. Theartsdesk.com, September 2009
93. Theartsdesk.com, September 2009
94. Siobhan McCarthy: Author interview
95. Andrew Bruce: Author interview
96. Judy Craymer: Author interview
97. *Mamma Mia! How can I Resist You?* by Judy Craymer, Björn Ulvaeus and Benny Andersson, Weidenfeld and Nicolson, 2006
98. Judy Craymer: Author interview
99. Judy Craymer: Author interview

## CHAPTER 7: "MUSIC OF THE NIGHT"

1. Academy of Achievement.org, June 2016
2. Richard Stilgoe: Author interview
3. The artsdesk.com, September 2009
4. Richard Stilgoe: Author interview
5. Richard Stilgoe: Author interview
6. Jonathan Allen: Author interview
7. Jonathan Allen: Author interview
8. Jonathan Allen: Author interview
9. Jonathan Allen: Author interview
10. Jonathan Allen: Author interview
11. Jonathan Allen: Author interview
12. Martyn Hayes: Author interview
13. Myra Sands: Author interview

14. Martyn Hayes: Author interview
15. Martyn Hayes: Author interview
16. *Unmasked: A Memoir*, by Andrew Lloyd Webber, HarperCollins, 2018
17. Richard Stilgoe: Author interview
18. Richard Stilgoe: Author interview
19. Richard Stilgoe: Author interview
20. Richard Stilgoe: Author interview
21. Richard Stilgoe: Author interview
22. Richard Stilgoe: Author interview
23. Richard Stilgoe: Author interview
24. Richard Stilgoe: Author interview
25. Richard Stilgoe: Author interview
26. Richard Stilgoe: Author interview
27. Richard Stilgoe: Author interview
28. Richard Stilgoe: Author interview
29. Richard Stilgoe: Author interview
30. Lynn Jezzard: Author interview
31. Lynn Jezzard: Author interview
32. James Paterson: Author interview
33. Claire Moore: Author interview
34. Claire Moore: Author interview
35. Claire Moore: Author interview
36. Claire Moore: Author interview
37. Claire Moore: Author interview
38. Janet Devenish: Author interview
39. Janet Devenish: Author interview
40. Janet Devenish: Author interview
41. Academy of Achievement.org, June 2016
42. Lynn Jezzard: Author interview
43. Lynn Jezzard: Author interview
44. Lynn Jezzard: Author interview
45. Janet Devenish: Author interview
46. *Unmasked: A Memoir*, by Andrew Lloyd Webber, HarperCollins, 2018
47. Lynn Jezzard: Author interview
48. James Paterson: Author interview
49. Martyn Hayes: Author interview
50. Martyn Hayes: Author interview
51. Alan Hatton: Author interview
52. Alan Hatton: Author interview
53. Alan Hatton: Author interview
54. Alan Hatton: Author interview
55. Alan Hatton: Author interview

56. Jonathan Allen: Author interview
57. Jonathan Allen: Author interview
58. Martyn Hayes: Author interview
59. Jonathan Allen: Author interview
60. Alan Hatton: Author interview
61. Alan Hatton: Author interview
62. Alan Hatton: Author interview
63. Alan Hatton: Author interview
64. Jonathan Allen: Author interview
65. Janet Devenish: Author interview
66. Christopher Tucker: Author interview
67. Christopher Tucker: Author interview
68. Christopher Tucker: Author interview
69. Christopher Tucker: Author interview
70. Janet Devenish: Author interview
71. Jonathan Allen: Author interview
72. Martyn Hayes: Author interview
73. Martyn Hayes: Author interview
74. *Behind the Mask*, BBC documentary, 2005
75. Martyn Hayes: Author interview
76. Claire Moore: Author interview
77. Claire Moore: Author interview
78. Claire Moore: Author interview
79. Claire Moore: Author interview
80. Claire Moore: Author interview
81. Claire Moore: Author interview
82. Chris Walker: Author interview
83. *Behind the Mask*, BBC documentary, 2005
84. Alan Hatton: Author interview
85. Lynn Jezzard: Author interview
86. Lynn Jezzard: Author interview
87. Martyn Hayes: Author interview
88. Lynn Jezzard: Author interview
89. James Paterson: Author interview
90. James Paterson: Author interview
91. Alan Hatton: Author interview
92. Lynn Jezzard: Author interview
93. James Paterson: Author interview
94. James Paterson: Author interview
95. Claire Moore: Author interview
96. Claire Moore: Author interview
97. Alan Hatton: Author interview

98. Lynn Jezzard: Author interview
99. James Paterson: Author interview
100. Lynn Jezzard: Author interview
101. Claire Moore: Author interview
102. Lynn Jezzard: Author interview
103. Lynn Jezzard: Author interview
104. Lynn Jezzard: Author interview
105. Christopher Tucker: Author interview
106. Christopher Tucker: Author interview
107. James Paterson: Author interview
108. James Paterson: Author interview
109. James Paterson: Author interview
110. James Paterson: Author interview
111. SAG-AFTRA Foundation, October 2017
112. Jonathan Allen: Author interview
113. Lynn Jezzard: Author interview
114. Jonathan Allen: Author interview
115. *Behind the Mask*, BBC documentary, 2005
116. Janet Devenish: Author interview
117. Lynn Jezzard: Author interview
118. Lynn Jezzard: Author interview
119. Lynn Jezzard: Author interview
120. Lynn Jezzard: Author interview
121. Claire Moore: Author interview
122. Claire Moore: Author interview
123. Claire Moore: Author interview
124. Claire Moore: Author interview
125. Claire Moore: Author interview
126. Claire Moore: Author interview
127. Claire Moore: Author interview
128. Richard Stilgoe: Author interview
129. Claire Moore: Author interview

## CHAPTER 8: "THE AMERICAN DREAM"

1. *The Story of Miss Saigon by Edward Behr and Mark Steyn*, Arcade Publishing, 1991
2. *The Story of Miss Saigon by Edward Behr and Mark Steyn*, Arcade Publishing, 1991
3. *The Story of Miss Saigon by Edward Behr and Mark Steyn*, Arcade Publishing, 1991
4. *The Story of Miss Saigon by Edward Behr and Mark Steyn*, Arcade Publishing, 1991
5. *The Story of Miss Saigon by Edward Behr and Mark Steyn*, Arcade Publishing, 1991
6. *The Story of Miss Saigon by Edward Behr and Mark Steyn*, Arcade Publishing, 1991

7. John Cameron: Author interview
8. Simon Opie: Author interview
9. Simon Opie: Author interview
10. *The Story of Miss Saigon by Edward Behr and Mark Steyn*, Arcade Publishing, 1991
11. Playbill, January 1998
12. *Cameron Mackintosh: The Musical Man*, BBC, 2017
13. Playbill, January 1998
14. Frances Ruffelle: Author interview
15. Claire Moore: Author interview
16. Peter Polycarpou: Author interview
17. Peter Polycarpou: Author interview
18. Peter Polycarpou: Author interview
19. Claire Moore: Author interview
20. John Napier: Author interview
21. John Napier: Author interview
22. John Napier: Author interview
23. Andrew Bruce: Author interview
24. Andrew Bruce: Author interview
25. Andrew Bruce: Author interview
26. John Napier: Author interview
27. John Napier: Author interview
28. Andreane Neofitou: Author interview
29. Andreane Neofitou: Author interview
30. Andreane Neofitou: Author interview
31. Andreane Neofitou: Author interview
32. Andreane Neofitou: Author interview
33. Claire Moore: Author interview
34. Claire Moore: Author interview
35. Peter Polycarpou: Author interview
36. Andreane Neofitou: Author interview
37. Andreane Neofitou: Author interview
38. Andreane Neofitou: Author interview
39. *The Story of Miss Saigon by Edward Behr and Mark Steyn*, Arcade Publishing, 1991
40. Peter Polycarpou: Author interview
41. Peter Polycarpou: Author interview
42. Claire Moore: Author interview
43. Peter Polycarpou: Author interview
44. Claire Moore: Author interview
45. Peter Polycarpou: Author interview
46. Simon Opie: Author interview
47. Simon Opie: Author interview
48. Claire Moore: Author interview

49. Simon Opie: Author interview
50. Peter Polycarpou: Author interview
51. Peter Polycarpou: Author interview
52. Claire Moore: Author interview
53. Peter Polycarpou: Author interview
54. Claire Moore: Author interview
55. Peter Polycarpou: Author interview
56. Peter Polycarpou: Author interview
57. Peter Polycarpou: Author interview
58. Peter Polycarpou: Author interview
59. Andrew Bruce: Author interview
60. theatermania.com, March 2017

## THE CURTAIN FALLS

1. Richard Stilgoe: Author interview
2. John Napier: Author interview
3. Arlene Phillips: Author interview
4. Simon Opie: Author interview
5. John Napier: Author interview

# INDEX